Edgar Cayce's
STORY OF THE SOUL

Edgar Cayce's
STORY OF THE SOUL

W. H. Church

A.R.E. PRESS
Virginia Beach, Virginia

Author's Note: In correlating Edgar Cayce's psychic vision of creation and evolution with the current scientific evidence, as well as with data drawn from biblical and other sources, I have found it advisable to adopt a largely interpretative and broadly paraphrased approach, with but a few exceptions. There are two significant reasons for this. First, despite its scholarly underpinnings and a meticulous concern for accuracy, my foremost aim with this book has been to make it readable and entertaining, as well as instructive. Verbatim quotations inserted in a book at frequent intervals visibly disrupt the flow and clarity of the narrative. Then, secondly, there is the language of the readings. Often eloquent and moving, it is nonetheless confusing to many modern-day readers because of its frequent use of quasi-biblical anachronisms and an awkward syntax that can sometimes result in misleading interpretations. These are pitfalls I have chosen to remove from the path of the unfamiliar reader. Meanwhile, wherever one of my references to the readings has suggested the appropriateness of backup attribution, the insertion of a raised numeral at that juncture will lead the reader to an identifying chapter note at the rear, giving the specific case number from the Cayce files. Finally, I wish to point out that the opinions expressed in this book are my own and are not necessarily endorsed by the Edgar Cayce Foundation or its affiliate organization, the Association for Research and Enlightenment.

The Edgar Cayce readings were copyrighted in 1971 by the Edgar Cayce Foundation, Virginia Beach, Virginia.

COPYRIGHT © 1989 by W. H. Church

This book is published by:

Association for Research and Enlightenment, Inc.
67th Street and Atlantic Avenue
P.O. Box 595, Virginia Beach, VA 23451-0595

Printed in the United States of America.

4th Printing, October 1994

ISBN 0-917483-15-4

For I.B.W.

Despise not prophesyings.
Prove all things; hold fast that which is good.

— Thessalonians

CONTENTS

PROLOGUE TO A JOURNEY

Come.

We are about to embark together upon a remarkable journey. It will take us into unmapped regions, to forgotten lands of former renown and great antiquity. Not imaginary landscapes, these, but a part of our evolutionary past. More real than any dream...

There we shall encounter godlike titans, pitiful monsters and strange mutations, all long since obliterated and consigned to myth and legend, as well as other beings not too unlike ourselves. To get there, our psychic guide must carry us through the etheric portals of the akashic records, where, we are told, all memory of the mist-shrouded eons has been permanently etched on the skein of time and space.

We go with a purpose, of course. We are off in search of our evolutionary roots. To find those roots, we must trace the origin, evolution, and destiny of the soul. For it is the soul, in fact, that is evolving—not matter, as is commonly supposed, except as dictated by the soul-entity's architect and builder, mind.

The journey will be full of surprises. We must learn to expect the unexpected. Like wise travelers, let us lighten our load by leaving behind us any preconceived notions or prejudices we might normally carry, and keep an open mind. It will aid us in crossing unfamiliar territory without mental or spiritual impediments. Many of our most cherished beliefs are apt to be seriously challenged along the way; and some, I suspect, will be demolished and replaced before we reach our ultimate destination.

Our goal is a a laudable one.

Evolution, as everyone knows, is a particulary vexing subject, surrounded as it is by so much heated controversy. Not only do science and religion hold fundamentally opposing views as to our origins, but within their separate camps there are feuding factions, as well; groupings and counter groupings, all agreeing to disagree with one another for lack of a common thread of interpretation. The result is a hopeless tangle of conflicting theories and opinions. Our aim, as we travel a psychic route back in time to ancient Lemuria and Atlantis, to Eden and Og and other sunken or vastly altered landscapes and civilizations of prehistory, will be to compare our astonishing discoveries with the existing multitude and muddle of unreconciled views, in the hope of reconciling them. In short, we shall seek a single, unifying theory of evolution to replace the present proliferation—an intelligent and workable synthesis, as it were, which conforms in principle with the basic tenets of both science and religion.

A big order, that. But it fits into the holistic scheme of things that was always the hallmark of our guide and mentor on this journey—Edgar Cayce.

Most readers will require no introduction to the man or his work. The world-renowned psychic, holistic healer, and New Age prophet is already known to millions. Today, less than half a century after his death, Edgar Cayce has already been the subject of several biographies, two of them international bestsellers. There has also been a veritable avalanche of articles and books written about the various aspects of his long and fruitful psychic career. These range from his numerous prophecies, many of which are already being fulfilled, to such popular present-day topics as holistic medicine, conservation practices, dream interpretation, reincarnation and karma, and esoteric astrology, to name but a few. But above all else, Cayce's contribution centers on his spiritual philosophy, which moves like a laser beam across his every thought, lighting up his words with a rare wisdom. We shall encounter its influence often in the pages ahead.

In some 14,000-plus psychic "readings," as they are termed, totalling more than 25 million words, Edgar Cayce has left us a legacy that has been only partially researched and explored, to date, and which promises to continue expanding mankind's self-knowledge for generations to come.

Meanwhile, before we begin to explore his psychic view of evolution, we need to know where Cayce stood philosophically with respect to science, and how different (and yet, how similar in certain basic ways) was his trance-state self, as the authoritative seer in psychic touch with higher sources, from the simple, soft-spoken country fellow from Christian County, Kentucky. The latter, we find, was a devoted family man and churchgoer, whose daily reading was mostly confined to the Bible, and who much preferred fishing and gardening, or his old hobby of photography (once, briefly, his profession), to being seen, heard, and sought after by an ever-curious public. Yet, like the pictures we have seen of a rumpled-looking Einstein with his violin and slippers, seeking inspiration for his scientific equations in music, I have before me a photo taken of Edgar Cayce in a rumpled jacket and old garden hat, bent over his hoe in an equal search for inspiration as he labored over the bean patch. We must cultivate our gardens, said Candide. And many of Cayce's waking-state visions came to him as he labored thus. For we must remember that this was not a simple man, any more than Einstein was, but a remarkably complex one, appearances to the contrary. Yet the psychic genius, like his scientific counterpart, always wore his greatness with infinite humility.

It will not seem surprising, then, to learn that Edgar Cayce had a properly respectful and appreciative attitude toward the various branches of science, and was able over the years to count a growing number of professional scientists and doctors among his friends. In his later years, in fact, several of his trance-state discourses (given in direct response to professional inquiry) were downright mind-boggling in their presentation of scientific data of the most advanced technical complexity, which only a scientifically trained mind could begin to grasp or interpret, and which admittedly mystified Cayce himself in his conscious state.

I think we may safely conclude, in light of the foregoing, that the Edgar Cayce story of evolution, as found in his psychic readings and presented here, is not intentionally hostile toward any of the basic assumptions of science. In supporting the religious notion of a directing Intelligence, or First Cause, behind all creation and subsequent evolution, the readings are admittedly at odds with atheism, of course. But how many scientists today are avowed atheists? They are in a distinct minority, and their numbers are rapidly declining in the face of the new physics now emerging, which is restructuring our whole scientific concept of man and the universe in quasi-metaphysical terms.

Moreover, going back through history, from Einstein to Newton, to Kepler and Copernicus and Galileo, we find that most of the truly great men of science have stood on the side of God—even when orthodox religion may have opposed them! Yet, if their religious beliefs have tended to be of a boldly original and cosmic nature, has this not also been true of virtually any of the world's great religious figures? Though time may have distorted their revealed teachings, pushing them into the mold of yet another orthodoxy, these have always been men—and women—with a cosmic vision, trying to lead mankind towards greater enlightenment through their unique glimpses of a higher truth.

And it was perhaps in this higher, cosmic sense of things, touching on the revelatory powers inherent in both science and religion at their inspirational best, that Edgar Cayce once observed of the two that they are as one when their purposes are one.[1]

Let us salute and embrace that unifying concept. But we could expand upon it somewhat. We could include the psychic and the mystic also.

This invites a look at some interesting examples.

Nostradamus, for one.

It is not well known, I think, but the 16th-century Catholic mystic, in his psychic precognition of a coming New World superquake in our present century (also envisioned by Cayce, of course, much later), appears to have discovered through spiritual insight what was to take science another four centuries to eventually observe and identify as the source of earthquakes, as well as volcanic eruptions and the gradual movement of continents. We call this brand new science "plate tectonics," after Tekton, the carpenter in the *Iliad*. Yet it would have been more fittingly named in honor of Nostradamus, who wrote in one of his quatrains depicting the cause of that prophesied quake: "Two great rocks shall long have warred against each other."[2] It forms a precise description, of course, of the invisible forces at work all along the extensive San Andreas fault-line in California today, where the under-riding Pacific plate has long been "warring" against the plate of the North American continent in an inexorable shoving-match destined to produce not only major quakes and possible inundations (as Cayce predicted), but volcanic eruptions, as well.

Yet another example of spiritually inspired prescience turns up in the writings of the 14th-century German mystic and religious genius, Meister Eckhart. "I am certain," Eckhart once declared unequivocally, "that a man who wanted to do so, might one day be able to walk through a wall of steel."[3] And what says modern science of such a seeming miracle? Why, it is now deemed quite possible—at least, in theory. For such is the spacing of atoms in any material object that man and wall might just conceivably come into such a rare juxtaposition of their respective atomic components as to enable the one to pass through the other without a collision. (Now, don't ask me to try it!) But did Eckhart, not at all meaning to trade in miracles, simply envision a time in man's ongoing evolution when he might thus master a natural law pertaining to energy and mass and motion?

Meanwhile, in the writings of Thoreau we find an interesting case of what Cayce once termed "occult or mystic science."[4]

The 19th-century New England Transcendentalist was quite emphatic about it, as he boldly contradicted the scientific orthodoxy of his day: "There is *nothing* inorganic," he stated flatly.[5] It was a strictly heretical position at a time when science had neatly compartmentalized all matter into "organic" and "inorganic" substances. Today, of course, in their illuminating study of subatomic particles and the whole universe within the atom, modern physicists have caused science to rethink its former premise and come down on the side of Thoreau. Nothing, after all, is really inorganic . . .

On the subject of the atom, we come back to Edgar Cayce.

In a reading on the use by the Atlanteans of the energy of the Sun, converted to atomic power, Cayce commented that this captive energy, once put to constructive purposes, was eventually turned into a channel for destructive ends and the unintentional breaking-up of the Atlantean continent. Then, prophetically, he added a warning that this same latent energy was again at hand, and about to be turned once more to destructive purposes.[6]

That was on July 22, 1942. The highly secret Manhattan Project for the development of the atomic bomb, under General Groves, had gotten under way following a March 1942 recommendation to President Roosevelt by Vannever Bush, chairman of the National Defense Research Committee. And Cayce, in that psychic reading on Atlantis, appears to have tapped unconsciously into this covert undertaking, which eventually led to the atomic destruction of Hiroshima and Nagasaki and the subsequent arms race by the superpowers.

It was, of course, a tragic abuse of Einstein's brilliant formula on the equivalency of mass and energy, discovered some years earlier: $E = mc^2$.

The great physicist was a creator, not a destroyer. He was also, to the chagrin of many of his fellow scientists of lesser stature, a self-avowed mystic and religionist. But let us allow him to speak for himself.

First, on mysticism: "The most beautiful and most profound

emotion we can experience is the sensation of the mystical. It is the sower of all true science."[7]

And on his own unique concept of religion, which he called "the cosmic religious sense," he wrote: "The basis of all scientific work is the conviction that the world is an ordered and comprehensive entity, which is a religious sentiment. My religious feeling is a humble amazement at the order revealed in the small patch of reality to which our feeble intelligence is equal."[8]

Surely, in Einstein's case, science and religion had merged as one, in a mystical union. He obviously shared Cayce's holistic view of things. So did another, of whom Cayce once said that he was the greatest psychic who ever lived.[9] His name: Jesus of Nazareth.

1

THE QUESTIONS THAT CHILDREN ASK

Chaos.

Then, suddenly, a cosmic bang.

In the blink of an eye, the universe is born. An exploding "something," out there somewhere, lights up the former nothingness . . .

It is the dawn of the material creation.

Out of the vast, scattering clouds of mindless matter—hydrogen gas and dust—emerge the earliest forms of life, as wheeling galaxies take shape in flight. Now stars and moons and planets begin to sow themselves in the rapidly expanding, virgin fields of time and space, where they are given initial nourishment by crashing asteroids and the lashing tails of interstellar comets.

Evolution has begun its slow, upward-groping climb.

So goes the leading scientific version of events, cupped in a nutshell. Other sources, other versions. We shall come to them in good time. Meanwhile, we have no cause to pick a quarrel with the top cosmologists. Their generally approved account of things, as far as it goes, is arguably as good as any other. (As far as it goes, be it noted; for the preamble seems to be missing. Science necessarily avoids preambles in such esoteric matters. It must. They fall in the domain of metaphysics or philosophy. Yet, without the preamble — But let's not get ahead of ourselves.)

Unknown forces at work! God or nature? Design or accident? Darwin or the Logos?

We are bombarded with conflicting answers which are apt to be confusing at this point. Let us proceed, then, with the questions.

Where did we come from?

Did we climb up out of the ooze, so to speak, or come down from the upper atmosphere to inherit earth? Evolving apes, or fallen gods? or neither?

Where—if anywhere—do Adam and Eve fit into the picture of human evolution?

Why, in fact, are we here?

Who are we, and what is our destiny? Is it linked to the destiny of the whole universe?

Is science or religion nearer to the truth about our origins? Can they both be wrong—and both right?

Is there a personal God? a personal devil?

What of death and the afterlife?

The pre-existence of the soul?

Reincarnation and karma?

Other earths in the universe?

Multiple dimensions?

The true relativity of time and space?

Finally, let us ask: Are we fully evolved now, or a species still in transition? If the latter, who will our successors be? Ourselves, returning?

Questions, questions. So many questions! Yet I have hardly begun to list them.

Basically, they are the questions that children ask. The ultimate questions about God, man and the universe, to which no one listens.

Yet, Cayce did. And he picked up the answers for us.

Come along, then. Our journey of discovery awaits us, under his psychic guidance. We have only to take the first step, and we shall be on our way.

Step, did I say? More like a quantum leap, to be exact. For, to begin aright, we must go back in time, to before time was.

BEFORE THE BIG BANG

God, the First Cause, moved, and the Spirit came into activity. In the movement, it brought Light, we are told. Then chaos.[1]

Light we can understand. It would appear to be the natural consequence of the First Cause revealing Itself in motion. For, all light is a form of vibration, or movement. But why chaos, as its aftermath?

This surprising sequence strikes us, at first, as paradoxical. If there was to be chaos involved in the primal movement of Creative Energy, we should have expected the reverse order of events: chaos—the void of the unmanifest—followed by a great burst of light, a cosmic vibration. In fact, just what the cosmologists quite properly seem to have envisioned as the beginning of things, in their rational perception of the divine pecking order (if "divine" it was, and not a mere "accidental happening" in time and space).

But let us accept that it was divine. Order is too much evident everywhere within our observable universe to permit the "accident" theory, as we shall later see. In which event, the Divine Originator must have had Its own logic, presumably.

But what was that logic? Read on. It is about to unfold.

The projection of the Light, we discover, was synonymous with the awakening Mind-force, or Universal Consciousness. Mind, in association with its companion, Spirit, brought into being the first creation: a *spiritual* universe, at-one with the

Godhead, and peopled with celestial ideas that took on spiritual form and substance, dwelling in a dimension of Mind requiring neither time nor space for their individual expression. (The material counterpart of this higher creation was still non-existent, at this stage, for there was no necessity as yet for its appearance.)

In the Cayce scripting of that initial event and subsequent happenings, we find a number of heretofore mystifying biblical passages corroborated and demystified. We learn, as both John's Gospel and Paul's Epistle to the Hebrews have obliquely suggested, that the "light" originally mentioned in Genesis was synonymous with the first- and only-begotten Son—Mind—the Word. And it was later He, as Mind the Maker, or the creative aspect of the Godhead (defined by Edgar Cayce as the First Cause, or "Father," as the Body; the Son, the Mind; the Holy Spirit, the Soul[2]), who brought into being another, separate universe, as the Infinite moved upon the finite in that place outside of Itself, called chaos.[3]

As to the reasons for such a second creation, as well as its consequences, I fear we are pushing too far ahead of ourselves. The answers will appear in due order, when we come to the War in Heaven and the revolt of the angels. (For angels, let us concede, are quite real, if not necessarily "angelic"! The record of their activities, both bad and good, has been spun on the etheric threads of *akasha*, along with man's.) Meanwhile, it is time to point to a fateful development. That same first- and only-begotten Son of God, through whom all the other sons were subsequently begotten, as well as the hosts of angelic forces populating the upper universe of spiritual thought-forms, now made a strange choice. He chose to materialize Himself in the lower realm of increasingly dense matter—His second creation—where the light must be shared with darkness, on planet Earth. But why? For a divine purpose, the records suggest. A purpose sacrificial in nature. Appearing again and again in physical manifestation, at the very last His cycle of earthly appearances ended in victory on a cross and in a grave. He arose, and returned from whence He came, that others in the earth might follow . . .

"Study the philosophical or theosophical data," Cayce once advised a woman who approached him as to how she should go about getting involved in spiritual work that would be complementary to his own.[4] On yet another occasion, one of Cayce's psychic readings made reference to the useful role played in the development of the mind of man by the philosophy presented to the world by Confucius and Buddha, or contained in the teachings of Taoism, as well as in those sacred scriptures of India that tell of Brahma.[5] He then went on to emphasize the need to correlate the scriptures of various lands, down through the ages, as a means of expanding our spiritual perspective in line with that holistic precept to be found in the Bible: "The Lord thy God is One."

It was sound advice, so let us take him at his word.

In fact, in the theosophical writings of H. P. Blavatsky, in the late 19th century, she presented as her motto these words, derived from an Indian source: "There is no religion higher than truth."[6] Who can fault that sentiment? Let us hold to it here, as we backtrack a bit to explore one of the many ancient parallels to the biblical version of creation. Such parallel versions, in fact, pop up in the religious legends of almost every major culture, where we find familiar truths concealed in myth and metaphor. Obviously the creation story has been around as long as time itself and has become a part of the collective unconscious of the entire human race. What better proof, then, as to its probable veracity? Painted in broadly varying colors, with differing brush strokes from land to land, and often with a cast of characters that appears on stage in scarcely recognizable and outrageous costume, we nevertheless know the parts too well to mistake the players—or the story.

Let us take the Hindu version for our example here. We shall find that it accords most closely with our familiar biblical account of things. Yet we might just as readily go further afield, of course.

To China, and the Taoist trinity. To Egypt, and Osiris. To Greece, and the Monad of Pythagoras. To Norse mythology. Or to the "Upper Adam" of the Hebrew cabalists, the many-colored "Logos" of the early Gnostic sects. But why confuse the issue with such multiplicity?

So we turn to the Hindu literature. Here, too, there are variations among the Puranic and Vedic texts. Let me simplify. Briefly, we find God identified in the beginning as Brahma, the Absolute Being. Yet he is also billed as the creative member (the Mind-force, as it were) of the Hindu version of the trinity, whose "mind-born sons" make their appearance, along with the *saptarishi*—angelic agents—in the first, or invisible, creation. Later, moving out from the interior realm of the Absolute Self, Brahma initiates the "cycle of necessity" by dropping the Cosmic Egg into chaos, from which the visible universe is hatched into being. Then, as Lord of the universe, Brahma enters this lower creation in bodily form to commence the Grand Cycle of evolution back to the Absolute, and to show to the struggling souls around Him the path of liberation from the treadmill of karma, rebirth, and *maya*—the illusion of separation and multiplicity.

In the *Bhagavad-gita*, a popular Vedic text, we find this embodiment of the Higher Self referred to as the Atman. Commentaries on the Gita, however, make it clear that we should regard the Atman merely as another name and form for Brahman, or Brahma—or Brahm, if you will. Purists, caught up in the notion of multitiered dimensions and divisions of the One, will of course argue otherwise, insisting upon the niceties of differentiation. Such philosophical nuances are out of place here. Not that we would choose to deny them, of course. But let us opt for the underlying Oneness. Different names and changing faces, perhaps, but the same divine Entity. That's what matters.

True also of the Christ.

In Cayce's psychic interpretation of the biblical version of events, we discover the Lord playing out His divine role as Wayshower through some thirty different incarnations in the flesh, always under different names, but ever the Christ. Later we will encounter Him in several of those historic appearances. One, however, can be disclosed here, in passing. This was the androgynous Adam—as He existed before the proverbial Fall. And the last, of course, we have already identified as Jesus of Nazareth. And in between? All but a handful remain a mystery.

Conceivably, though, one of them may have been an incarnation in ancient India, under the Brahmanic name. For the Cayce readings tell us that the biblical "Savior," whether in fleshly manifestation himself, or appearing as that invisible Christ impulse directing others in tune with the one Universal Consciousness, has influenced *all* those forms of philosophy or religious thought throughout history which have taught that God is One.[7] In any event, we may readily imagine Him as the Teacher of the Vedic cosmogony and philosophy, who upon His passage from their midst was subsequently deified and mythologized by reverential Hindu scribes, who had glimpsed His divinity. It is a plausible scenario. Yet we need not insist upon it, of course. All the same, it would certainly explain, as nothing else can, why two of the world's leading religions, so distinctly separate in cultural and geographic terms, nonetheless offer an account of creation so remarkably similar.

And there is yet another aspect of their parallelism for us to ponder: the Word. OM. In the Hindu lexicon, "OM" is the vibratory sound and symbol of Brahm. It is also referred to as the "Audible Life Stream," an occult term that may be equated, in essence, with the Voice of Creation—the Word. (Sound, like light, we are reminded, is merely a mode of energy or vibration.) Repeated over and over during the act of meditation, OM (pronounced "Aum" or "Ohm") is the traditional Hindu mantra. Its audible repetition is believed to raise the bodily vibrations in such a manner as to rouse the sleeping *kundalini* energy resting like a coiled serpent at the base of the spine, as the meditator moves into an altered state of consciousness. Once awakened, this transforming "energy" is said to dart upward through the body along a prescribed path, activating certain spiritual centers until it may reach the highest of these, which has an esoteric association with the pituitary gland at the center of the brain. If this pinnacle is reached, a blissful condition of Oneness with Brahma, or God, is supposedly experienced by the meditator. This exalted state of being is termed *samadhi*. It is comparable, of course, to the "rapture" of Christian saints and mystics, who have achieved a condition of meditative union with God through the raising of the Christ Consciousness within—an identical transformation process, obviously, but simply under different metaphorical terms of reference. In psychological language, this same meditative state has been called "cosmic consciousness."

The Cayce readings have a lot to say on this profound subject. Without losing our heads in such deep water, we shall nonetheless dip briefly into that unplumbed pool of wisdom in a future chapter, as our journey takes us there. And we shall find that our acquaintance with the matter plays a necessary part in the soul's gradual evolution back to its Source, and that it is in fact a subject intimately related to the complex symbology to be found in the Apocalypse of John.

Meanwhile, with more specific reference here, where we have stumbled upon a rather obvious parallel between the biblical "Word," and the Hindu "OM," Cayce once remarked that speech is the highest vibration in the human body. In this same connection, he recommended use of the *spoken* word in prayer as being more effective than its silent counterpart.[8]

What unimaginable feats, we might reasonably ask, far more marvelous than bringing down the walls of Jericho with shouting and trumpets, might not the Lord have performed in the beginning through the immense vibratory powers of His spoken Word? Then one utterance was presumably enough to push into being a whole universe! But I submit to you the awe-inspiring notion that in the Mind of God, a billion times a billion ideas is no greater than one. And therein, it logically follows, lies the great secret behind creation: its Oneness. An atom equal to a universe.

And *Mind* informing and governing all, the macrocosmic and the microcosmic, right down to the very least particle of sidereal dust...

To resume our journey, we must now follow our psychic guide down through the vast, mist-shrouded halls of *akasha* to where the War in Heaven is about to erupt.

Over what?

Self-will. Or, to put it in a more metaphysical context: the divine gift of free will, misdirected. In short, *selfishness*. Turning away, or separating oneself, from God.

And the culprit in this heavenly ruckus? None other than that former Prince of Light, Lucifer—known in the earth today by a number of less flattering names, such as the Tempter, Satan, the Devil, Dragon or Serpent, Prince of Darkness, all symbolic of the malevolent influence of free will, misdirected.

The first-created of the seven archangels and all their angelic hosts, Lucifer was also reputed to be the most beautiful to behold: a veritable "angel of light." Perhaps it is for this reason that his name, meaning "light giver," and his initial rulership became associated in legend with Venus, the morning and the evening star. (An apt metaphor, depicting his early rise and his later fall.) This mythic notion can probably be traced to that well-known passage in Isaiah, "How art thou fallen from heaven, O Lucifer, son of the morning!" The words, of course, were addressed in the form of a prophetic warning to Nebuchadnezzar, King of Babylon, who sought, like the misguided Lucifer, to exalt his throne "above the stars of God. . ."[9]

Yet this Venus-Lucifer theory must topple, even as did Lucifer himself. Venus, as well as all the other planets and the whole of the manifest universe, had not even come into existence when Lucifer and his minions were driven from the presence of God and into the abyss. There, in the emptiness of chaos and stripped of all heavenly splendor, Lucifer and his fallen followers drifted aimlessly in their own darkness, presumably, without a visible kingdom or rulership until the second creation was set into motion.

This lower universe of matter now formed an arena where the contending forces of light and darkness—good and evil—might meet anew to resume the unfinished struggle, in a place well-removed from the sanctity of the Infinite Being, though not altogether beyond the redeeming influence of its deflected Light. Here the dethroned Lucifer, with his trembling hordes, was to take on a new name—Satanail, or Satan—and a vastly different rulership, as the Prince of Darkness. His power and influence were to be restrained, however, by the fact that he must perpetually contend with the ever-watchful presence of the Upper Forces, operating under a divine fiat to impose the necessary balance. Thus, the free will of any of the sons of God who might elect to separate themselves from the Maker and take on the evolutionary experience in the lower universe of matter would remain intact, allowing them to turn back eventually to the spiritual universe from whence they came, and reclaim their divinity.

So the battle goes on today, the readings agree with the theologists, though now waged largely in human minds and hearts—and souls, of course.

But what of its actual beginnings? Separating the factual from the purely allegorical may pose a problem for the fastidious-minded. Yet let ours be the broader perspective, which recognizes that factual and allegorical, reduced to their essence, may be one.

Turning first to the theosophical teachings, we need not be surprised to find that Hinduism can again provide us with an instructive parallel. The Vedic version of the Lucifer story finds Moisasure, the Hindu Lucifer, becoming envious of the Creator's resplendent light, so that he decides to lead his legion of subservient spirits against Brahma in a declaration of spiritual warfare.

But Shiva, the third person in the Hindu trinity and lord of the forces of dissolution, hurls Moisasure and his rebel spirits out of the celestial abode into the region of eternal darkness.[10]

In our next account of events, let us look at both the apocryphal writings and the Bible. Then we shall turn to our psychic source.

Regrettably, however, there is nothing in our story, thus far, to lure the scientist to share in our celestial pursuits. The reason? Lack of empirical data, of course. No natural laws involved here for observation and theorizing. The framework of science does not permit philosophical speculation, and rightly so. One day, however, if science can eventually learn how to tap into the akashic records as currently only a few of the psychically gifted can, scientific observation of heavenly as well as earthly phenomena may become a distinct possibility. Moreover, the means for such a scientific breakthrough may be closer to hand than is realized. First, it is evident already that science is proceeding at a vastly accelerated rate toward previously unimagined new horizons. Fresh discoveries abound. Recently, two astonishing new scientific disciplines have emerged: one is called the science of chaos, the other is even more improbably dubbed the science of experimental metaphysics. One is dazzled by the obvious daring they both imply, in a heady departure from the scientific determinism of the past. Meanwhile, in a series of readings on what he termed etheronic energy and etheronic wave forces, Cayce pointed the direction for a bold new science to follow if it would unravel one of the higher mysteries of the universe: the nature of *akasha*.[11] Synonymous with the mysterious "ether" long ago dismissed by science because its existence eludes detection, it is actually a *mental* force in its essence and permeates all space.

Among the apocryphal gospels, there is one attributed to Bartholomew, in which the apostle holds what must be perceived as an allegorical dialogue with the Devil.[12] It is a meeting forced upon Satan at the Lord's command, in which he is made to speak to Bartholomew of many things, including the nature of his creation and his ultimate fall, following his refusal to obey a command from the Archangel Michael to drop his prideful pose and be angelically worshipful, as he was created to be.

Satan repeats to Bartholomew his boastful response to Michael:

"I am fire of fire, I was the first angel formed," he reminds his brother archangel, who, though chief captain of the hosts, was formed second ("created by the will of the Son and the consent of the Father"). And though there were five other archangels besides these first two, sibling rivalry is known to be strongest always between the two leading offspring in any larger number.

When Michael tells the recalcitrant Satan that God will be wroth with him, the reaction is nothing short of open rebellion.

"God will not be wroth with me; but I will set my throne over against His throne, and I will be as He is."

But, God, of course, was very wroth indeed. Satan was cast out of Heaven, with all of his angels. And he plotted thereafter to avenge himself upon the man in the earth, who had been created in God's image. (Which was to be later, of course, in Adam's day.)

After Satan's unwilling confessions to Bartholomew, he is allowed to depart. But he mutters bitter words about having been "tricked" into talking before his appointed time. No doubt he had found the whole episode humiliating. Devilishly humiliating, one supposes . . .

In another apocryphal account, contained in the "Secrets of Enoch,"[13] it is the Lord himself who tells how He created the order of the ten troops of angels, commanding that each should stand in his order. But Satanail, having turned away with the order that was under him, "conceived an impossible thought . . . that he might become equal in rank to My power."

The outcome was inevitable. He had to go.

He went—but not voluntarily.

In the Gospel of Luke, we have his departure rather graphi-

cally depicted in the Lord's very own words, after He has listened
to the returning seventy joyfully recount their experiences in
casting out devils in His Name. "I beheld Satan as lightning fall
from heaven," Jesus tells them of the original ejection.[14]

And the ejector? We turn to these words from Revelation on
the subject:

"And there was war in heaven: Michael and his angels
fought against the dragon; and the dragon fought, and his angels,
/ And prevailed not; neither was their place found any more in
heaven. / And the great dragon was cast out, that old serpent,
called the Devil, and Satan, which deceiveth the whole world: he
was cast into the earth, and his angels were cast out with him."[15]

Into the earth, was it? Well, not at once, surely. First, into the
abyss—wherever that was. For here we are reduced to a language composed mainly of symbols. The earth, as already noted,
was not yet created when that resplendent archangel-turned-
dragon fell. Nor did he "fall," in any literal sense. Nothing to drop
through, or into. Neither time nor space had yet come into
manifestation, remember. In a boundless universe of purely
spiritual thought-forms, what need for those visible props or
limitations, which would later be imposed upon the Lord's
second creation? No, Satan and his fallen minions must have
found themselves locked in a kind of nether realm, a spiritual
vacuum of unmitigated night and non-beingness.

Chaos, we would call it. That which came into creation right
after the Light. And for a good reason, apparently. It was to form
the ground for the second creation and the expression of the pairs
of opposites. For, without such a choice, of what use was the gift
of free will to the soul? And how else would it know it had
separated itself from its Maker?

Which brings us back to Satan.

Was the creation of this angel-turned-monster an accident?
Surprisingly, such accidents in creation are possible. That stunning piece of information was plucked straight from the akashic
records by Edgar Cayce.[16] And verily, did not God repent in

making man? So we are told, in the Bible. (If true, a humbling reminder of our innate deficiencies.)

But the ways of the Lord are often inscrutable. And to support a growing suspicion that Satan's plight, though clearly self-inflicted, may nevertheless have fitted into the Divine Pattern from the beginning, let me quote a confirming excerpt from Isaiah. It is the Lord Himself who is speaking through His prophet:

"I am the Lord, and there is none else. / I form the light, and create darkness; I make peace, and create evil: I the Lord do all these things."[17]

It is a hard saying. How are we to interpret it?

I think we may already have a handle on its meaning. That bit about free will, as already noted, and the need to provide the soul with a choice through the creation of the pairs of opposites in a bipolar universe of matter. But let me elaborate. And to do so, we had best see what Edgar Cayce has dug up from the akashic records.

In the spiritual universe, we discover, all force is One; and that One is *positive*.[18]

The Mind-born sons, projected into being through the will of Mind the Maker, were in His image (*His individual selves*, says one reading, quite explicitly[19]), which meant that they were celestial thought-forms—divine cells, as it were, in the Body of God, suddenly made aware of their individuality. Each a universe within himself, and capable of manifesting creativity in his own right.

Androgynous beings, they contained within themselves all of the elements and characteristics required to reproduce spiritually through thought-projection, even as their Maker. They had no need, therefore, to develop any type of sexual polarization as a part of their nature. Rather, they drew their creativity from the God-force. (This may serve to demystify the Lord's comment, in Matthew 22:30, concerning the resurrected souls in the earth, who shall neither marry nor be given in marriage, but be as the angels!)

God is Love, we are told. And spiritual bliss is derived from union with God. Creativity is the inevitable result.

The Mind-born sons, as long as they maintained psychic union with their Creative Source in the Oneness, could still be separate, yet not "separated." God, however, in desiring their companionship, had bestowed upon the sons the gift of free will, that they might choose to remain in His Presence or separate themselves. For, without that choice, the sons would be in the same category as the angels, who, though created a little higher in the beginning, must remain as servants (although exalted ones, to be sure), attendant upon the Creator. On the other hand, the sons were endowed with a unique heritage, if they chose to earn it, raising them above the very highest of the angels.[20] By perfecting themselves through the cycle of spiritual evolution, they would become full-fledged co-heirs with the first Son, and co-rulers with Him of the universe, in an unending pattern of spiritual creativity and growth. (For, growth is the eternal mandate of Mind, as someone once wisely observed.)

Asked on one occasion to describe the cycle of spiritual evolution, as contrasted with man's evolution in the flesh, Edgar Cayce's answer was an oblique one. Evolution in the spiritual plane, he pointed out, cannot be properly viewed from another plane.[21] Presumably we will have to wait until we can reach that level to find out.

Meanwhile, puzzlement arises over another point. And inasmuch as Mr. Cayce is not readily accessible to provide an answer, let us attempt it ourselves. It concerns the fact that Lucifer, the first-created of the archangels, was apparently endowed with a quality intended by God to be reserved for the sons alone: the gift of free will, or choice. Was this one of those "accidents" mentioned earlier? Perhaps. Or perhaps it was a part of the Lord's hidden agenda... In any case, without Lucifer's willful disobedience, how else might there have arisen cause for the dropping of the Brahmic "Egg," as it were, and the creating of that lower universe? And without that saving event, where in heaven's name might all of us separated souls now find ourselves? In the abyss, most likely. Instead, here we are: groping our slow, painful way back upward to the Mind of the Maker, which—so we are assured—is our destiny, unless we foolishly will it otherwise.

Man in his original state, or *permanent* consciousness, our source points out, is *soul*, with a spiritual body like unto the Maker's. And here in the flesh, the soul is the God-part in us. The fleshly consciousness in materiality was only brought about so that the soul might become aware of its separation from the God-force. And it was Satan, or Lucifer—*as a soul*, it is said—who "made those necessities," through his own fall, for this condition to be brought about.[22] Nor does he repent of his ways. Thus the constant warring of the flesh with the spirit, as a replication of that original rebellion in heaven.

"As above, so below," runs the Hermetic axiom.

And even as there is a personal Savior in the earth, whose Name we can call upon at will, so is there a personal devil too.

Yet the readings, in recounting that primordial battle in the Unseen Forces between the Archangel Michael, servant of the Light and Lord of the Way, and Lucifer, Lord of Rebellion and Darkness, conclude on a cautionary note. It is suggested that all of the present evil in the earth should be regarded impersonally, as various *influences* with which we must contend, rather than the work of any specific personality. In fact, the attempt to personalize evil, or error, if we let it come to that, is more apt than not to point to ourselves.

And why so?

Each of us here in the earth plane entered voluntarily, as a soul seeking fleshly experience in a realm of consciousness apart from God.

We, too, fell.

CRACKING THE COSMIC EGG

Our cosmic origins in an egg?

We must treat it as a metaphor, of course. Apt enough, to those ancient sages who invented it, in an age that knew nothing about such complicating matters as quantum mechanics or relativity. But times change, and with them their symbols. We can no longer nurture the obsolete notion of a nesting God or a hatched-out cosmos. Let us leave the dropping of over-sized eggs to the long-extinct pterodactyl and look for a more up-to-date symbolism to signify the birthing of our universe.

We find it in the geometric point.

Centered in its own weightless nothingness (it exists at zero gravity, take note), this inert and invisible point of ours represents an undreamed-of energy potential suspended in an as-yet-unmanifested timespace. Perhaps no larger than a very tightly compressed atom, such as might be formed by a suddenly collapsing universe overwhelmed by its own crushing gravity or brought down by the disintegrating action of antimatter particles, it now begins to swell like a nascent bud after a long winter. In this nanosecond of inner movement, it suddenly pushes out of itself with all of the force and velocity of a genie released from its bottle after eons of inertia. There is a vast explosion of long pent-up matter—an unimaginable Big Bang that is still resonating throughout the farthest reaches of the ever-expanding universe as the former geometric point races uniformly outward in all directions, becoming a boundlessly widening circle in timespace. Even today, numberless new stars and nebulae and whirling galaxies continue to take shape in the outermost ripples created by that initial nanosecond of celestial movement.

What has just been described, in fact, exceeds the purely metaphorical. In the minds of most of the Big Bangers, it is precisely The Way It Happened . . . and will continue to happen, as our self-sustaining universe keeps on expanding indefinitely, they say.

Indefinitely? Well, here's where the dominant school of quantum theory collides head-on with general relativity. Envisaging an unstoppable gravity, Einstein predicted the ultimate collapse of this finite universe, in an exact reversal of its beginnings. He was derided for his views, in conflict with quantum theory, and dismissed as old-fashioned. But if the current proponents of supergravity are confirmed in their latest speculations, the unstoppable Einstein (like his gravitational forces) will be proven the ultimate winner. And it accords with our psychic view of things, as will soon be demonstrated. A kind of Alpha and Omega sequence, one might say, borrowing that apocalyptic term in which the Lord proclaims Himself the beginning and the end of the finite creation.

Rather surprisingly, that biblical allusion takes us right back to our Brahmic Egg. Was it perhaps abandoned a tad too hastily? For the egg, like the serpent and other symbols familiar to the religious teachings of both East and West, has a concealed as well as a commonly revealed interpretation. In Hinduism, the egg becomes an esoteric symbol for the "No-Number," or the oviform zero, before the *Adi-Sanat*—the "Number," or "He is One"—is added, whereby it becomes the fertile ground for the multiplicity of numbers in Brahm's visible creation.[1] In Western tradition, the life-giving "egg" loses its oviform shape to become a sphere, or circle. It is the symbol of Eternity, to which the centerpoint is added to signify the Logos, or Word—that Creative Energy which brings Eternity into finite manifestation. This same circle with the geometric point in its center is also the popularly recognized emblem for the Sun (the Son).

Modern physics, in attempting to trace the origins of the universe back to that invisible compression-point preceding the Big Bang, brings science uncomfortably close to the governing tenets of religion. Matter merges into spirit, the natural into the supernatural. Similarly, a theoretical "mind of the universe" dogs the dangerously metaphysical probings of particle physicists as they appear to have discovered a self-organizing principle behind the seemingly random and chaotic behavior of subatomic particles. Some physicists, well aware of the quicksand rising beneath their feet, have taken refuge in the elusive aphorisms of Buddhism and Taoism, where there is less risk of being charged with the unpardonable scientific sin of "religiosity." (It was a charge that might have been Einstein's undoing but for his undisputed genius.) This turn to Eastern mysticism has resulted in a rather fascinating synthesis of views, expressed in a growing number of books in this unusual genre, which is not quite science or religion. Or, rather, it may perhaps be termed a philosophical mixture of the two . . .

It was back in the early part of the 17th century that Sir Francis Bacon first proposed the proper parameters for scientific inquiry, categorically declaring that "we do not presume by the contemplation of nature to attain the mysteries of God." It was a particularly wise distinction to draw at the time, for it cut two ways: it implied that the Church should not meddle in science. But essentially it was addressed to a growing need to clarify science's perceived role, which has changed very little until quite recently. In consequence, scientists have dutifully concerned themselves over the passing centuries with their sole, legitimate task of uncovering and proving the laws of nature, leaving the mysteries of God to the speculations of the preachers or the mandates of the popes. Not too surprisingly, this long mutual isolation between science and religion has bred a mutual distrust as well, often fed by dogmatism on both sides. However, the time has now come to breach both walls—the isolation and the distrust—and seek a common ground. I think we are learning at last that God is as much in the laws of nature as anywhere. Why shouldn't the scientist begin—as, indeed, he is now doing—to discover Him there? And why shouldn't the religionist become more scientific in his interpetation of the nature of God, exchanging the supernatural for the divinely natural? There is another problem, of course: scientific findings are necessarily tentative, whereas religious pronouncements are absolute. But as Cayce once expressed it, Truth is a *growing* experience. Religion, as well as science, must be subject to constant change and growth as we evolve toward God.

In fact, we have seen religious absolutism take quite a tumble in the past century of scientific progress, as fundamentalist Christian positions on certain basic matters of biblical interpretation have been proven radically untenable: the age of our earth, for instance, or the probable length of man's tenancy here. Not that science has come up with any certain answers as yet, but the evidence to date has been strong enough to unseat fundamentalist assertions in these areas by an exceedingly wide margin. It is only a matter of time until dogged fundamentalist resistance must crumble in the face of new truths, even as the Copernican Revolution of an earlier century eventually brought an obstinate pope to his senses.

As Gandhi once sagely observed, Truth is God. But as seekers of Truth, who have not yet realized God, "religion of our conception is always subject to a process of evolution and reinterpretation. Progress toward Truth, toward God, is possible only because of such evolution." Wise words. And it was in this context of spiritual growth, perhaps, that Cayce more than once asserted that the true "church" must lie within us, rather than in any static organization, however useful the latter may prove to be, and even necessary to some as a "centering" force despite the inevitable drift toward dogmatism.

On the other hand, science has sometimes been just as dogmatic about holding to unproven positions. The Darwinian theory on the origin of species is a prime case in point. Still no more than a debatable theory, it is too often exalted to the status of proven fact. And in this instance, it is likely to be science rather than religion that may find itself forced to retreat in time, making certain major concessions as it softens its hardline position. Not that man hasn't evolved, of course, or that he isn't still evolving. But from what? and toward what? Those are the critical questions. And what of the soul of man, which so vastly affects the whole scheme of evolution? Science is well within its rights to doubt the soul's existence, but not to go beyond doubt to denial. In fact, one of science's own has recently labeled science "the art of doubt."[2] It is a distinction for all scientists to heed carefully whenever they are tempted to overstep themselves and become dogmatic.

One of the hazards of scientific dogmatism is the embarrassing habit long-discredited views sometimes have of regaining their lost respectability as a new generation of scientists stumbles upon new facts. As a case in point, certain discarded notions once put forward by the French biologist Lamarck which contradict popular biological dogma about the randomness of evolution have just been resurrected by a team of Harvard biologists. The surprising results of their experiments on bacteria, published in the September 8, 1988 issue of the British journal *Nature*, indicate that these one-celled organisms are capable of controlling their own genetic mutations, in full accord with the old Lamarckian theory. (Whether a multicelled creature like man can do the same still remains unproven, but logic tells us that what a one-celled bacterium can accomplish on its own is surely not beyond the innate wisdom of every living creature, including man.)

Meanwhile, even as the scientists display signs of waxing increasingly metaphysical in looking at the atom and the universe, thus moving into the backyard of religion, some religious debaters have attempted to encroach upon the private turf of science with a misnamed "science" of their own, called creation science. But while it may reflect in some respects an inadequate understanding of basic scientific principles, thus disqualifying itself as a true scientific discipline, it nevertheless serves to demonstrate that science and religion can no longer expect to preserve mutually exclusive domains immune from crossovers. And in all honesty, is not a cross-fertilization of ideas in these two rival realms just what is needed at this critical evolutionary stage? For a new root race is now in the making, we are told, whose world cry will be for greater unification at every level.

Our theme here is oneness.

Science and religion form the twin props of our modern civilization. Each has its separate function, of course; but so do human head and heart, though the one cannot survive without a degree of cooperation from the other. This interdependency needs to be recognized and acted upon, or the welfare of the whole body is at risk. It is like intellect and emotion: we need them both, in a balanced interplay, or we are in danger of becoming a split personality, heading toward self-destruction.

A perception of the totality of things is what I am getting at. Despite the wonderfully fertile minds and imaginations of our better scientists, aided as never before by an almost limitless technology at their disposal, science's innate contempt for spiritual values creates a "blind" side that blocks much potential progress. How long can an independent-minded science hope to hide from or dismiss the spiritual realities pushing up right under its probing fingertips, so to speak? Sooner or later, it must face the evolutionary necessity (a necessity to which only a relative handful of scientists is now awake) of acknowledging the existence of a universal Mind-force, or God, behind everything it is presently examining with such willful inattention to its underlying nature. Having done that, science must then develop an interdisciplinary set of goals and guidelines on that unifying premise. The resultant progress for mankind, both spiritually and materially, will be nothing short of phenomenal, enabling us to create an earthly utopia if we wish.

As for religion, its self-corrective task would appear to be a bit harder—but what is impossible to God? Religion is a house that is badly divided against itself, and it is a wonder indeed if God can find a resting-place beneath its falling rafters. All of the major religions of the world need to unite, in spirit if not in individual practice, on a theme common to each: "The Lord thy God is One." Then, working in tandem with science around the world, this unified religious body can make an organized effort under a common ideal, seeking to eradicate the poverty and ignorance they have too often unwittingly fostered in the past, through self-serving and socially retrograde policies. The needs of the inner man cannot be met by ignoring the outer.

Working together, we reap the fruits of oneness. And oneness, said Cayce, is what evolution is really all about. Whatever separates any one of us, holds the others back; and that which unites us, raises up the whole body of mankind. Jesus, in addressing the spiritually hungry who had gathered to hear His words on one of the final days before His last supper, articulated this universal Law of Oneness in the form of a startling prophecy. Its fulfillment may be an ongoing process, even now. "I, if I be lifted up from the earth," said He, "will draw all men unto me."[3]

Mind is the builder, we are told, and our thoughts are continually materializing themselves at a multitude of levels. One of those levels, rather incredibly, has cosmic implications. It involves the resonance factor. For it is an aspect of the Cayce philosophy that our human evolution is linked to that of the universe as a whole, and that our combined thoughts and actions, if of a negative character, can set into motion a discordant resonance that affects not only the Sun (where it may trigger sunspots)[4] and the various planets within our immediate solar system, but will reach to far more remote star systems within our own galaxy and beyond. This resonance factor is set into motion, theoretically, through a vast, etheric web of harmonic impulses connecting one part of the universe with every other part, much like the circuitry of nerve cells in the human body. And when the collective human consciousness on earth is out of harmony, the planetary organism may be presumed to resonate with an off-key pitch, as it were, adversely affecting the "music of the spheres." In a reciprocal effect that accords with the principles of resonance, our altered pitch comes bouncing back to us as a discordant impulse because of our improper attunement. Its effects upon the planet can take the form of earthquakes, solar storms, plagues and the like, until the planetary resonance factor adjusts itself to a more harmonious pitch. And this depends, of course, upon the collective consciousness of man, to whom the rulership was given in the beginning with a command to "subdue" the earth—and, by implication, that which earth symbolizes: the lower self.

It is a plausible theory, with acceptable links to some of the latest scientific propositions. At the same time, it remains in basic accord with biblical tradition.

Let us look at some related theories, which are drawn directly from the world of modern science.

"God does not play dice with the universe."

Of all of Albert Einstein's oft-quoted aphorisms, that one is perhaps the most famous and the most often quoted. It is also the most frequently debated among scientists of conflicting persuasions, even to this day.

It was debated from the very moment it was uttered, in fact.

"Stop telling God what to do!" was the instant retort of an angered Niels Bohr. The talented Danish quantum theorist hotly resented Einstein's flat rejection of his proposition, later to be tested and confirmed by other physicists, on the seemingly chaotic and random character of the world of subatomic particles. Einstein and his orderly God were the apparent losers. Lawless electrons won the day. Based on the free electron's unpredictable behavior in repeated experiments, the conclusion seemed to be clear: nothing in the universe can be predicted with certainty, inasmuch as the atomic particle is the essence of all matter. (Never mind that the very act and mode of observing the electron under artificial conditions in the laboratory may interfere with its normal behavior, causing it to jump erratically from one orbit to another, or change suddenly from a particle to a wave, and back again.)

At any rate, particle physicists have now begun to realize that the pioneering work done by Bohr and others in their early exploration into the little-understood world of quantum systems did not go far enough to merit any final conclusions. In fact, newcomers in the field have come up with some fresh discoveries of a rather startling nature. Current research shows that the chaotic free electron can also exhibit an astonishing self-organizing ability, and what we might here presume to call a form of "consciousness" that actually enables it to respond to the mental stimuli of the observer. Result: out of chaos, sudden order. The random mode of the laboratory electron shot from an electron gun, at first playing a free-willed game of chance arrangement and rearrangement in blind Darwinian fashion, shifts suddenly to a predictable and orderly pattern of behavior under the watchful eye of a human observer (the physicist, in this instance).

This perceived interaction between the observer and the observed, which lies at the heart of the "new physics," carries profound implications that are unsettling to science. First, any suggestion that the human mind may exercise a form of control over the atom would appear, as a necessary corollary, to validate biblical tradition concerning man's God-given dominion over all creation in the beginning. Also, it introduces the probability of a matching role, in this relativistic universe of ours, between the mind of man and that of a higher Intelligence (whether or not we label it "God").

In summary, one must conclude that the electron-chasing game has raised for science some vexing questions of a purely metaphysical character, which are normally perceived to be beyond the competence of physical science to answer. Yet a tentative hypothesis has nonetheless been put forward by the proponents of that brash and breakaway new science of experimental metaphysics, mentioned earlier. Brash and breakaway? Well, not altogether the latter, alas. We shall see that the old science continues to intrude upon the new and innovative, holding it back with most of the familiar strictures. Indeed, our so-called "experimental metaphysics" eschews any adventurous overtones that might carry spiritual or religious implications, thus keeping metaphysics grounded in matter, much like a bird with clipped wings. As a consequence, an otherwise promising theory never quite manages to get airborne. In pinpointing its basic flaw, I am reminded of what Blavatsky once wrote about Darwin: "Darwin begins his evolution of species at the lowest point and traces upward. His only mistake may be that he applies his system at the wrong end."[5]

The hypothesis in question appears to rest on the implicit supposition that a kind of subliminal consciousness factor, a wholly natural phenomenon devoid of any supernatural causes, is an evolutionary aspect of the physical universe. As nearly as science can interpret it, this cosmic "mystery of consciousness," as it is termed, has been slowly evolving into beingness over the eons of time, out of the primordial matter set loose in space in the beginning by the Big Bang, or whatever it was. At its apex today is the fully awakened consciousness of man—the most advanced thinking species in the cosmos, and specially brought into a condition of higher awareness by the mysterious consciousness-force of the cosmos to serve its own evolutionary ends. For the universe—so goes the theory—needs the mind of man as an observer, inasmuch as *nothing may be said to exist until it is observed*. (That latter statement is a root premise of the proposal.) Man's role in this capacity is to help perpetuate and carry forward the advancing evolution of the observed cosmos, even as man himself requires the cosmos for his own ongoing evolution. In short, it is a symbiotic arrangement, such as occurs throughout the world of nature, where one life-form develops a mutual dependency upon another for their joint survival. But here the process of symbiosis appears to have reached its highest state, its most perfect form. For the conscious observer is the offspring of that which he observes. Their pantheistic union forms what is termed a "metaphysical dance" between the mind of man and the universe of matter.[6]

The imagery may be appealing; the metaphysics is less so.

One must ask, in all humility: if there was not the observing Mind of the Creator in the beginning—and, indeed, throughout all subsequent time—how did an unobserved universe manage to survive and evolve on its own until man's arrival some billions of years later? Furthermore, how can modern science assign any validity to the Big Bang theory of creation, in a mindless beginning of things in primordial matter, with no one around to hear it go off or to observe that birthing event? Remove the First Cause, and you must remove its effects. No Prime Observer, nothing to observe. Simple as that. Mechanistic explanations won't do.

I prefer the view as seen from the imaginative pages of Genesis. Despite the hyperbole of its largely symbolic language, it somehow makes more sense, and its overall metaphysics is much sounder. Science should take another look. Perhaps a modern-day synthesis is possible. We can keep the Big Bang, but add Spirit and Light—the Mind-force. They might all fit together. As for that symbiotic relationship between man and the physical cosmos, it is only a temporary liaison, if we may rely on the Word of God. For we are told that man is imbued with a soul-self that lives on and on, and which will outlast the visible universe of matter. But while he is here, man has been given dominion. He is the legitimate keeper of the cosmos for the duration, with a mandate to protect and nurture all of those worlds that may temporarily serve his evolving needs, and to become an active participant in the ruling of the universe through his gradual mastery of the universal laws.

(An aside to the reader: In an age of acute gender consciousness, let it be clear that the preceding references to "man," and any similar references that follow, are intended solely in a generic sense, and should be understood to apply equally to "woman." If it is an offending usage to some, I apologize. But in subject matter such as ours, the generic term of reference remains scientifically correct and allows no practical alternative.)

Cayce often spoke of the Oneness of all Force.[7]

Implicit in such a oneness must be an underlying order to all things. If nothing else, we know from observation that eventual order emerges out of the most chaotic of events, from a volcanic eruption to the breaking up and remolding of a continent as the earth purges and renews itself. Similarly, it is obvious that order of a most marvelous and exquisite sort must rule the microscopic world of the atom and the subatomic particle; and their occasionally erratic behavior may have a rational explanation far beyond the physicist's ken. Who are we, to see "chance" at work when some unknown law can cause seemingly random or chaotic particles of matter to coalesce into such lovely objects as millions of geometrically perfect snowflakes, or the lacelike patterns of frost on a windowpane?

Science has already demonstrated that mental stimuli from the thought waves of the physicist can control the wayward electron in the testing chamber. Clearly, then, there is some form of primitive consciousness within the electron. And that consciousness has shown its willingness to take direction from a thinking presence within its proximity—direction that may even have been subconsciously transmitted and subconsciously received. But where or what is the Unseen Force informing the atoms that construct the snowflake, as it takes on its wondrous geometric formation in the upper atmosphere? or assembling the living cells in each upthrusting blade of grass, with its unique individuality? Stretch your mind for a moment to where the whirling galaxies are gathered in outer space, like so many titans, each obedient to its marching orders from—Whom or What?

There is no need to be evasive with the answer. It has been staring at us all along. Let me reiterate it in clear terms: there is a Creative Mind-force and Lawmaker (call it whatever you will) informing and governing every niche and corner of the universe. It has been there from the beginning, because the beginning was in Itself. And since there must be a law to everything in creation, it established the universal laws even before lighting the Banger or speaking the Word that set it all into motion.

The above philosophy, based on spiritual concepts revealed to us by our psychic source, may appear to be too esoteric for the rational scientific mind to consider seriously. Yet, as pointed out earlier, the world of science has been undergoing a sea-change of late, coming up with esoteric notions of its own as it begins to interact with the New Age consciousness. In one of science's more prestigious journals, there was recently published a mind-stretching little article by an astrophysicist, whose views are not too far removed from pure metaphysics. His article contains evidence enough, if one can accept it, that a law-enforcing Intelligence went right to work at the very instant the physical universe was created.

The subject-matter of that article? Cosmic strings.[8]

And what are cosmic strings, you ask? Possibly they are some type of thought-form or etheric "pre-matter." (But that, I must confess, is my own private notion.) They are identified in the article as "exotic, invisible entities"—thin, gyrating threads of enormous strength and energy, though now decaying for the most part, which remain from the fabric of the newborn universe. In that first instant of creation, they were flung out into every direction of space like a giant webwork of violently twirling, looping strings. Their design was marvelous and precise. Moving at about the speed of light with rhythmic pulses, their loop-ends were perfectly constructed to sweep raw matter into spinning clumps that were to spawn the galaxies.

What have we here? A growing cult of scientific mysticism? In theory after theory, we see science abandoning itself to mystical premises. It is as if all the known laws of nature had suddenly begun to give way to unknown forces. And that may be precisely what is happening. For a New Age is virtually upon us, and the whole body of mankind is being propelled by irresistible forces into an era of revolutionary change and awakening beyond our present comprehension. The scientist is quite naturally caught up in it, like everyone else. But what he is experiencing, really, is less a mystical transformation, if he but knew it, than a spiritual one. However, he is reluctant to come to terms with that fact.

Let me summarize:

First, a Big Bang—unseen, unheard; yet, somehow credible to scientists everywhere as the most acceptable creation theory. Then chaos, observed in a testing chamber. And out of chaos, order. A self-organizing universe proposed, as the theory of choice among particle physicists. Next, symbiosis: a metaphysical dance between mind and matter, at the cosmic level. And, finally, those cosmic strings: suppositional threads of invisible energy strung throughout the universe, by means of which some unidentified Genius in the beginning of timespace flung out the seed-material to form the galaxies . . .

Pure mind-stuff, all of this. The stuff, as well, of respectable scientific journals. Not that I am mocking it, mind you. And not that I disapprove in any way. Quite the contrary. But one can't help wondering: if this is science, what is so unscientific about probing the paranormal, or accepting as a working premise the existence of a God-force and a soul-entity to explain those many mysteries about man and the universe that are otherwise inexplicable?

There is a whole world of spiritual science waiting to be explored. Where to begin? To measure a circle, as someone once said, one begins anywhere.

4

THE SIX DAYS OF CREATION

Day One.

Darkness was upon the face of the deep. Let there be light, said God, and there was light. God called the light day, and the darkness night. And the evening and the morning were the first day.

That, we are told by the author of Genesis, is how Day One, of the six days of creation, began and ended. (The seventh, we recall, was a day of rest.)

But how long is a day, by heaven's clock? A Day of Brahm, says Hindu tradition, speaking of God-measured time, is about four-and-a-half billion years. Time enough for Rip van Winkle to sleep into Eternity, while God was just getting started about His business . . .

Seven days, altogether. Some 30 billion years, if we apply the Brahmic calculator. And if we don't? Well, we have other choices at our disposal.

First, the literal view. The literalists, thumping upon their Bibles in unyielding opposition to any symbolic kind of interpretation of events, insist that the Word be taken at its word. Seven days a week doth make—no more, no less. (Without meaning to be disrespectful, we must find ourselves wondering how the literalist handles dreams and parables.)

Each should interpret the matter to his own comprehension, suggested a conciliatory Edgar Cayce, when asked for his view.[1] But for his own part, he did not hesitate to side with the symbolists, quoting that familiar old adage: "A thousand years are as but a day, and a day as but a thousand years in the sight of the Lord." What the humble psychic knew, of course, with his extraordinary insight, was that time cannot be relevant to the Creator. Not a thousand years, not a billion. All time is one, he was fond of saying, just as all space is one, in the realm of Spirit, where all is the present—the Eternal *Now*—in God-consciousness. Or, to express it in more absolute terms (which the finite mind cannot fully grasp, said Cayce, in its separation from the Infinite), there is in reality no time, no space.[2] These are merely concepts of our finite consciousness. Mind the Maker brought time and space into being as necessary dimensions of the physical creation—the "stage props," as it were, for our evolution in a relative world, a relative universe. Another dimension, added by the Maker, was patience. For, as stated in Luke, "In your patience possess ye your souls."[3] (It was one of Cayce's favorite biblical themes, encountered again and again in his psychic readings.)

Which brings us, at last, to the final time-related viewpoint to be considered: that of material science.

Geology, in concert with the other earth sciences, now has a fairly firm fix on the age of our planet, which is set at about 4.6 billion years. The age of the universe, dating back to the Big Bang, is considerably less certain. Until rather recently, scientists were estimating about 15 billion years, but that figure is being continually shoved further back into the rolling mists of an unknown timespace. Our constantly improving telescopes enable the human eye and mind to contemplate in outer space the ghostly images of shining celestial objects so many billions of light years into the vanished past that it leaves the observer baffled and boggled.

The most recent and surprising revelation has been the sighting of two primeval galaxies some 17 billion light years away from earth, and believed to represent a distance about 95 percent of the way back in time to the so-called Big Bang. The mechanism used for this latest sighting was not an ordinary telescope, but an array of powerful new infrared detectors developed for the military, and made available to a team of University of Arizona astronomers.[4]

On less substantial evidence, one isolated voice of authority in the field of astrophysics—a widely respected professor of astronomy at the University of Chicago, named S. Chandrasekhar—has expressed his intuitive opinion that the age of the universe may range from 70 to 100 billion years.[5] (We are reminded of those Brahmic calculations, cited earlier. They no longer appear so exaggerated, perhaps.)

In any event, time and space out of mind confront us. Not to mention that third element, patience. Clearly, those six days of creation, setting earth and man into motion and filling up the firmament with stars (a firmament far more vast than the glorious ceiling of the Sistine Chapel, on which Michelangelo labored for much of a lifetime), had to have kept the Creator a lot busier than any literalist could hope to explain to us by pointing to the watch on his wrist or the calendar on the wall.

In summary, a Brahmic day of rest was more than merited.

Moving from science back to Cayce (or, as we might term it, from physical science to psychic science), we find the language changing, as well as the basic outlook. But despite the obvious gap between Cayce's spiritual perspective and the opposite orientation of the scientist, as well as a disparity of half a century or more between Cayce's psychic revelations and the latest scientific theorems, we can detect at times a surprising thread of similarity running between the two. It suggests to us that the two may be moving on parallel tracks toward some point of eventual convergence, much like Einstein's theoretical lines in space.

Precisely so, in fact.

Recalling what Cayce once said, foreshadowed events point to the inevitability of such a convergence between the worlds of spirit and matter as technological advances carry the ceaselessly probing scientist into ever more rarefied realms of research. Everything in the material universe, as Cayce put it, is patterned after that in the spiritual, though in a deflected form, much like a shadow manifestation.[6] And inasmuch as natural laws have their origin and higher counterpart in spiritual laws, the discovery of the lower law draws one simultaneously nearer to an intuitive grasp of the higher, from which it was derived. Once having attained that level of spiritual understanding of the laws of the universe, man is well on his way to becoming the master of the cosmos–and of himself. There are risks, however, in acquiring too much knowledge with too little understanding, as the Atlanteans were to learn to their undoing. . . (We shall observe their catastrophic fall in a future chapter.)

Meanwhile, as to that thread of similarity we were talking about, let's look at some examples.

The first concerns the Big Bang theory of creation. If a proper "bang" it was, we may be sure its most notable aspect was a vast central vibration—that essence of both sound and light—which was sent traveling spontaneously outward in every direction through the newborn fields of timespace, and has never stopped. On this, science fully agrees, of course. It continues to track the waves of primeval sound and light throughout our expanding universe. Well, then: What said Cayce, long before talk of a big, vibrating bang had sent out shock waves into the world of modern science? His psychic vision of our universal origins differed but little. But that little was a lot, spiritually speaking. All comes, he said, from One Central Vibration—the Word, the Light—taking different form in its continuously unfolding manifestation throughout the universe.[7]

In amplification, he went on to state that all vibrations are part and parcel of the Universal Consciousness; that all force in nature, all matter, has its existence as a form of vibration, which is life itself. This includes the body-physical of man. Describing electricity and vibration as one and the same energy, Cayce defined vibration as the movement or activity of a positive and a negative force, creating the electric patterns of life found in the smallest atomic particle—thus, even in something as seemingly "lifeless" as a stone. All vibration, he concluded on a profoundly metaphysical note to which science should lend a listening ear, must eventually, as it energizes into whatever material form it takes, pass through a stage of evolution and out.[8] It is as true of a budding leaf in springtime, destined to follow its seasonal cycle of self-fulfillment, as it is of a man or a decaying star. But the evolution of matter, in the case of man, is subject to mind, as the "builder," and to the soul. For it is the *soul* of man that distinguishes him from all the rest of creation. The soul is the God-seed in man, and is that which survives him, reincarnating again and again in its gradual growth toward the Oneness . . .

Meanwhile, those particle physicists who are today engaged in a metaphysical waltz with the atom might gain much important insight from the following thread of similarity with their own research. Each and every atom in the universe, said Cayce, has its relative relation with every other atom.[9] Again, he was speaking of the Oneness of all Force, but this time applied, interestingly enough, at the microcosmic level of the atomic particle, thereby demonstrating the pervasive oneness of the least, as well as the greatest, in the divine scheme of things. And therein, if you please, lies the nucleus of a startlingly simple "unified field theory," such as Einstein was seeking, though it might radically alter the future course of science. Cayce also spoke of the *mind* of the atom—a statement that closely parallels the latest scientific theorems. Along this same line, he once defined all physical healing as a process of attuning each atom of the body to an awareness of the Divine within—a reference to that resident soul-entity, which sets man apart from, and above, all other evolving life-forms in the universe.[10]

The consciousness of the individual atom, like the larger Universal Consciousness, has long been an accepted reality in esoteric circles. Predictably, it will soon become a well-established premise in particle physics and related scientific disciplines. It is an observable fact that the atom is a universe in itself, complete with its own orderly system of rotating satellites around its nucleus, as if under the harmonious direction of some form of interior intelligence and law, which, in turn, may be presumed to replicate and carry out the higher law and intelligence of the Universal Consciousness itself.

In summary, if the six days of creation had produced nothing more than a single atom, they would have achieved a miracle. Except that I reject the so-called miraculous or supernatural. It is my notion, based on the Cayce philosophy, that what we perceive to be supernatural is only the natural, not yet understood. But there is the divinely natural, and there is the earthily natural. The one relates to the finite forces, the other to the forces of Infinity.

5

THE SEVENTH DAY

On the seventh day, God rested.

Yet it was not so much a rest, perhaps, as it was a transition. The Creative Forces are never wholly at rest: both Cayce and our telescopes tell us that newborn stars without number are still springing up like buttercups in the far-off, misty meadows of outer space.

In interpreting that passage from Genesis, Edgar Cayce saw it as an allegorical depiction of the very first act of grace—a blessing from the Creator, as it were, upon His own handiwork. Specifically, he described the so-called "rest" as a contemplative phase, in which Mind the Maker paused to let His purpose flow through everything He had set into motion, *so that it might be perfected in itself.*[1]

A self-perfecting universe, including man. Let that be our premise. Evolution with a spiritual impetus, rather than a material one. Darwin undone by the prior action of the Logos. Divine fiat replacing blind chance. And suddenly a need, it seems, to rethink the accepted theory of natural selection, along with genetic theory, in evolutionary terms of a very different order than poor Darwin ever dreamt of . . .

Evolution, it has been rightly said, does not create anything, it only reveals it. Its origins lie outside of matter, in the Mind of the Creator. The evolution of all ideas took place in God-consciousness first, before materializing. Evolution in the physical universe got its visible start when Spirit first pushed itself into matter, in coordination with the creative, energizing forces of Mind, becoming what we see in this three-dimensional world of ours as the kingdoms of the earth: the mineral, the vegetable, and the animal, in their various stages of expression.[2] Each of these three lower kingdoms, in turn, preceded man (the lord of creation) in their arrival here. And each was, and is, imbued with the spirit-force—but not the soul. The soul-force was reserved for man alone.[3]

Within each of the three kingdoms, we find what Cayce termed a "group mind," or collective intelligence. The group mind becomes individualized in varying degrees, most notably among the more advanced species in the animal kingdom, but does not extend beyond the conscious and the primal unconscious mind-forms. (Once, when specifically asked if animals have that unlimited mental "storage area" we know as the subconscious, Cayce responded with a firm, unequivocal "no.") It is only man, it seems, who has been gifted by the Maker with the three-tiered intelligence embodied in the subconscious, conscious, and superconscious forces.[4]

At the same time, it is the destiny of *all* creation, our psychic source informs us, to reach a condition of universal Oneness with the Creator, continually growing, growing, toward that common ideal.[5] Man observes the cycle of change everywhere about him, and he terms it evolution. And so it is, in essence. Yet sometimes there may be *de*volution, as well. For the process of change appears on occasion to be a curiously fluctuating one, which would tend to belie the heavenly purpose at its root. But this is only because separating forces and disruptive influences are continually at work, here in the earth plane, through the contention of those opposing powers of light and darkness, good and evil, life and death, which were set into motion in the beginning of timespace.

Spirit, entering into what we know as the visible world of matter, represents a quite different condition or phase from its original activity in the spiritual universe. There, all form and substance remain purely spiritual, or positive. Matter, antipodal to Spirit, has no claim to, or place in, Infinity; but, paradoxically, having evolved as an idea or concept in the Mind of the Creator, matter requires the activity of Spirit to give it expression. Its existence as a finite and negative force can only be made real, or "realized," as it is given its own state and condition of being, external to the God-consciousness. Thus, the need for matter, as a thought-conception, to be "materialized," whereby it becomes a ground for the indwelling mind-force to be made aware of its separation from God. Materialization takes place through polarization of the finite-negative energy with the mutually repelling and attracting energy found in the positive-infinite force of Spirit. In short, as the Infinite moves upon the finite, in the invisible realms, the act of interpenetration of the negative force by its positive opposite creates an atomic or cellular reaction. This activity, in turn, draws about itself a nucleus that enables matter to emerge in a visible state, taking whatever externalized form and nature is desired by the controlling mind-force that has called it forth—whether that of the Son and Maker, as in the beginning, or of the other sons and co-creators later on . . .[6]

For, truly, as the Edgar Cayce readings repeatedly admonish us, *thoughts are things*. And they do indeed externalize themselves, in time, for weal or woe. Thus man, as a collective organism, continues to mold and influence the evolution of the planet and himself, albeit unconsciously at present, and remains a co-creator unawares . . .

That seventh day must have been approaching nightfall when the Creator finally arose from His contemplative rest. An afterthought seems to have occurred to Him. Judging by the length of a Brahmic day, which has been set at some four-and-a-half billion years—just about equal to the presently estimated age of planet Earth, by an interesting coincidence—only mere minutes of daylight remained, relatively speaking (measurable in Brahmic time as only some millions of years, perhaps less). Reaching hurriedly down to earth, the Maker scooped up a handful of dust and made that second man, mentioned in Chapter Two of Genesis. Then He set the man-creature back down on earth, among the rocks and vegetation and animal-life that had preceded him, in a garden called Eden, with a few last-second instructions on how to behave himself.

It was all a rather impromptu affair, it seems. Almost as if the lower universe of matter had not been planned, initially, as a place of tenancy for any creature endowed with a living soul, such as God had breathed into the earth-man of Eden just before abandoning him to his own resources.

That mist, you know. It arose so unexpectedly. What did it mean?

We have it on the authority of the opening chapter of Genesis that a perfect man, in God's image and likeness, had already been created. What need for another?

No need at all, in fact.

In fact, we learn that they are one and the same entity, in differing states of consciousness. A higher consciousness, and a lower one. A state of original grace and blessedness, and a subsequent state of separation, temptation, and, with the fall that seemed bound to ensue, *dis*-grace.

If we pierce the veil of symbolism, we discover that the Genesis story of creation, first told in Chapter One and then repeated in a strangely altered version in Chapter Two, is a classic presentation of the inverse worlds of Spirit and matter—the one deemed real and permanent, the other illusory and transitory. We find the theme echoed again and again in the myths and legends of every land, epoch, and culture, from the Aztecs to the Eskimos, the Hindus to the ancient Greeks. Fanciful myths at times, maybe. Broadly embellished legends, some of them, without a doubt. But taken together, they all add up to something that can't be dismissed with a shrug: the inherited wisdom of the race, whose ancient origins are programmed in our genes.

But back to Genesis now, as interpreted through our psychic source.

As the evolving earth became a dwelling-place for matter, Cayce tells us, then matter first began its ascent in the various forms and stages of physical evolution—*in the Mind of God*.[7] And therein lies the explanation for the original material creation, as recounted in that opening version presented in Chapter One of Genesis. It had its initial existence in the Mind of the Maker, and was a flawless conception, with its crowning achievement the Archetypal Man, or androgynous "Upper Adam" (created "male and female," says Genesis 1:27), an image of the Maker Himself.

What went wrong, we must ask, to cause the perfect mental concept to turn out so differently in its actual materialization, as is presumably represented in that second account of man's earthly creation from a fistful of clay?

Well, to reach a plausible explanation, we must remember that evolution in the earth plane had been ongoing for a while, before the advent of Adam. (He may already have existed as a perfect mental concept in the Mind of the Maker, but we are thinking of a time that preceded his physical appearance.)

There is the evolution of the soul, our source tells us, and evolution of the mind; but there is *no* evolution of matter, except through mind itself, which is the builder.[8] This leads us to a bit of speculation concerning the activity of free will and choice, among the sons of God, who were Adam's predecessors. And this includes that first-begotten Son, Mind the Maker Himself, who was destined to take on flesh, as Adam . . .

Come then. Let us see.

We are at Chapter Two of Genesis. After the Lord has given His blessing to the finished creation, and sent His purpose flowing through it all, something untoward happens. Enter, the rolling mists of material consciousness. What is meant by this inimical intrusion? But perhaps we have forgotten that the creation of a material world, a material universe, gives the ruling Prince of Darkness equal play with the forces of Light in this lower domain . . .

Anyhow, from the akashic records our psychic source has picked up an incident unrecorded in Genesis. It probably explains that mysterious mist and much of what may have happened to corrupt the so-called "paradise" of Eden some while before it was turned over to the hapless Adam's custodial care.

It is rather late in the Brahmic seventh day—though not yet time for Adam's arrival—and earth has long been settled in its orbit. Already it is evolving the material manifestations of life, up through the Mesozoic era, and on into the Tertiary period of our own Cenozoic era—geological terms that may mean little enough to the layman, but which imply a time only some millions of years distant from the present, as compared with earth's 4.6 billion-year-old history.

Suddenly there arrives a fateful moment.

The Son, the Maker, decides upon an experimental entry into

this unfolding lower world of His own making, first projecting in—

But wait. We are pushing ahead too fast, I fear. What transpired, not only in that initial entry but in two successive ones preceding Adam's arrival in the flesh a bit tardily on the seventh day, must be reserved for the several chapters that follow.

Suffice it to say that it all countermanded the Will of the Father.[9]

If only that mist had not arisen . . .

DESCENT OF THE GODS

In the upper firmament could be heard the faint, melodious humming of the spheres, each heavenly note in perfect harmony with that of its nearest neighbor throughout the whole of the ever-expanding canopy of newborn stars.

Over the rolling waters of the lower firmament, where giant seabirds rode on the oceanic winds with outstretched wings and hungry, searching beaks, there now came the curious rumble of newborn continents in formation on planet Earth. Pangea, the single landmass that had originally formed at dawn, had long since broken up into drifting segments, even as the dinosaurs had come and gone in the scorching heat of mid-afternoon, allowing the better-adjusted mammals to emerge in their place.

Earth, on this seventh day, was now well along in its present Phanerozoic eon, which had begun some half a billion years previously with the Cambrian period of primeval rock formation, and was already approaching the much more advanced Miocene cycle of its evolution, some 24 million years B.P. (Before Present).

As all of this was happening, the gods of the universe rejoiced.

Co-laborers and co-creators with the Maker, these Mind-born sons were watching from afar as the heavenly purpose continued to pour through all of the multifarious forms of unfolding creation, in the deepening afternoon of that seventh day. Meanwhile, angelic forces were hovering everywhere, in eager attendance.

In the beginning, as Spirit had first pushed Itself into matter, the sons had seen rolling mists of hydrogen gas emerge out of nowhere and suddenly coalesce into a single, exploding mass of incandescent atoms. It was just as Mind the Maker—the Word— had willed it. Thus, they had witnessed the primeval universe of matter take shape before their very eyes—the myriad observers, and the singular observed.

(Hydrogen, as the principal element of the universe, undoubtedly accounts for a comment by the sleeping Cayce to the effect that water is the mother of all material creation, forming some three-fourths or more of the total contents of the human body, of planet Earth, and of the oceans of astral matter comprising the body of the universe as a whole.[1])

The role of the sons, we may assume, had been to help along the evolutionary process with various thought-form projections of their own, all in conformity with the Maker's blueprint, as it were, and holding to the universal laws He had set into motion. Everything, at first, was patterned after the spiritual, as we have already noted, but in a deflected form, as befitted its material counterpart. Only in one respect did the Maker reserve unto Himself a totally exclusive role: it concerned the decision whether or not to people the worlds of the lower firmament with a higher being, as lord and ruler over the lower kingdoms of matter, and embodying soul and spirit in a house of flesh that would be governed by the Mind-force—subject to free will and choice, of course, in the conduct of its rulership.

"Such a being would be a god, like ourselves," said the sons to one another, wondering what the outcome might be in such a case. "Why should not some among our own be appointed the rulers?" And even as they reasoned thus together, the Maker was reasoning within Himself.

Looking down on planet Earth, as only one of a myriad of

worlds in the unfolding universe of matter, He saw an immensely beautiful object: a shimmering blue and white bauble spinning in space, as it caught the full reflected glory of the light on its sunward side; but on its hidden side, He knew it moved in darkness. And it was the dark side, of course, that worried Him. There, where the Tempter would be lurking about, in the night-side forces . . .

Free will and choice. God's gift to His only-begotten Son; and a mixed blessing, as it was meant to be, providing Him with a set of options—companionship with the Father, or a separate godhood. (For it was a loving Father's wish not to bind His Son with the same bond of obedience He might require of a servant.)

Similarly, the Son had bestowed the same gift upon the other sons—those divine cells, as it were, drawn from within His own spiritual body, who thereby became sons of God in their own right. Co-heirs and co-equals, yet given full freedom to abrogate their divine heritage at any time, if they so chose, through the free-will movement outward, and into a separate godhood within self.

And yet, it was to contain and counteract the similar sin of the fallen Lucifer and his outcast minions, of course, that the Maker had created the material universe, with its contending dualities. Only through exposure to the conflicting pairs of opposites (those mutually repelling forces, such as light and darkness, good and evil, spirit and matter), as well as those opposites that mutually attract one another, seeking a harmonizing equilibrium in unity (as represented by yin and yang, in the separated sexual forces), could a fallen god, like a fallen angel, be made aware of its separation from the Oneness and the Light.

Now, in truth, the earth, like the other worlds still appearing throughout the manifest universe, was not necessarily intended as a place of tenancy for the soul.[2] The eventual creation of an earthly soul-vehicle (represented by the "man" of Genesis) would be dependent upon the need to meet a situation that had not yet arisen among the unfallen sons of God. But in His wisdom, Mind the Maker had nevertheless conceived an as-yet-unmanifest prototype in His own image. This ideal soul-man could be projected, should that need arise before the seventh day ended, as lord over the physical creation. The stewardship of the universe would become his responsibility, guiding matter through its full evolutionary cycle, as well as shepherding any strayed or fallen souls back to their unfallen celestial estate, if they so willed, in accord with the Maker's purpose. Meanwhile, the Maker waited. Some private reservations, perhaps. Yet many millions of years still remained to that seventh day. What the Maker did not then have reason to foresee, of course, was that He Himself would eventually have to fulfill that earthly role, as the archetypal man projected in the flesh . . .

There is no law, said Cayce, causing any soul to separate itself from the Godhead.[3] Moreover, there are those spirit-entities (one does not actually become a soul-entity, we learn, until physically entering the universe of matter) that have never participated in physical consciousness at all, but have remained ever at One with the First Cause.[4]

What, then, was to induce the Maker Himself, at about this time, to slip momentarily and go astray? Satan, no doubt, had set a cunning trap for Him; and He fell right into it...

Listening to the Mind-born sons, as they contended among themselves as to the proper stewardship of the lower firmament, an interim plan occurred to the Maker. It involved an experiment that would not altogether violate the Will of the Father, for it would not imply full separation from the Source, but would mean only a partial descent into the realms of matter.

As spirit-entities in astral form, He and any of the sons who chose to accompany Him would descend into the ether surrounding planet Earth and become firsthand observers of the evolving thought-forms they had jointly willed into materialization. Not as active participants or rulers would they go on this occasion, but as observers only. It would be primarily a "learning" experience, educating them in the ways of material laws at work in the evolution of a material universe, as they moved unseen in the air or on the billowing waves or spirited themselves in the rocks and vegetation.

It was in this manner, then, that the first root race came into being. All quite innocently enough, the gradual descent and fall of the gods had begun.

How, one might reasonably ask, could the sons of God have descended into matter, that first time around, without actual self-materialization? The explanation was given by Edgar Cayce once, indirectly, when he explained that the body-celestial of the cosmic spirit-entity has those matching attributes of the physical, but with the cosmic added, wherein hearing, seeing, and understanding become as one.[5]

In yet another of his psychic readings, which has some relevance here, we find our psychic guide referring to the stages of evolution as sometimes ascending or descending in the form of an arc.[6] That metaphor is matched in the theosophical writings of H. P. Blavatsky, who tells us that on the descending arc of evolution it is the spiritual which transforms itself into the material; whereas, on the ascending arc, it is of course the material that goes through the transformation process, gradually reasserting its spiritual selfhood. "All things had their origin in spirit," she writes, "evolution having originally begun from above and proceeded downward, instead of the reverse, as taught in the Darwinian theory."[7]

She did not mean to reject evolution as a valid theory, but only to set it running upon a quite different track. "If we accept Darwin's theory of the development of species," she concludes, "we find that his starting point is placed in front of an open door."

It is the door at which material science can find no answers. Matter, left to itself, has no traceable point of origin.

But what, we must ask ourselves, is the "game plan" of Spirit? Why the descending and ascending arc of the evolutionary pattern? Meister Eckhart has given us this golden key with which to unlock a deep mystery: "God is Intelligence," the medieval mystic tells us, "occupied with knowing Itself."[8]

What better explains man's evolutionary relationship to the Godhead than that?

We find Eckhart's illuminating words echoed in the Edgar Cayce readings, which tell us that we are gods in the making. Or, as once stated: "We are God, not yet come into our heritage."[9]

Precisely. That sums it up. All of the mystery and meaning of creation and evolution are made plain in those few simple words of spiritual revelation. Creator and creation are One, engaged in an ongoing process of Self-realization.

And so, perhaps, that initial descent of the gods, in search of experience, was not such an altogether bad thing . . . ?

In fact, our psychic source strongly suggests the illusory nature of evil. Only the good lives on, we are assured; whereas bad is only good gone wrong, or a temporary turning away from God.[10] Evil, Cayce once said, only has its appearance "in the mind, in the shadows, in the fears" of those who do not yet know the light in its entirety, or who have not yet experienced the awakening of the higher self.[11]

But what does all of this philosophizing do to the Devil? Why, it would appear to banish him once again—but this time by making of him an unreality, so to speak.

Such a metaphysical view of Satan may seem solid enough, by the time we have reached the end of our evolutionary journey together. At present, however, as we are about to rejoin the falling gods in the next chapter, on their further descent into the realms of matter, we shall find that Satan works his mischief still.

As for those luckless gods, a reminder: they are none other than ourselves, as we then were.

LAND OF THE LEMURS

In their initial descent to terra firma, where did the sons of God probably alight? And approximately when?

Where would be anywhere. Their phantomlike astral bodies knew no material restrictions. They could thrive equally well in any ecosystem, whether it be in the air, under the water, or on land. As invisible as any spirits, their presence could be sensed but not seen; and so they had no enemies to fear—unless they were the lurking spirits of the darkness. However, if we were to venture a guess as to the preferred location of their landing party, we would select the now-extinct continent of Lemuria as the major freefall zone of that first root race. As to why, one had only to look around at the virginal beauty of the place: an early forerunner of Atlantis and Eden, its luxuriant vegetation and multifarious life-forms in a setting of verdant, rolling hills and meandering streams of purest water made it a veritable replica of the upper paradise.

Now, as to when.

A bit problematical, that. The akashic records are somewhat hazy on the subject. But in general terms, we can place that original descent within the latter half of the Tertiary period, probably about midway in the Miocene cycle. In other words, some ten or twelve million years ago. A valid reason exists for picking that approximate point in prehistoric time. It will become evident as we proceed.

In the middle of the 19th century, when bioevolutionists were eagerly looking at their rigidly fixed maps for possible land-bridges of a bygone era that might confirm Darwinian theory on the migration of species in early times from one continent to another to explain the carryover of evolutionary traits, scientists in certain quarters became somewhat overbold in speculating on the former existence of now-vanished continents, such as Plato's legendary Atlantis, or a similar sunken landmass in the Pacific or Indian Ocean. Not that they supported the theosophists or other promoters of psychic and legendary lore in this regard, of course. That would have been most "unscientific." But from their own rational perspective, such hypothetical crossing-points were a justifiable invention to validate their proliferation of unfounded hypotheses.

One of those happy map-hunters was a zoologist named P. L. Sclater. He had observed the lemurs of Madagascar, and he began wondering aloud how this unique species of mammal ever got locked into such an isolated island habitat, out in the Indian Ocean. The primitive lemur, a nocturnal little creature with distinctly monkeylike characteristics, belonged at the bottom rung of the primate ladder. Yet it was already being seriously viewed as a possible prosimian forerunner of the genus *Homo sapiens.* Now, it so happened that a long-sunken continent of vast latitudinal dimensions (depending upon one's view of it), stretching across the South Pacific from the Americas to the Indian Ocean, had already been envisioned by some. Others, such as the German naturalist, Ernst Heinrich Haeckel, and a fellow naturalist, Alfred Russel Wallace, both of whom were to climb aboard the Lemurian ark later on with separate hypotheses, placed the lost continent in the confines of the Indian Ocean. But whatever its location, it took Sclater to give the lost land a sense of reality by inventing a name for it: Lemuria.

Later, in the early 20th century, when it ultimately came to light that the lemur was not, after all, unique to Madagascar, the Lemurian hypothesis, which had already mushroomed to encompass other mystery-shrouded species as well, suddenly became an embarrassing hot potato that no scientist wished to touch. And so it has remained ever since. But let us go willingly where science fears to tread. And we may thank one of its forgotten own, P. L. Sclater, for corroborating psychic fact with that name he thought he had invented—Lemuria.

Yes, a curious synchronicity there. Perhaps the good Sclater was psychic without ever knowing it? or perhaps he had tapped, if only for a magical instant, into the universal mindstream of the collective unconscious? Anyhow, although the geographical dimensions of his hypothetical "Lemuria" did not altogether jibe with the psychic version, the *name* did. Edgar Cayce, in trance state, was to refer alternately to the sunken Pacific continent as both "Lemuria" and "Mu," with the latter designation also identified with its leader at one period. In its latter days, however, when Mu's son Muzuen ruled, most of the original continent had already vanished into the sea, well ahead of the final demise of Atlantis. What remained, apparently, was a remnant population at its western extremity, then called the Gobi land, which actually extended from what is now Indo-China, northward to the Gobi Desert (then a fertile land), as well as detached colonies of Mu descendants on the opposite side of the ocean, in the Andean cordilleras and—surprisingly—in the now-inland plateau region of the American Southwest, both areas apparently representing Lemuria's easternmost extremities in former times. However, as Cayce explained it, the poles were then reversed, so that north and south were turned about in respect to their magnetic roles, thus altering the compass orientation of east and west, as well.[1] But if the compass changed, the earth's spin axis did not; and the Sun continued to follow its familiar course.

Modern science not only confirms such periodic flip-flops in earth's geomagnetic polarization at rare intervals, but lesser and more frequent polar shifts in between, which may relate to crustal displacements, as will be discussed in a future chapter. Additionally, current knowledge of plate tectonics, which traces the formation and movement of continents and the gradual spreading of the ocean floors through thermal activity along the mid-ocean ridges, suggests that the Pacific Ocean of an earlier age was in all likelihood less wide and of a rather different configuration than it is today. Lemuria, in that event, would have been a continent of somewhat more modest proportions than 19th-century visionaries imagined it.

Finally, we come back to that name: Lemuria. Or Mu. (Mu, incidentally, was the revealed name of the lost continent in the early 20th-century writings on the subject by the somewhat eccentric Col. James Churchward.[2]) We are indebted to W. Scott-Elliot, a turn-of-the-century occultist of the theosophical school, and author of *The Lost Lemuria*,[3] who reminds us that there is a second meaning to the word *lemur* (or *lemures*, in the plural), and it is a meaning which strikes me as being more applicable to the lost continent than those little nocturnal mammals still inhabiting the island of Madagascar, in the far-off Indian Ocean. Specifically, lemures are said to be the "spirits of the dead." The ghosts of those early gods, perhaps? Wandering phantoms from that first, experimental descent to earth in astral form? But, no. Led by the Maker, they came as observing spirit-entities, and they left as such. More likely, then, the "lemures" in that place were the trapped ghosts of their immediate successors there, whom we shall meet shortly . . .

Meanwhile, we note another odd piece of synchronistic data: in both the Chinese and Japanese languages, the character *mu* denotes a "void," or "nothingness." But dismiss it, if you wish. I don't want to be accused of carrying the oddness of things too far.

Not yet, it seems, can we close the records on Lemuria.

Once more the gods descended to earth, in an early return. This time, however, those who chose to enter exchanged the spirit-bodies of their former astral projection for denser etheric forms that would enable them to draw closer, through a lowered vibratory rate, to the physical life-forms all about them. And they came again to Lemuria, of course.

This was the second root race, containing many returning from the first. No longer content to be mere observers, this time they sought a more active role. They would become direct participants, experiencing firsthand the nature of matter. In short, they would set themselves up as the rulers over the lower kingdoms that had preceded them here in this curious world, subordinate to Spirit. After all, were they not the sons of God? They would therefore exercise their divine heritage on earth.

However, they were not joined this time by the first Son. He had withdrawn Himself into the sanctity of the Spirit. There He waited and watched from afar—and presumably wondered to Himself, with certain misgivings, just what the outcome might be, now that He had initiated this chain of unforeseen events. (His own next return, made necessary through the transgressions of the Mind-born sons in the earth, would not take place until the third cycle, with the emergence of the mighty Atlantean root race.)

Unlike the lost continent of Atlantis, portions of which are expected to rise again, and may already be surfacing in the vicinity of the Bahamas, Lemuria is apparently gone forever, except for its faint, shimmering image limned upon the skein of time and space, in the akashic chambers.

It is just as well, perhaps.

The Lemurians, of whom Edgar Cayce said but little, apparently left behind them a dark trail of abuse and bestiality in their rapid and undisciplined descent into matter. As a result, it is no cause for wonder that the adopted "home" of those fallen gods, along with the ill-conceived civilization they built upon it over a stretch of many millennia, was consigned to eventual destruction and oblivion, even as the more favored Atlantis was just beginning to be inhabited by the somewhat wiser gods of the third root race—to be led, later on, by the first Son Himself.

In its earlier phases, it seems probable that the Lemurian culture may have shown some promise of a happier evolution, long before its downward-gravitating cycle had gained momentum. This sense of early promise is revealed in an unusual reading Edgar Cayce gave for a very old soul who, prior to her subsequent appearance in Atlantis during its opening epoch, had apparently been one of the early members of that etheric second race, the Lemurians. In adapting themselves to their material environment, social instincts quickly developed. Clans were formed. Though living in trees and caves at first, like the birds and beasts, they had soon evolved bodily forms not too unlike our own. And like the later Atlanteans, they were endowed with a third, or psychic, eye. Meant as a point of contact with their celestial origins, its usefulness soon ended. But back to the entity in question: she was told that her artistic drawings on the wall of a cave in what is now the ancient and arid plateau region of the American Southwest might still be seen—though the markings were some ten million years old![4]

That reference gives us a tentative dating for the original Lemurian culture, predating the much later Gobi rule under Mu, in an offshoot culture paralleling the Atlantean epoch. Its significance, for that reason, is hard to ignore. And it poses questions we cannot presently answer concerning the pace of evolution in Lemuria's early stages, prior to its subsequent phase of devolution and degeneration as the sharp curve of the descending arc began its rapid downward slide.

Meanwhile, the fact that more favorably evolving pockets of the Lemurian culture, situated at the eastern and western extremities of the doomed continent, were spared the final cataclysm, suggests gradations that may have existed in the rate and level of descent. Presumably not all of the devolving gods had completely abandoned or forgotten their higher origins. As for the survival of that high plateau country in what is now a portion of Nevada, Utah, and Arizona,[5] it may represent a sheared-off portion of the Lemurian continental shelf that overrode a sub-ducting oceanic plate of basalt, which set it down in its present inland location astride the newly rising American continent, as Lemuria sank. At any rate, geologists have noted the great antiquity of those ancient rock formations in the American Southwest, with the Grand Canyon said to be some 1.7 billion years old, whereas the bulk of our continent is considerably younger.

Judging by the theosophical writings on the subject of Lemuria's devolving curve, most of its etheric occupants descended through fairly precipitous stages into bestiality, in time reaching the same level as the beasts themselves. Material entrapment began with the projection of monstrous thought-forms for their sport and pleasure, strange admixtures and genetic variations modeled on the existing animal and plant life already on the continent when the gods first arrived. The contaminating effects of their activities soon disrupted the evolutionary process in other parts of the planet and had to be stopped. The once-lovely Lemuria was turning into a nightmarish place, infected by the rapidly multiplying sins of its disgracefully fallen occupants. (Those rolling mists, again . . . !)

They had to go. They went.

Churchward, in his highly romanticized version of that lost civilization of Mu, or Lemuria, lets his "evidence" rest primarily upon debatable artifacts in other lands, such as the Maya temples of Yucatan, which he unhesitatingly attributes to the wisdom and workmanship of wandering Mu colonists—those survivors, presumably, of the volcanic holocaust and subsequent sinking of the mother continent. Among other dubiously assigned relics, he leaves us with the mysterious stone statues of an ancient race of giants on Easter Island, first found in 1722 by a Dutch trading vessel, as a telltale remnant of Mu's vanished culture. His attribution is highly doubtful, based on more current archaeological evidence. All the same, those grotesque monoliths, staring vacantly out of a murky, prehistoric past, may at least impart to us some faint cognition of what misdirected creative energies can breed. They are ghostly reminders of greatness gone awry . . .

Strange gods, in abundance. They are gone now. But they have left their mark in many places, more often than not as a warning against repeating their mistakes.

Before we can close this chapter and set sail together on the next leg of our evolutionary journey, which will carry us out past the Pillars of Hercules to the long-lost Atlantis, we must address a nagging conundrum.

Upon comparing the theosophical literature on the progression of the root races with Cayce's cataloguing of events, we find that similarities and differences, alike, confront us. Let us concentrate on the former, while acknowledging that the latter may reflect little more than a matter of interpretation.

I will be brief about it. I shall not get too technical. Generalities will suffice, for the most part.

In the Eastern-oriented view of the theosophists, as we have already noted in earlier chapters, old East Indian (and Tibetan) texts are the major source of information. On the other hand, we find the psychic readings of Edgar Cayce drawing upon more universal sources than the traditional written wisdom of either East or West. It is not an approach that attempts to invalidate the latter, of course, but rather to simplify and clarify the esoteric record in most cases by cutting through the elaborate symbolism that springs up around much occult literature, as well as surrounding a great deal of the Christian dogma relating to our origins.

In full agreement with the esoteric school, Cayce's psychic readings confirm the existence of seven stages of development,[6] as our evolutionary journey takes us from heaven to earth, and home again, along the cyclical pathway of the seven root races. Of the latter, the first two have already been accounted for—namely, the astral and the etheric, or Lemurian, root races, on the descending evolutionary arc. (Each of these root races, like the remaining five, involves a series of subraces, as well. Let us acknowledge their relevance, perhaps, to the archaeological record, but not to this narrative. We may therefore skip over them, as our psychic mentor did, before us.)

In the theosophical interpretation, the first, or astral, root race entered a place called the "Imperishable Sacred Land," regarded as the first continent. Conceivably, this might have been what modern science now refers to as the primordial landmass, Pangea. And conceivably not, of course. The esoteric wording suggests a far more ethereal landscape than even Pangea might have supported. For our part, as noted, we have placed that astral race, like its etheric successor, in the virginal Lemurian terrain, with its rapidly evolving life-forms—unlike the more ancient and primitive Pangea. (And while our placement is not specifically confirmed anywhere in the Cayce readings, no alternate location is anywhere suggested either. So Lemuria looms as the most obvious choice; it is the only continent Cayce mentions as an antecedent to Atlantis.)

Returning to the theosophical record, we find that the second, or etheric, root race descends only to what is termed the second, or Hyperborean, continent; it is not until the third round that Lemuria is reached, by their reckoning. So, based on those same calculations, the Atlanteans become the fourth root race. And this is where the theosophists end up one number ahead of the Cayce ledger in tabulating the transition of the root races up to the present.

Specifically, the Cayce readings follow up the Lemurian race with the Atlantean, which becomes the third root race. Adamic man follows as the fourth (our present root race, now ending), with the fifth about to emerge as we move over the cusp of the incoming Aquarian Age.[7]

The theosophical position, on the other hand, contends that the incoming new race will be the sixth—the returning etheric, on the ascending arc of our evolutionary development—to be followed by the astral, or seventh, in the final cyclical phase of our homeward journey. A bit precipitous, that chronology. An etheric age does not yet seem quite ready to overtake us. But we need to remember that this Aquarian Age placement for the sixth root race was made back in the 19th century, without benefit of our more sobering 20th-century perspective. In any case, we share with the theosophical tradition an acceptance of a cyclical pattern of events, through seven planes or stages, as the evolutionary arc first descends, then reascends.

Agreement also exists that Atlantis marked an evolutionary transition point, as the close of that root race resulted in the emergence of our own. For it was not until Adam's advent, as well as his subsequent stumble, that the fallen race of gods could reverse its downward course at last, and begin its painful rise and long ascent as the race of man ...

8

BEYOND THE GATES OF HERCULES

Plus ultra. More beyond.

Those two words, plucked by a curious twist of events from an old legend, became the inspiring motto of the early pioneers of science several centuries ago, led by the intrepid Francis Bacon, who had a philospher's instinct for the right phrase.

The phrase conveys a worthy sentiment: To the bold and venturesome, more always lies beyond the existing limits. As seekers after new horizons ourselves, let us approve and applaud such a mind-stretching view. But it is the underlying legend, more than the motto derived from it, that merits keener attention. In fact, by a stroke of sheer serendipity, it leads us to yet another and more ancient legend, which we may take to be true, whereas the first may be purely fanciful.

The first tale is told concerning the twin pillars of Hercules. Supposedly flanking the Strait of Gibraltar, where the familiar waters of the Mediterranean Sea give way to the limitless depth and breadth of the vast Atlantic, it is said that the pillars carried the hero-god's warning inscription: *Ne Plus Ultra*—"No More Beyond." Ever bold and fearless himself, such a surprisingly timorous message makes it sound very much as if Hercules might have known some dark and terrible secret about that larger sea... If so, what *was* it?

Ages later, at any rate, that same circumspect inscription was to be incorporated in the coat of arms of the ruling house of Spain, under a depiction of the fabled pillars. There it remained, we are told, until the time of Columbus' daring venture across the vast weed-beds of the Sargasso Sea to the mysterious continent awaiting his discovery: America. But soon thereafter, the outdated negative was deleted from the heraldic emblem, so that it henceforth read: *Plus Ultra*—"More Beyond."

So much for the first legend. On to the next.

It concerns the oft-told story of the sunken Atlantis, originally revealed to us in words of tantalizing realism by the Greek philosopher Plato, writing some twenty-four hundred years ago. It is a legend, we suspect, which may have lain behind the somewhat later one telling of Hercules' cryptic warning on those mythic pillars of his. In truth, the pillars probably never existed as such, although their counterparts were real enough—namely, the great rock of Gibraltar, on the European side of the strait, and the steep rise of Mt. Acho on the African side, in what is now Morocco. And it was presumably from these two natural battlements, if Plato's tale be true, that invading hordes of desperate Atlanteans in the closing days of their once-great empire were driven back by the warriors of Hellas to their own doomed, earthquake-ridden shores. Yet, even as their ships hove near, there were vast subterranean rumblings as the last island remnant of mighty Atlantis erupted in a terrible shudder and sank beneath the waves, creating a massive eddy of water that must have sucked up all luckless ships for many miles about, pulling them into a common grave. So great was the earthquake, in fact, that it even shook the whole of the far-off Mediterranean basin, claiming the lives of most of Hellas' brave warriors still encamped at their promontories overlooking the Gibraltar Strait.

The legendary Hercules, if he truly lived, may well have been privy to the awesome events of a single day and a night in those deep, silent waters out yonder. And needless to say, it would have provided ample justification to put up a couple of pillars with an implicit message to all future ships about to exit through the Mediterranean's portals: "No more land beyond these gates. Take heed, lest ye perish too!"

As for the much later Columbus, had he but known it, he sailed right over one continent to reach another. That eerie Sargasso Sea, recognizable by its vast expanse of floating patches of tangled seaweed, is the reputed burial site of Poseidia, best-known and largest, as well as the loveliest, of the several islands that constituted the once-extensive island-continent of Atlantis in the final stages of its destruction.

Turning to the Dialogues of Plato,[1] we start with the *Timaeus* for this opening account of the lost continent of Atlantis, and find the story resumed in the *Critias*, which follows. Unfortunately, this remarkable narrative stops short of its completion, for reasons not made clear. Some have assumed that Plato may have planned to take up the unfinished tale at a later date but found his pen stilled by death.

Whatever the case, Plato's convincing version of events, as far as it goes, is substantially confirmed by the psychic record of Atlantis that can be pieced together from several hundred of Edgar Cayce's readings touching on the subject, as well as by corroborating accounts to be found in the esoteric literature of both East and West, which we shall be examining in proper turn. Additionally, scientific evidence of the former existence of a highly evolved civilization here on earth, dating back to prehistoric times, continues to mount and is impressive. We shall take a close look at some of the gathering facts.

Meanwhile, in the *Timaeus*, we find Socrates' disciple Critias being persuaded to tell those present—including Plato, of course—the strange tale of Atlantis, which came to his ears by a succession of oral transmissions, as was the tradition in those times. It had all begun with a visit to Egypt several generations back by a celebrated Athenian sage named Solon (ca. 640-559 B.C.), who learned the story from the lips of a priest at Sais. Years later, Solon was to relate the extraordinary tale to Critias' great-grandfather for safekeeping, by whom it was transmitted in turn to his son, and thus in time to Critias himself. Plato, convinced of the truth of Critias' earnest tale, thenceforth ensured its perpetuity by committing it to writing.

The original narrator had begun by explaining to Solon that many great civilizations had come and gone in ages past, of which there was no present trace because a great flood had destroyed all records, and the memories of the hard-pressed survivors had soon grown dim. This later cataclysm had apparently occurred not too long after the final destruction of Atlantis by a series of violent earthquakes, an event that took place some nine millennia before Solon's time, or what would presently be about 11,600 years ago. (Mark that date well. We shall be reverting to it more than once in the pages ahead. It is highly significant, for it falls closely in line with several related datings.)

The once-mighty Atlantean empire described by Plato in the days immediately preceding its watery demise was still a relatively large but, by then, a morally declining and a geographically weakened island-state situated out beyond the Pillars of Hercules. This points us in the direction of the Azores. Are they perhaps a mountainous Atlantean remnant, once submerged and now risen again, along with Madeira and the Canary Islands, further to the south and east? At any rate, all of these are the protruding peaks of underwater seamounts, which are most numerous along the broadly arching curve of the Mid-Atlantic Ocean Ridge. That ridge, noted for its volcanic and seismic activity, marks a spread-zone in the ocean floor; it encompasses the underwater Azores Plateau, where mysterious tower-like structures have been "sound-photographed" by a process of echo detection. Elsewhere along the ridge, the ancient remains of land-grown plants have been recovered in core samples taken from floor areas as deep as two miles below the ocean's surface.[2]

Plato, we are reminded, actually referred to latter-day Atlantis as a chain of several large islands, which one might cross from the one to the other, and thus pass westward to a vast, unnamed continent beyond the Atlantean lands. Very curious, that. And powerfully convincing, in this author's opinion. If an Egyptian priest, some 2,600 years ago, was sufficiently knowledgeable about the geography of the world beyond his own country's borders to speak of the as-yet-undiscovered Americas, why should we doubt the truth of his story of the lost Atlantis? He must have had ancient maps or manuscripts at his private disposal, or gathered his wisdom from some higher source . . .

As for that reference to an archipelago, rather than a single island-continent, we find it corroborated in Cayce's psychic description of Atlantis in its closing phase. The original continent had broken up about 52,700 Before Present, leaving a chain of five major islands until the occurrence of a second great upheaval, estimated to have taken place about 30,000 B.P. Thereafter, until the time of its final sinking—a catastrophe that actually appears to have occurred in widely separate stages, rather than a single eruption—only three major islands remained, which Cayce identified as Poseidia, Aryan, and Og. Of these, Poseidia was the first to go.[3] It presumably sank some centuries ahead of the other two. In fact, warning tremors may have begun as early as 12,600 B.P., a full millennium before the last inundation, generally placed about 11,600 B.P. At any rate, the earliest evacuations from Poseidia appear to have taken place in 12,600 B.P., and continued for several centuries thereafter, into the reign of Araaraart II, in Egypt.

We have already placed Poseidia in the vicinity of what is now the Sargasso Sea, with its westernmost extremity marked today by slowly rising land in the area of the Bahamas—most notably at Bimini atoll, where underwater archaeologists continue to map and analyze strange rock formations first seen from the air in 1968 (even as Cayce had predicted, back in 1940).[4] These are believed to be the remains of ancient roads, walls, or other manmade structures. And it is in this general area, we are told, that long-buried records of the once-flourishing Atlantean civilization, placed in a sealed pyramidal temple by priestly initiates of Poseidia as the end drew near, may be unearthed in our time.[5]

As for the islands of Aryan and Og, we might take our cue from Cayce's wording, and assign the midway position to Aryan.

This leaves Og as the easternmost isle, directly confronting the Mediterranean. It was that remnant of Atlantis known to the Athenians. Presumably it was the last to perish.

Interestingly enough, we find an isolated reference in the Cayce readings to ancient Persia as the "Aryan land," in the early post-Atlantean epoch, suggesting that colonists from the island of Atlantis bearing that name may have settled there. Similarly, the name Og appears in the readings as a designation for a portion of what is now Peru, and which had formerly been ruled by a people known as the Ohums, whom we shall encounter in a later chapter. Apparently certain Atlantean emigrants, fleeing from Og to the remote and primitive Andean cordilleras in advance of the final destruction of their homeland, carried with them not only a remnant of their superior culture but the transplanted name of their former island home. We are reminded of those New World colonists many millennia later, who sentimentally renamed former Indian territories to suit themselves, such as New York, New Amsterdam, and the like. It is the age-old habit of migratory peoples everywhere, particularly if they happen to hold the upper hand over the locals . . . as the Atlanteans usually did.

Most of the members of the Atlantean priesthood, along with others who were followers of the sacred teachings of the Law of One, chose to evacuate well ahead of the final catastrophe. It was a broad-ranging diaspora that ultimately led to the extinction of the Atlanteans as a united race, power, or world influence. Specifically mentioned among their various points of dispersal were Egypt, Morocco, the Pyrenees, the Yucatan peninsula and Peru, as well as various parts of North America not blanketed by glaciers (for this was just prior to the ending of the last Ice Age, set at approximately 11,000 years ago). With reference to the latter, the plateau region of the American Southwest is mentioned, where the newly arriving Atlanteans presumably intermingled with much earlier colonists from the long-sunken Lemuria. Also, in a secondary migration out of Yucatan later on, some hardy Atlanteans came by a long and arduous trek north-ward to that extensive area of the American Midwest marked today by the mysterious remains of the mound builders.

Yet the primary influx of Atlanteans into North America consisted of the outlawed sons and daughters of Belial, whose troublemaking ways had precipitated not only this last and final disaster, but the two preceding upheavals that had reduced Atlantis by gradual stages from its former greatness and glory, setting the stage for its ultimate ruin amid a watery grave. Unwelcome, it would seem, in those areas settled by the more peaceable sons and daughters of the Law of One in their orderly exodus, the hedonistic sons and daughters of Darkness had presumably hung on until the very end. Then, in a desperate, last-minute attempt to wrest living-space for themselves by seizing the property of others (as Plato's record suggests), they appear to have launched unprovoked attacks upon the more primitive inhabitants of what is now Europe and Asia Minor. There is no evidence, however, that these attacks, which were probably aerial in nature, ever succeeded. But if repulsed, we may specu-late that the invaders left much death and destruction behind them. This is deduced in part from the vitrified remains of ancient forts in Scotland, Ireland, Brittany, and Austria, where some-thing akin to powerful lasers once streaked across the stones with deadly aim, fusing the blocks and turning them to molten glass.[6] The Atlantean "death-ray" at work? Cayce once mentioned the existence of such an awesome weapon in their arsenal, which marks them as the likely culprits. In light of their highly ad-vanced technology, the Atlanteans could strike with impunity at any target. But in the end, it seems, the frustrated followers of Belial had but one option open to them: turning to the largely uninhabited continent to the west, those who did not go down into the sea with the sinking Atlantis now hastily took refuge in an unknown wilderness.

Did that harsh experience change their wicked ways some-what? One would like to think that it had a tempering influence upon them. In fact, we find some circumstantial evidence to that effect in the Cayce readings. First, we are told that the noble and fearless Iroquois were among the direct descendants of those last of the wayward Atlanteans. And in a "life" reading* Edgar Cayce once gave for a woman who in a prior incarnation had been Narwaua, a princess of the tribes of the peacemaking Algonquin chief Powhatan, the surprising news came to light that the arrival of the English colonists among the American Indians had marked the coming together again, for the meeting of self, of the former children of the Law of One and those rebellious children of Belial who had escaped many millennia ago to the continent they now regarded as their own.[7] If true, it reveals deep psychological insights into the ensuing rivalries that soon developed between the white settlers and their red-skinned brethren, who lost in that experience. Yet the latter, despite certain savage practices, were in many ways morally superior to the unscrupulous newcomers, who took away their lands in cunning barter or outright battle. One may view their eventual defeat, though perhaps karmically inevitable, as both sad and ironic.

A closing note to muse upon: Whereas the Atlanteans were the original red race, this racial characteristic was lost or modified in time through intermarriage with those of other races throughout the ancient world with whom the proud exiles were obliged to co-exist. Yet there was a notable exception in the case of those children of Belial who kept the racial strain largely intact as they evolved into the various tribal groupings of the American Indian. (Only in the Southwest, where browner skins and smaller, rounder heads bespeak a Lemurian infusion, are the North American Indians notably "different.")

We return again to Plato, this time picking up that portion of his story to be found in the pages of the *Critias*. Whereas the *Timaeus* tells us only of Atlantis' final days, the *Critias* relates its auspicious beginnings. It also recounts in brief its rapid development toward the ideal state under its early leaders, who were of godlike mien.

Not surprisingly, one of the first names we encounter is that

*A psychic discourse relating to an entity's past lives.

of the god Poseidon, from whom the principality of Poseidia undoubtedly derived its name. (Although Plato's relatively brief history of Atlantis does not mention Poseidia by name, it occurs with some frequency in the Cayce readings; and one esoteric source, which we shall be examining a bit further along, tells us that the citizens of Atlantis in its latter days, when Poseidia was the unquestioned seat of power, were alternately referred to as Atlans or Poseidi.) In Greek mythology, Poseidon personified the fertilizing power of water, and we find him to be synonymous with Neptune, god of the sea. It is perhaps appropriate, then, that it was the sea itself, in time, which reclaimed Atlantis as its own . . .

The descending gods of the new root race divided the earth into lots, we are told, and Poseidon fell heir to Atlantis. There he met and fell in love with the beautiful Clito, the only daughter of one of the original earthborn men of that region—descendants, presumably, of the previous root race, and thus of godly stock themselves once, though long since stripped of any memory of their divine origins through countless centuries of fleshly associations.

With the fair Clito, however, who had grown up in isolation with her parents atop a high mountain in the center of Atlantis, there may have been a harking back, as it were, to a purer, more etheric lineage, so that Poseidon was thus attracted to her. Through their union, Poseidon begat five twin pairs of male offspring. He then divided Atlantis into ten parts, or principalities, giving the overall rulership to the firstborn of the first set of twins, whose name was Atlas. In fact, Plato points out that this firstborn son received a name from which the surrounding Atlantic Ocean was to get its designation, as well as Atlantis itself.

After describing at rapturous length the natural wonders of Atlantis, its numerous architectural marvels, and its many other unparalleled accomplishments under a united and enlightened leadership, Plato comes at last to the sad account of its eventual decline and fall. For many generations, he tells us, while the "god-strain" was still strong within them, the Atlanteans were both a vigorous and a virtuous people, achieving much and remaining obedient to the laws established under Atlas' rule. Wealth and power meant little to them, though they had both in abundance. But then, almost too gradually to notice at first, a subtle change took place. Here are the words of Critias, the narrator, on the dismal subject: "As the god's part in them began to wax faint by constant crossing with much mortality, and the human temper to predominate, [they] began to behave themselves unseemly."

Unseemly indeed. Acts of downright wickedness and depravity are hinted at. (Those rolling mists, once more. . .)

Yet it is precisely at this instructive juncture, as if overwhelmed by what remained untold, that Plato's moral tale comes to an abrupt end.

Nevermind, let us turn to the akashic records.

Our psychic source can now provide us with the balance of the story, with whose watery ending we have already been made familiar. Much, however, occurs in between. And it is only by means of examining the entire chain of events that we can come to a proper comprehension of the evolutionary cycle that has brought us to where we are today. Today, in fact, we stand once again at the dividing of the way, even as we did in Atlantis. And which way will it be? The way of the flesh, or the way of the spirit? God or mammon?

The choice never changes. But the lessons of the past can serve to guide us in our future actions if we will but heed them. Let us proceed, then, with our evolutionary journey back to the lost Atlantis. And as we go, it may prove useful to bear in mind the words of the Preacher, in Ecclesiastes: "Is there *any* thing wherof it may be said, See, this is new? It hath been already of old time, which was before us."[8]

Truly, there is nothing new under the Sun. This is because the evolutionary cycle begins and ends in the Mind of God. On the descending arc, the thread of total ego-experience unwinds itself, and on the ascending arc it is gathered up again, along with the lessons gained.

The time is at hand for the gathering-up process. Unless, of course, we allow those confounded mists to interfere, as in the past—

Throughout Edgar Cayce's psychic career, the entranced clairvoyant would surprise his listeners from time to time by mentioning certain books or publications which most of them knew he had never read, or even seen, in his waking state. After all, with the extremely limited time available to him for study of any sort, and the lack of any scholarly inclinations on his part, Cayce's reading time was devoted almost exclusively to his beloved Bible. Thus, when a book title cropped up in one of his readings, it was cause for special interest and attention.

Such a case occurred in February, 1932.

A series of readings on Atlantis had been proposed. The suggestion came about because Atlantis had been mentioned increasingly, of late, in reference to the prior incarnations of many of those who came to the Virginia Beach psychic for life readings. In the first of what was to become a total of thirteen psychic discourses about the fabled continent, Cayce's opening remarks alluded to "those few lines given by Plato" (an under-statement, in fact), as well as "references made in Holy Writ that the earth was divided"—relating, of course, to Genesis, and the birth of Peleg, one of Noah's descendants.[9] (The name Peleg, in fact, means "division," perhaps signifying a branching off of Noah's heirs, as well.) Then the sleeping Cayce went on to mention "the writer of Two Planets, or Atlantis—or Poseidia and Lemuria," a then-obscure esoteric work that had purportedly been psychically dictated to a 17-year-old boy named Frederick S. Oliver by its deceased author, a former Atlantean adept who identified himself to Oliver as "Phylos the Thibetan," then dwell-ing in "Devachan," or what is more commonly referred to as the Other Side. The book was first published in 1899 under the title, *A Dweller on Two Planets*. It has subsequently gone into many editions, remaining in print to this day.[10]

Although Cayce did not necessarily endorse Phylos' extraordinary story, or Plato's either, for that matter, adding that their credibility as individual versions of life in Atlantis must be left to the reader's judgment, it is nevertheless noteworthy that much of the contents of *A Dweller on Two Planets* (relating to a time frame stated as "10,700 years before the Prince of Peace") is in fact corroborated by Cayce's own psychic information dealing with that general period.

Of course, students of both Phylos and the Cayce material will have noted that these two sources differ considerably from a philosophical perspective. Phylos assigns to the Law of Karma a high degree of fatalism and bleak inevitability. This does not at all accord with Cayce's Christ-oriented view, wherein the Law of Grace is ever operative and able to erase the karmic burden that Phylos regarded as an age-old millstone weighting him down because of his Atlantean sins and other shortcomings. (But perhaps, in part, Phylos' 17-year-old amanuensis, in transcribing the old Atlantean's tale, was letting himself be subconsciously influenced by the grim Victorian moral climate of his day.)

Yet this philosophical difference is not too important, I think. What is far more significant is the number of areas in which Cayce and Phylos, in totally separate and independent versions, give us strikingly similar accounts of the Atlantean culture in the period preceding its final collapse. For this reason, in presenting the Cayce story on the subject, I shall occasionally interject appropriate cross references to Phylos' version by way of corroboration. References to the theosophical literature will also play a part in the unfolding story that follows.

THE FIRST THOUSAND YEARS

Some two hundred thousand years ago, as ancient Lemuria was already heading gradually toward extinction as a failed experiment, the first arrivals from the androgynous third root race began descending upon the virgin soil of an unnamed continent specially prepared by the gods of the universe for their occupancy.

The continent would become known, in time, as Atlantis.

As for its evolving occupants, they were destined to bring into being a civilization unmatched on earth before or since. So great was their remarkable technological prowess that they could quite literally reach out among the stars, and harness the power of faraway Arcturus, as well as the energy of the nearby Sun. Many of their extraordinary accomplishments are only now being rediscovered as we move into our own great Aerial Age of Aquarius, corresponding with what Cayce termed the "aerial or electrical age" in Atlantis, at the height of its powers.[11] Yet it was technology run amok, in the end, without the necessary spiritual controls; and so it proved to be the undoing of the proud Atlanteans. This, and the shameless carnal pursuits of those undisciplined sons of Belial, whose accelerated activities wrought untold mischief... But their rightful place is toward the end, rather than here at the beginning, of our story.

In the beginning, the luminous soul-beings of the new race, arriving in the earth plane as thought-form projections at first, observed their new environment with mingled wariness and wonder. Moving through the unfamiliar sea of air, they were like cautious swimmers entering an underwater world of beckoning delights, who nevertheless sense that unseen danger may lurk behind each colorful stem of coral or shadowy frond of kelp. And so it did, of course. Indeed, they had been forewarned. They must not for an instant abandon their celestial links, or all would be lost. But can children who have come upon a forbidden play-ground be expected to act for long with the cool detachment of gods? And so it was that many among their innocent number, fashioning for themselves fantastic thought-patterns modeled in part on the beguiling animal and vegetable life they witnessed all about them, found these idea-images attracting physical atoms to themselves. Thus, instead of remaining at the fourth dimensional level of purely etheric mind-creations, the forms materialized, taking on the elemental substance of the earth in which they now dwelt. In this way, the originally free and luminous soul-beings found themselves grotesquely trapped in matter of their own making. And it was from their pathetic number that subsequent legends sprang up, telling of mermaids and satyrs, of unicorns and other curious beasts and half-beasts—all very real, alas, in those ancient days. Most, however, escaped a similar fate by materializing in human form, though androgynous. And it was they who became the true Atlanteans.

In order to remain in psychic touch with their divine Source in the formative stages, they evolved a third eye. This psychic "eye" (which eventually disappeared as its original function altered, to be replaced by the human pineal gland at present) could be made to appear wherever desired on the body. Eventually, however, its location became "fixed" at the back of the head. It was used for purposes of psychic "visualization," enabling the entity to draw on the higher Mind-force for all of its material and spiritual needs in the earth plane. In this way, the early Atlanteans lacked for nothing. As to bodily form, this varied according to individual desire, ranging from those of giant stature to midgets; but the ideal height and form were very much as at present, with the color at first able to change with the environment, in the manner of the chameleon, but stabilizing with the further evolution to become, in time, the red race.[12]

In what we might term its primitive or "pre-Atlantean" phase, before the emergence of the first of its mighty rulers in the days of Poseidon and Atlas, or the enlightened reign of Amilius at what was to become the all-time zenith of Atlantean civilization, the new continent was being busily colonized. Already it promised to become what Cayce was to call "the Eden of the world," and home to a most unusual race of androgynous soul-beings. More peaceful, we are told, than the other peoples of the universe, these early Atlanteans evolved quickly, using their natural psychic gifts to master the elements in ways their predecessors, the Lemurians, had never dreamt of. They soon learned how to make maximum use of nature's storehouse for their unfolding needs at every level. In fact, the greater development of what would today be called occult, or psychic, forces occurred during the first thousand years of Atlantis' evolution.[13]

Yet, in comparable terms, this would have been more like a hundred years today, or perhaps a single generation. For the physical form was then composed of purer elements, and its atoms were less compressed or "hardened," so that great longevity was the general rule. Indeed, some of the early androgynous sons may have survived for several millennia before passing into the Interbetween, or crossing over to what has been termed the Other Side. Later on, as the life-span tended to shorten, rejuvenation became possible. The energy of that known as the great Tuaoi crystal, set to a low vibration, could revivify the cells of the body; in this manner, many restored their ageing bodies to youthfulness again and again. Among the initiates, however, longevity was more often achieved by entering the silence in prolonged periods of spiritual attunement with the One. (Even today, we may do the same. Keep the pineal center active through meditation, counseled Cayce, and it will be possible to remain physically young.)

Meanwhile, we must leapfrog over a hundred thousand years, to arrive at the early rule of the "Upper Adam" or Amilius—the Maker, in short—who made His androgynous entry into Atlantis about midway in its two-hundred-thousand-year-old history.

Our account of that era opens with an ancient legend.

THE LEGEND OF LILITH

It is a curious and a covert tale, the story of Lilith. Much of it remains shrouded in deep mystery, which is further deepened by conflicting time frames and interpretations, as well as lack of detail. Part fact, part fantasy, the story hints of bestiality and simian-like offspring, but also of innocent intent at the outset—even of rescuing seraphim.

Perhaps the most compelling version is to be found in Hindu

mythology, although Lilith is not mentioned there by name, as occurs in the Talmudic allegory of Jewish tradition. Additionally, dark allusions to Lilith exist in Gnostic and medieval Rosicrucian doctrine, where her name is associated with Adam's as his first wife and a begetter of "devils" in the beginning of time. It would appear, however, to be a misleading and exaggerated interpretation, if we may rely upon what Edgar Cayce had to say on the subject when asked to explain how the legend of Lilith might be connected with the Atlantean projection of Mind the Maker as Amilius (alias the fourth-dimensional "Upper Adam," androgynous prototype of the later, flesh-form Adam of Genesis).

Let me now proceed to put together the bits and pieces from various sources, withholding Edgar Cayce's account until the last, where it will enable us to resolve the conflicting differences and extrapolate the underlying truth of the legend.

In Hindu mythology, the seed of our present human race were the sons of God, who, during the root race associated with the Atlantean epoch, had devolved into semi-divine, androgynous beings, self-imprisoned in bodies that had physiologically changed, becoming human in appearance. In this form, they began taking unto themselves wives who were indeed fully human in appearance, and fair to gaze upon, but in whom lower, more material, soul-entities than themselves had incarnated. These entities, nevertheless, are described as having been originally of sidereal origin, leaving us to speculate whether or not they may have been a devolved remnant of the etheric second root race, which preceded the Atlanteans. Called "Khado" (or *Dakini*, in Sanskrit), Lilith may be regarded as their prototype. All of these legendary "Khado" were credited with the art of walking in the air, which may have marked a "throwback" to their forgotten origins as fallen members of the etheric Lemurian race. Known for their great kindness to mortals, they nevertheless lacked any ability to reason, and were reportedly imbued with animal instinct only. In Hindu tradition, what was later mistaken for monkey worship was simply a form of respect for the lower primates, who are still believed by many Hindus to be a degenerate subphylum of man—the bestial offspring of that ancient sexual congress between the early Atlanteans and the "Khado."[14] Presumably, many in India may also look upon the "abominable snowman" of the Himalayas, called *yeti*, in much the same compassionate light, ascribing karmic consequences for the human race because of our ancient role in begetting these "lost" creatures, devoid of reason.

Meanwhile, in the Talmudic version of events, Lilith is introduced to us as Adam's first wife, before God had created Eve as his legitimate companion. She was a charming creature with long, wavy hair—in brief, a female hairy animal, in the general appearance of a woman. From Adam's unnatural union with Lilith—so runs the Talmudic tale—sprang a subrace of speechless beings, not unlike the apes of our present day.[15]

Although the Jewish, Rosicrucian, and Gnostic accounts have interpreted events in terms of the biblical Adam of a much later period, rather than his androgynous prototype (known in cabalistic lore as Adam Kadmon), their similarity with the prebiblical Hindu version, as well as certain elements of the Cayce interpretation placed in the days of Amilius, which follows next, serves to lend accumulating credence to the Lilith legend—whatever its proper interpretation. But before examining what Cayce had to say on the matter, there is an interesting footnote, so to speak, drawn from the apocryphal tradition. After his unholy alliance with Lilith, one of the six-winged seraphim is said to have hurried Adam to the Acherusian lake, where he was washed in the presence of God. Sin is not mentioned, however, for Adam presumably had no prior awareness of guilt . . .

In the early days of Amilius' rule, the separation of the sexes had not yet begun to take place. Though male in their outward aspect, the androgynous sons of God embodied within themselves the nature of both male and female in one person. By turning to the Creative Forces, they could become channels to bring into being androgynous progeny after their own kind, imbued with a double soul as well as a double-sexed body. In this way, sexual intercourse was unnecessary as a means of propagation. Moreover, by remaining free from carnal desire, they not only kept open the channel of spiritual communication with the Higher Forces from which they had originated, but they were able to avoid any impure relationships with the sons and daughters of men—fallen souls from the last root race, or early forerunners of their own, who had lost their celestial heritage and taken to copulating in the manner of the beasts around them.

Unfortunately, however, there was another side to the creative capabilities of the androgynous sons. It involved turning within, rather than turning to the Upper Forces. In a psychic process best described as "mental imaging," they could will into manifestation almost any object of a physical nature. Thus, their everyday needs were readily met, and it could perhaps be said that this visualization process wrought no harm, and even brought a degree of progress, in strictly material terms. Yet it had a potential for abuse, of course, particularly in application to lifeforms. This became evident when the androgynous sons, observing the enchanting thought-form now often seen in company with their leader, Amilius, soon discovered that it lay within their power, also, to generate such a creature from out of themselves, at will. Yet it was a far more complicated process than simple visualization, as used in materializing inanimate objects out of the ether. Thoughts are indeed things; but the "things," in this instance, had to be fashioned in living mimicry of flesh-and-blood models built up slowly in the mental forces of their double-sexed creators, in a process Cayce identified as "progeneration." It took as long as "four-score and six years," we are told, to fully materialize one of the "things," as they came to be called, quite literally.[16] Proprietary feelings must have run deep and strong. Whether of a form divine or grotesque, the hapless creature who emerged was destined to permanent servitude.

All of which leads us back to Lilith.

Was the projection by Amilius of this ravishing thought-form meant to produce no more than a mere "thing," a soulless automaton to serve his personal wants? It would seem otherwise, for we are told that he brought her into being "out of self" as "the first of that that was made," *to be the helpmate and companion.*[17]

Incidentally, note the phrasing: "the *first* of that that was made." Clearly, in producing Lilith, Amilius had set the precedent for bringing the so-called "things" into existence: a mistake, in retrospect, with tragic consequences. Yet whereas Amilius had only sought to create a helpmate and companion, "that there might be no change in the relationship of the sons of God with those relationships of the sons and daughters of men," we have already noted that his higher motivation did not seem to prevail among the other androgynous sons who chose to bring forth living thought-forms of their own. Most of these projections and their subsequent offspring, in fact, became mere drudges—slave-laborers—leading the way to an increasingly class-conscious society in Atlantis in future generations. Moreover, as separation of the sexes began to become a common choice among the sons, there was the gradual commingling with the sons and daughters of men, even as Amilius had feared, while the abuse of the "things" for purposes of sexual gratification took on ominous and tragic dimensions in a later era.

Meanwhile, as for Amilius' created companion, there are some troubling questions about her.

First and foremost: Did she have a soul?

The Cayce readings, addressing this subject, tell us that the "things" were of the animal kingdom, whereas only that created by the Creator was endowed with the soul.[18] But did Mind the Maker, having descended into the limiting dimensions of earthly existence as the androgynous Amilius, retain enough of His power to imbue His lower-level thought-form creation with a soul? In light of His higher purpose in creating Lilith, it might seem probable. It is made even more probable by the fact that some of the repentant Atlanteans—those who were to become faithful adherents of the new teaching introduced by Amilius, called the Law of One—later set about purging the so-called "things" of their numerous impurities, so that they might become fit habitations for both mind and soul forces, in an evolutionary process. (If Amilius had not pointed the way as an Exemplar, would they have taken such a humbling step of their own accord?)

But now, another question: Is the legendary image of Lilith as a prolific sexual partner of Adam (or of Amilius, as the Upper Adam) to be believed?

We may look upon it as a largely mythic element of the story, perhaps. It would appear to be inconsistent with Amilius' given purpose, which was to create a helpmate and companion who would enable Him to preserve His sanctity as the Son of God, free from the contaminating influence of the sons and daughters of men. For it was probably at about this time that Amilius had first observed that many of the androgynous sons had begun to separate, becoming two, like the lower mortals. Their next step was inevitable. And Amilius, to avoid falling victim to the same fate, may then have decided to create Lilith as an alternative. For certainly the projection of a thought-form helpmate or companion—unlike separation from His "other self," or female counterpart, which would have entailed a permanent loss of the celestial oneness of being—could, at first, have struck Amilius as a plausible way around the growing dilemma, whatever His later regrets. Moreover, as an idealized mental image, one may suppose that Lilith must have manifested many of the divine qualities, upon her full materialization, whether or not she was imbued at the outset with either a soul or the gift of human reason.

All that aside, however, one must still raise the final, and unanswerable, question: Did the semi-mortal Amilius, though He had been the divine Son and Maker in the beginning, at last find Himself yielding, like the other androgynous sons around

Him, to the earthly temptations of carnal desire? If so, the Prince of Darkness must have been secretly chuckling . . .

AMILIUS AND THE LAW OF ONE

Divisions arose in the land. Some aggressively defended the separation of the sexes and the experimentation with human and animal sexuality, others bitterly opposed such willful innovations.

Amilius was greatly troubled. His heart weighed heavily within Him. After cleansing Himself, He withdrew from the sight of the people. Transporting Himself in secret to one of the high and sacred places overlooking all of Eden, in Poseidia, which was the seat of His rulership, He communed for many days with the heavenly hosts and the Holy Spirit.

When Amilius at last descended again, His countenance was shining with the brightness of the Sun. The people saw, and they came together as one, laying aside their disputes temporarily. For they knew that their Leader must have been to the upper heavens and back, and they eagerly awaited whatever oracular message He might be bringing to them from the gods above.

The words Amilius spoke to them were direct and simple. With their utterance, He was to establish forever on earth the one true law that had been set from the beginning to govern all the universe. And to those Atlanteans who heeded Him, it henceforth became known as the Law of One.

In this manner spoke Amilius:

"Listen as I tell you of the heavenly law, and obey.

"Oneness is the law of all that is. For the Lord thy God is One. All of you emanate from the One, and must return to the One. Oneness is the law that binds the universe together, and holds the stars in place; for all force is a unified force, even as time and space, and the multitude of dimensions, are one in Eternity.

"That One is the Light, and the giver of life. Its visible symbol is the Sun above your heads. Yet the thousands of suns throughout all time and space are but as one, even as all souls are one, though many in number—as numerous as the stars.

"Yet, know this: all flesh is not one flesh, and the impure may corrupt that which is pure. Night and day do not mingle, but each follows its separate course for a reason. Separation from the life-giving Light, by any willful or unclean act, is to cast yourselves into the outer darkness, and to be no longer a part of the One. Therefore, turn not away from the Light. Make it the eternal magnet of your thoughts and actions henceforth. Worship only the One. Center yourselves, like the Sun's rays, upon the source from which you draw your own inner life and light. Become not children of darkness, who think the light is in themselves, and who follow in the ways of increasing selfishness and separation.

"Therefore, now, declare yourselves sons and daughters of Light, and children of the Law of One."

For a long time thereafter, while Amilius ruled, adherence by the majority of Atlanteans to the teachings of the Law of One brought great progress and enlightenment to the land.

It was during this time that the priesthood was established for the perpetuation of the law. A white-turbaned fraternity at first (though some of the androgynous daughters were later admitted as priestesses), these sons of the Law of One became known as the White Brotherhood. Cayce says of these Atlantean initiates that they had the ability to transport themselves in thought or in body;[19] and in *A Dweller on Two Planets*, Phylos similarly alludes to astral projection as a common occurrence among these "Sons of the Solitude," as they were alternately called, telling us that they had the ability "to lay aside the gross body of earth as one would an overcoat" and project themselves wherever desired.[20] Control of the sacred stone spheres, which were to be found in every temple throughout Atlantis, and of the mighty crystal, or Tuaoi stone (identified by Phylos in late-Atlantean terminology as the "Maxin-Stone"), was entrusted solely to this elite group of spiritual guardians.

In its essence, the Tuaoi stone was a giant energy accumulator of pure quartz crystal. But in its original usage it was far more than that. In the beginning, it was the source through which there was the spiritual and mental contact with the Unseen Forces.[21] Similarly, the circular stones that were placed on the temple altars or in the courtyards, and which varied in diameter from as small as a few inches to as large as eight feet, were of a highly polished granite that carried "the magnetized influence upon which the Spirit of the One spoke" to the early Atlanteans during their religious services.[22] In a much later age, toward the very end of the Atlantean era, many of these sacred spheres were transported by a Poseidian leader named Iltar, of the house of Atlan, to the safety lands of the Yucatan peninsula, and some to what are now Guatemala and Costa Rica.[23] In the latter-named country, great numbers of these mysterious stone objects, still seated upon altar-like beds made of river stones, have recently been unearthed in the jungles, totally confounding their modern-day discoverers, as reported in *Science Digest* (June, 1967). As for the Tuaoi stone, which sank with the rest of Poseidia some twelve millennia ago, Cayce indicated that it may one day come to light again, as portions of the sunken continent begin to rise once more in the vicinity of the Bahamas.

Housed in a special temple, with a domed enclosure that could be rolled back to reveal the heavens, the Tuaoi stone was of a large cylindrical shape, cut with many prismatic facets in such a way that its capstone could gather and centralize the power or force concentrated between the bottom end of the cylinder and the capstone itself.[24] (Referred to in one of the readings as "six-sided,"[25] it is assumed that this terminology may simply have been Cayce's way of identifying the material as crystal quartz, which has a hexagonal cross section.) Specially tuned to incoming vibrations from far-off Arcturus—identified by Cayce as that center about which our own solar system moves[26]—as well as the nearby Sun, it is not surprising that the Tuaoi stone later came to be called the "Firestone," although this was at a time in the changing Atlantean culture when the stone's function had become of a partly technological, rather than a purely spiritual, nature.

Once, when asked to name the point at which the great Atlantean civilization had reached its zenith, Cayce responded that this would depend upon whether or not the questioner was referring to the common perception of progress, in terms of material advancement, or to spiritual achievements. If the latter, it was clearly during Amilius' reign, some 98,000 years before the entry of Ram, or Rama, into India.[27] Hindu chronology places Rama at approximately 8,000 to 7,500 B.C.,[28] so we may conclude that Amilius' reign had its beginnings about 108,000 years ago. And how long did it last? We have no record as to its termination. It would be fair to estimate, however, that it was a very long reign indeed.

The "Golden Age" of Amilius, moving from its relatively primitive beginnings, used its peaceful rule and spiritual impetus to forge a mighty nation of unsurpassed accomplishments. Toward the end of his era, Amilius had already succeeded in pushing Atlantis into the beginnings of the aerial or electrical age, which was to follow. Initially, air travel in early Atlantis had been by means of balloons fashioned from the skins of pachyderms and lofted by helium gas—a tad primitive, perhaps, by our modern-day standards, but proof enough of Atlantean ingenuity. And they lost no time in advancing to far more sophisticated modes of travel, outstripping our own proudest achievements. It was under Amilius that Atlantean adepts discovered the controlling principle of what were termed the "nightside" or negative forces of nature, which are antipodal to the positive forces. For example, in understanding how the forces of attraction and repulsion come into play throughout the universe, gravity and anti-gravity could be balanced against one another, allowing great weights to be lifted or lowered easily, and with the most delicate precision. Indeed, all of the present-day mysteries of particle physics, electromagnetism, solar power and other cosmic energies were intuitively understood by the Atlantean adepts in that early era. Consequently, using metal alloys not yet discovered by modern man, in combination with certain of the

nightside principles at their command, they were able to construct wingless spacecraft that moved at incredible speeds
through outer space, or as readily traveled under the seas. (Not
only do the Cayce readings tell us of these things; they are
corroborated in the pages of Phylos' book, written in the 19th
century, long before the advent of air travel, infrared photography, television, and other modern-day innovations, all of which
were considered commonplace in Atlantean society long before
its fatal demise, we are told.)

Is there a lesson here for us? At any rate, it was toward the
close of Amilius' reign, even as great material strides were
bringing to the Atlanteans an undreamed-of prosperity and a
plethora of physical comforts and luxuries, that dissensions and
divisions again began to erupt throughout the land. They had
their roots, as might be expected, in the increasing moral deca-
dence that accompanies the rise to power of any self-indulgent
society as it forsakes the spiritual and ethical restraints of its
traditional values. Meanwhile, those among the pure androgynous lineage who held to the old standards fought a losing battle
as they did their best to persuade their wandering fellow-
Atlanteans to return to the teachings of the Law of One. But the
latter continued to pursue with wild abandon their pleasure-
seeking and licentious ways, which became more and more
unspeakable.

Finally, the children of the Law of One turned to the ageing
Amilius. His grief was great, as He listened. There was little,
however, that He could do; for He knew His time was already
come. Yet, before departing, He ordered establishment of the
first sacrificial altars in the land, as a means of remembering and
honoring God with the firstfruits from the harvest henceforth. It
was His hope, perhaps, thereby to remind the people to place
God ahead of self. Instead, in a perversion of purposes that was
in keeping with the rapidly deteriorating moral situation, the
altars came to be used in time for blood sacrifices.

Amilius was followed in time by Esai, who was the Atlantean ruler in charge during the period of the nation's first great upheaval, said to have occurred about 50,700 B.C. The ruler during the secondary phase of the progressive self-destruction of Atlantis, set at approximately 28,000 B.C., is not known. However, a ruler named Ani is mentioned in connection with Atlantis' closing days, from 10,600 B.C., onwards, until the last evacuee had left and the highest pinnacle of the final island gone under, some centuries later. . .[29]

As for the days of the god Poseidon, and the division of Atlantis into the ten legendary kingdoms under his ten princely sons, with Atlas, the firstborn, as the reigning monarch, we would assume a very ancient time-frame indeed in the 200,000-year-old existence of the fabled continent. It seems likely, in fact, that Poseidon may have been an early forerunner of the third root race, chosen by the upper gods to populate the promising new land prepared for their evolutionary experiment. If so, the civilization he presumably founded, as a legendary prototype of the later Atlantis, may have risen and fallen long before Amilius' mid-term arrival.

As for the latter, as the "Upper Adam" descending to earth, one wonders if He may have foreseen that His long, cyclical role as the Savior of the earth-bound souls had only just begun?

THE FIRST UPHEAVAL: 50,700 B.C.

During the reign of Esai, Atlantis was destined to evolve into an amazingly rich and powerful society of technocrats. But even as its scientific progress was reaching unparalleled heights, so was its spiritual ascendancy ebbing.

Neighboring states, all much weaker than the mighty Atlantis with its formidable arsenal of advanced weaponry, were easily cowed into submission as the Atlanteans freely roamed the whole planet as if it were their own preserve. Yet, as already noted, it was a society decaying relentlessly from within. Let us take a closer look at what was going on.

Some of the symptoms of deterioration were more subtle than others, of course. They might even have been interpreted as evidence of greater progress by the worldly minded. And that, of course, was precisely where the trouble lay.

Take space travel, for instance.

Whereas the initiates of old had been capable of traversing the nearby reaches of the universe through the application of their natural psychic abilities alone, now only a few chosen ones retained such occult powers. On the other hand, space travel in airships that Cayce once compared to the flying wheels described by Ezekiel at a much later date was now commonplace.[30] (Phylos, too, notes this technological mastery of interstellar space by Atlantean science.) And although such travel was under the control of what would today be termed the air fleet, the motivative force emanated, surprisingly, from the former Tuaoi stone.

The ancient crystal still remained exclusively under the sacrosanct control of the priesthood, as in the beginning. However, its original usage as a means of communicating with the forces of Light for spiritual guidance was now largely derided or ignored by the general populace, in what was considered an age of scientific enlightenment. Instead, the awesome power of the stone had been modified and redirected to serve a more practical purpose in the everyday lives of the increasingly materialistic Atlanteans. Referred to now as the "Firestone" (an appropriate reference to the phenomenal capacity of the mighty crystal to gather and store vast quantities of solar energy), its multitudinous rays were harnessed and channeled in such a manner as to fuel virtually every mode of transportation throughout the country, whether it was the air fleet, the submarine fleet, the pleasure crafts on the surface of the waters, or the various forms of land travel then in use. Moreover, not to be neglected in the conversion of what were formerly spiritual instruments to the changing needs of a more technological age, the polished granite spheres of varying sizes now apparently provided the necessary electromagnetic connection between the central "powerhouse," or the Firestone, and the individual motor-element of the thousands of crafts, trains, or whatnot, in which the spheres were placed. The propulsion mechanism appeared to be a simple matter of individual attunement in a control panel at the receiving end to adjust the in-flowing power and speed requirements, as needed.

If it had ended there, the material uses to which the celestially powered Tuaoi stone was being subjected might have been regarded as relatively harmless, however regrettable. But there was another and more ominous use—a use of a much more shameful nature. Whereas the energy of the stone could be life-saving, and was used by the Atlantean elite to regenerate and rejuvenate their bodies often, thus enabling some of them to live to a very great age indeed before taking flight to the afterlife, its higher vibrations could deal instant death and devastation to any material target.

The nature of the weaponry that made use of those higher vibratory forces emanating from the stone was known as the death-ray.[31] Similar in principle to an ultrapowerful laser, it could be set to emit death-dealing cosmic rays at varying rates of intensity and depth, as needed. Its creation had come about, initially, to ensure the defense of Atlantis' shores against foreign invaders; but rumored word of this formidable weapon had proven sufficient, in itself, to ward off any would-be invaders, whose technology was far behind that of Atlantis in virtually every respect.

Consequently, the death-ray remained largely untested. But now a threat of quite another sort, right within its borders, confronted the nation. Citizens in several of the outlying provinces of Atlantis, where the terrain was more mountainous and relatively uncultivated, began to report the increasing menace to their livestock and themselves from rapidly proliferating packs of fearsome beasts of all kinds. Many of these were the grotesque offspring of earlier thought-form creations interbreeding with already-existent animal species in the earth. Indeed, in many parts of the world far less developed than Atlantis, this rapidly multiplying threat from monstrous creatures originally of their own making[32] had reached crisis proportions among the badly frightened and disorganized tribes that then constituted the embryonic nations. (In Egypt, however, an enlightened leader named Asapha, still relying on primitive airships and backward communication facilities that had once marked the very earliest phase of Atlantis' technological development, was making efforts to form and convene a world council of leaders from all of the major tribal groups around the beleaguered planet to discuss the common threat that faced them and propose a solution. The surprising outcome of Asapha's efforts will be covered in the next chapter.)

Meanwhile, the far more advanced Atlanteans were proceeding independently to eliminate the threat from their land. At first they desisted from use of the awesome death-ray, trying less hazardous techniques. Explosives were dropped by air over visible targets moving in the open fields or on the mountaintops, while land-mines were set at the entrances to suspected lairs. But there were deep pits in the earth where many of the beasts dwelt in large numbers, and these could not be reached with surface explosions. Therefore, some of Esai's counselors proposed use of the awesome death-ray, which could easily penetrate into the deepest pits and caverns. But Esai temporarily decided against that largely untested and controversial weapon. The temple priests of the Law of One urged him to proceed instead with less drastic means, even recommending unified appeals to the Higher Forces for spiritual assistance. As for the cosmic death-ray, the priests cautioned Esai that its indiscriminate use against the marauding animals could prove quite as deadly in the long run to themselves as well as to the future ecology of the planet— concerns that had not been given proper consideration, in the beginning, by the creators of the weapon.

It was sobering advice, and matters might well have rested there. However, there had arisen an increasingly powerful and bellicose faction among the Atlanteans in those days. Excoriating Esai and the priesthood for their timidity, they petitioned vociferously for more vigorous and decisive action. They demanded that the death-ray be used without further delay to rid the country once and for all of the threat from the beasts known to be hiding in the deep caverns in the very bowels of the earth, as it were.

The leader of this opposition group was a charismatic figure named Belial. A cunning troublemaker, he was the offspring of a former priestess of the Law of One, who had left her activities in the main Poseidian temple to become a mistress and patron to one of the beguiling sons of men.[33] Belial, with his mother's aid as chief priestess, had built a magnificent temple of his own in a calculated effrontery to the children of the Law of One. He then persuaded many citizens to join him in forming a political movement against Esai and the organized priesthood on a number of strongly debated issues, among which the death-ray was only one.

Perhaps the most controversial issue was the continuing progeneration of the so-called "things," which most of the priesthood had long opposed on the grounds that the shameful treatment of these hapless creatures as soulless sex objects or as chained and hobbled workers in the mines and fields was a violation of the enlightened teachings of the late Amilius. In fact, some of the more influential among the sons and daughters of the Law of One had succeeded in convincing Esai that special electrotherapy clinics and instructional centers should be established throughout the land for the purpose of treating as many of these malformed creatures as possible, bringing them nearer to normal human standards—spiritually and mentally, as well as physically—so that they might be set free to join the rest of society.

To Belial and his followers, many of whom owned large numbers of the enslaved beings, such a program posed a double threat. First, they greatly feared and resented the prospect of being made to give up the unpaid laborers who accounted for much of their revenues, as well as those of more attractive form who were obliged by the bonds of ownership to serve their sexual needs. But additionally, there was the deeper fear that some of these miserable creatures, if ever set free, would turn on them and kill them. In chained and hobbled form, they were readily controlled; and with realtively undeveloped mental faculties, at present, they were not equipped to reason or disobey, but remained quite docile. In stature, however, many of them were virtual giants, while others had the appearance of grotesque semi-beasts, with horns and tails, with hairy shanks and sharp, cloven hooves, or perhaps hawklike beaks and claws, among some of the endless variations conjured up by their heartless or whimsical-minded creators. To what extent the children of the Law of One, by means of electrosurgery in the clinics or mental and spiritual training in the instructional centers, could reshape the malformed bodies of the "things" remained a matter of speculation at that incipient stage. But to Belial and his likes, who had long abused the creatures, there was no way of erasing their fear of retribution if they were to become free members of the Atlantean society, in time. Revenge might be very much on their newly awakened minds. Besides, it was well known that a large number of the "things" had escaped in the past, and were now presumed to be among those beasts hiding in the deep places of the earth. If others were to be "liberated" in the future, they might, regardless of outward changes in their appearance, join their brethren in the pits and caverns, and incite them to unprecedented violence.

But, first steps first. The deep hiding places must be cleansed of the monsters.

With that objective, Belial presented an ultimatum to Esai, backed up by his growing band of militant followers. Either Esai must instruct the initiates in charge of the Firestone to activate the power modules in the death-ray guns, and use the unleashed cosmic energies to eradicate the beasts in the lower caverns throughout the land, or Belial himself would take over control of the stone in the chief temple of the Law of One. It was a threat Esai did not wish to challenge, knowing that Belial had already won powerful forces to his side. He gave in. The long-delayed bombardment of the deep pits and caves with the death-rays could now begin.

Asal-Sine, the initiate in direct control of the Firestone, though somewhat ambivalent at the outset as to its use to empower the deep-fire lasers, found himself gradually falling under the persuasive influence of the charismatic Belial. The promise of power, in a changing order of things, proved to be his undoing.[34]

At Belial's suggestion, Asal-Sine gradually raised the power level in the prismatic attunement, so that the death-rays would have sufficient penetrative power to go into the very bowels of the earth, where Belial was convinced some of the most threatening of the monsters might still be hiding.

It was more effective than anyone might have imagined.

Not only were the poor, cowering beasts eliminated in all of their lairs, but the whole continent erupted in seismic activity and destructive fire. Volcanic upheavals rained death and destruction on much of Atlantis, and broke up the mighty continent into a fractured landscape of separate islands, five in number.

One might have thought that such a holocaust would have taught the likes of Belial a humbling lesson, but such, alas, was not to be the case.

In time, Atlantis recovered, and resumed its former ways. But if the beasts were no longer a threat, the same could not be said of the wicked sons of Belial.

Their numbers continued to multiply. And as their numbers grew, so grew the seeds of mischief they were sowing.

THE SECOND UPHEAVAL: 28,000 B.C.

Belial. Baalilal. Baal.

What do these names have in common? All reek of evil incarnate, for one thing. And for another, they look and sound too much alike to be unrelated. As a matter of fact, we can double that list of suspiciously similar names. Let us add Baalzebub (or Beelzebub, as he is more commmonly but less properly called). And Balaam. And Baalbek.

All of a kind, rather obviously. A kind to be shunned like the devil himself, in fact. Nevertheless, we may find it instructive at this point, before proceeding any further along on our journey, to pause sufficiently to sort them out.

In the Edgar Cayce readings on Atlantis, we find the first two names—Belial and Baalilal—used interchangeably, it seems, to identify the same entity, whom we have already had the dubious pleasure of meeting. Now, as to the Baal connection. In further reference to that period of the first Atlantean destruction, one young man received a reading from Mr. Cayce in which he was told that he had been among "those that worshiped Belial," or the satisfying of physical desires of every nature;[35] while yet another, who had aided in the preparation of the explosives, learned that he had "followed the law of Baal" rather than the Law of One.[36] These two references serve to establish with reasonable certainty that Belial and Baal were originally synonymous. Baal, in Hebrew, is said to mean "owner," or "master"; and in biblical times, Baal was worshiped as the fertility god by the Canaanites. Worship rites, even as those in ancient Atlantis, were orgiastic and sensual, and they often included blood sacrifice. All forms of the "black arts" were secretly practiced.

In the Old and New Testaments, meanwhile, and also in Jewish apocalyptic literature, we encounter the terms "son of Belial," or "man of Belial," denoting a lawless opponent of the Messiah. And in Revelation, there is a reference to those that hold the doctrine of Balaam, sacrificing unto idols and committing fornication.[37] Whereas Balaam was a Midianite soothsayer, his affinity to the ancient Belial, and the ongoing worship of Baal, is apparent. As for Baalzebub, or Beelzebub, the biblical "Lord of the Flies," we can trace his origins, too, to Atlantis. In a Cayce reading covering the latter days of the doomed continent, we are told of "the destructive influence" that still continued to arise "from the sons of Belial through the activities of Beelzebub."[38] We might well interpret that excerpt to imply that Beelzebub, as the apparent inheritor of Belial's mantle, was either a descendant or a reincarnation of the founder of the cult of Baal—perhaps both.

And what of Baalbek?

This brings us uncomfortably up to date. It is Baalism with a modern twist. In Lebanon's notorious Bekka Valley (*beka*, with ironic suitability, meaning "split," or "fraction"), the ancient town of Baalbek is the site of the oldest-known Temple of Baal, which went through a number of transitions in Roman times, but never quite lost its original significance to the locals. It is in this same infamous area today that the terrorist Hezbollah group of Iranian-supported fundamentalist Shi'ite Muslims carry on their lawless plotting—but all in the name of Allah, rather than Baal ... And if these zealots observe none of the former orgiastic rites of their hedonistic predecessors, they make up for that oversight in their redoubled zest for bloodletting.

Satan, it would seem, has always been able to identify his own, in every age, and put his mark upon them.

In the days just preceding the second breaking up of the land, a crisis erupted. Atlantis stood on the verge of civil war. The rebellious sons of Belial, true to their troublemaking namesake of an earlier era, sought to overthrow the rule of the Law of One and replace it with their own lawless rule.

The basis of their discontent was a gradually diminishing work force of slave labor, as the rulers permitted the priest class to accelerate its efforts to regenerate more and more of the unfortunate "things," thus enabling them to evolve unhindered as full-fledged members of Atlantean society.

At the same time, the number of androgynous soul-beings endowed with the original powers of progeneration once common to all had been steadily diminishing over the passing centuries and millennia of exiting and re-entering souls, in an ever-changing evolutionary environment where the etheric bonds grew continually weaker as the material atoms became further solidified and strengthened in a world composed of matter-substance. This posed a particular dilemma for the sons of Belial, who had never had progenerative powers themselves but had always relied upon their seductive charms to woo over to their corrupt ways as many as necessary among the androgynous soul-beings to create for them replacements for their dying or "liberated" slave forces. But to their increasing consternation, it was no longer possible to find a sufficient number of recruits.

As an alternative, they tried to pry from cooperative elements among the children of the Law of One the secrets of progeneration, which they believed were obtainable from the great white stone and the associated spheres, through which the initiates were known to speak with the Higher Forces. But, failing dismally in this, they seized weapons and airships and, breaking Atlantis' long record of peace with its neighbors, began making warring raids upon the relatively defenseless populations in nearby lands, bringing back great numbers of captives in chains to serve them. Those who refused to serve were conveniently turned over to the priests of Baal as blood sacrifices. Such sacrifices, in fact, were deemed necessary. Times were increasingly hard, with the overworked land becoming less and less productive. The mines, too, yielded less and less, though the workers were forced to dig deeper and deeper by their ruthless masters. And so it was believed in time by the sons of Belial that the only way to reverse this ominous state of affairs was to start offering human sacrifices on the altars, which they began to do in frighteningly prodigious numbers. Protests and pleadings from the rulers were to no avail. The sons of Belial, emboldened by rising support for their tactics, did as they pleased, with typical contempt for any outside authority. Moreover, it was subtly pointed out that those of the Law of One seemed no more able than themselves to meet the pressing needs of the people. Supplies of every sort became harder and harder to come by. Greed, long unchecked, was exacting its price.

The tensions inevitably worsened. Yet the ruling council continued to vacillate, avoiding decisive action. There was no Abraham Lincoln among them to rally the masses around a just cause, and put down the forces of Baal. Indeed, one of the Cayce readings on that sad, defeatist era suggests that a spiritual malaise had settled over the whole nation, allowing lawless elements to gain the ascendancy over the forces of One.

These words on the matter, spoken by the entranced Cayce to a former Atlantean initiate, sum up the pathetic situation for us quite succinctly: "The entity gave way, not to that of sin but ... rather to that of holding peace than using righteousness in power to destroy those willful in the flesh."[39]

A "righteous" war? To be sure, one should ever be able and willing to lay down his or her life to defend a just principle or protect essential freedoms.[40]

The Atlanteans chose to do nothing. Nature, however, had other plans. Higher forces went to work, as the land once more trembled and shook from one end to the other. When the tumult was over, many saw in what had happened the warning hand of God. Of Atlantis' five islands, only three remained: Og, Aryan, and Poseidia.

Lifting themselves up out of the rubble, some went on about their business. Others prayed, while yet others cursed. Still others packed, in preparation for the first of the evacuations to safer lands.

THE FINAL UPHEAVALS: 10,600 B.C. to 9,600 B.C

The final sinking of Atlantis was covered at the outset of this chapter, and was refered to as an event that probably occurred in several phases over a period of some centuries.

But if the disbelieving sons of Belial lingered until the end, with many losing their lives in the ultimate cataclysm, there seems little doubt that it was Iltar, a son of the Law of One, who led the very first resettlement group, heading for the Yucatan peninsula in 10,600 B.C., effective with the first warning tremors. (We shall follow him there in a later chapter.)

Some fled to the Pyrenees, others to what is now Peru, where we shall catch up with them eventually and trace their latter-day activities. Morocco, too, is mentioned as one of the safety lands chosen by the emigrating Atlanteans in those final days. And there may have been other places, not recorded. Meanwhile, many, many of the initiates went to the sun-drenched land of Egypt, traveling under divine impulsion to that favored spot, which was destined to play a crucial role in mankind's future evolution.

But let us go back a bit in late-Atlantean history to about 12,000 B.C., which places us at approximately the midpoint of the Age of Virgo, sign of the Virgin.

There was a God-sent Entity who incarnated in Atlantis at that time, some fifteen hundred years before the commencement of its final, phased destruction. And not improbably, it was meant to be His destiny to save the land and its people from its impending fate, pointing out to them the errors of their ways. His entry point was that same idyllic garden spot on Poseidia where all of the great initiates of the past had chosen to center their activities, and where still stood many of the ancient temples built to commemorate and perpetuate the teachings of the Law of One, as established there by Amilius, the Upper Adam.

The place, of course, was in the sacred groves adjoining the city of Eden. And the identity of the newcomer? He was the earthly Adam, projected into the three-dimensional sphere by his own "Oversoul," Amilius, and given a flesh-form, androgynous body in the beginning, which the Oversoul itself then occupied.

It was an auspicious send-off. Why, then, did He fail in His self-chosen mission of salvation at that first attempt, causing Him to be expelled from Eden? And where did He go, this remorseful Adam, with His twin soul and companion, Eve?

We shall find out, in time, as our evolutionary journey unfolds.

A proud and an accomplished race, the Atlanteans had evolved quickly, risen far, achieved much; but their gradual undoing can perhaps be attributed to the very quality that made them great: their extremism.

Cayce offered some revealing insights on this typical Atlantean trait, with its karmic implications for old Atlantean souls re-entering the earth during our current evolutionary cycle. For many of them will again be destined to occupy high places, with renewed opportunities and responsibilities (as was also the case during the days when Jesus walked in the earth).[41]

All reincarnating Atlanteans tend to be extremists, with exceptional abilities for weal or woe. They either excel, or are apt to make a mess of things. Endowed as a rule with remarkable mental powers, many of them also come under the strong influence of the planet Uranus, which governs the psychic forces and the extremes. This gives them unusual usage, in any chosen direction, of both spiritual and mental laws.[42]

Surprisingly, in a reading given during World War II, Cayce made the comment that there was not a leader in *any* country, *any* clime, whether friend or foe, who was not then an Atlantean. Equally surprising, and indicative of the extremist's capacity for self-sacrifice in any cause he strongly believes in (whether right or wrong), the Virginia Beach psychic noted in mid-1943 that there had not as yet been a single hero in the war, living or dead (or on either side, presumably), who was not a former Atlantean.[43]

Certainly Atlantis produced many heroes, as well as many villains, during the long period of its cyclical rise and fall. Toward the end, the chief heroes were those children of the Law of One who managed to save for posterity the records of Atlantis. This included a full history of their ill-starred continent, along with secret revelations concerning the mastery of the nightside forces to construct the mighty crystal, build their gravity-defying spaceships, and perform many other technological wonders that are still far beyond our grasp today.

Those records, we are told, were hidden deep in pyramidal chambers, in three separate places, where the manner of their concealment has apparently been able to guarantee their preservation until such time as they may be brought to light once more by New Age initiates when the time is set.[44]

Under the Gizeh plain, in Egypt, is one of the chosen locations, where the Egyptian records and relics were also entombed for future discovery, along with the Atlantean. Another set of the records was carried to Yucatan by Iltar, and placed in an as-yet-unearthed pyramid that lies beneath more recent Mayan ruins. Then, finally, in the pyramid of records now buried under the slime of the Sargasso Sea, in a portion of the long-sunken Poseidia expected to rise again near Bimini, lies the original set, accompanied by numerous artifacts, and sealed in place by the great Atlantean sage, Hept-supht.

His name, appropriately, meant "Help-keep-it-shut." He was later to play a similar role at the sealing ceremonies in Egypt. As a returning Atlantean in the New Age close ahead of us, he is named as one of three former initiates who will be personally involved in uncovering those same sealed records.[45]

The scientific evidence of a great civilization predating our Stone Age ancestors is hard to come by. Particularly when that ancient world lies, for the most part, buried under a deep bed of silt on the ocean floor . . .

Yet, now and again, strange reminders come to light. Clear enough evidence, if we will accept it, that highly advanced civilizations have preceded us here, and gone their way.

From a bed of solid rock, in Dorchester, Massachusetts, a bell-shaped vessel of an unknown metal turns up in 1851. It merits a passing reference in *Scientific American* before it passes into obscurity. In Austria, in 1885, a cube-shaped block of ancient metal with curious incisions upon it is found in a deep-layer bed of Tertiary coal. Following some disputatious scientific mumblings, it goes into the Salsburg museum and out of the minds of insufficiently curious scientists. Meanwhile, out in California, a traveler picks up a piece of auriferous quartz and accidentally drops it, splitting it open. Inside, a perfectly straight cut-iron nail, slightly corroded. No scientific takers on that one, back in 1851. A similar find in Kingoodie Quarry, North Britain, at about the same time. On this occasion, the nail, quite eaten by rust, is found projecting from a freshly dug chunk of stone deep in the quarry bed. Much speculation, but no firm agreement. Case dismissed. Then, an astonishing thing: an optical lens of purest crystal turns up among the ancient baubles unearthed in the treasure-house at Nineveh, in 1853. No way on earth or in Babylon to explain it. Finds its way to the British Museum as a curiosity, but gets nowhere at all as an archaeological specimen from an unknown culture. . .

All of the preceding are but a few examples of the many inexplicable objects that have ever so fleetingly puzzled the world's scientists in the past, and have even received passing mention (at least some of them) in their most prestigious journals before being swept hurriedly and forever under the rug. We are indebted to that indefatigable old eccentric, Charles Fort, for having carefully gathered them all up again for republication, with some delightful tongue-in-cheek commentary, in his 1919 minor masterpiece, *The Book of the Damned*. (Damned data, that is. Damned to oblivion.) This highly original work was followed by several others in the same genre, all gently—and some not so gently—chiding the scientific community for its notorious aversion toward any data that remain outside their commonly agreed-upon range of reference.[46]

Yet today, with our increasingly sophisticated instruments for aerial and underwater observation (though still crude, we daresay, by former Atlantean standards), there exists room for new hope. A better equipped and more enlightened physical science may one day surprise itself, and us, by confirming what the world of occult science has long taken to be an indisputable fact:

Atlantis *did* exist.

In fact, modern science has just taken a startling leap in this direction with a new theory on the crossing of distant species.

Many of those hybrid creatures of mythology, such as satyrs, centaurs and the like, said by Cayce to have inhabited the earth from the early days of progeneration in Atlantis, where they were known as the "things," are now deemed to have been more than mere chimeras. We are told, in fact, that they may have been quite real. New research findings, reported in the July 1989 issue of *Nature*, suggest that a unique form of sex—the transfer of genes in a process identified as conjugation—may actually be possible between organisms separated by a vast evolutionary distance, and may even involve what is termed "trans-kingdom" sex (i.e., animal-vegetable transfer of genetic information by way of bacterial cells and yeast, for instance) to create exotic hybrids.

Exotic indeed! Let us leave them alone. Their only proper place today is where we can still find them: safely locked away in our strange inheritance of legends, whose continuing "reality" is now limited to the akashic scrolls. . .

THE SHIFTING OF THE POLES

In 1981, as it passed over North Africa, a high-flying radar scan of planet Earth from aboard one of America's space shuttle flights picked up a curious pattern.

The radar evidence was unmistakable: buried beneath the desert sands of the now barren, featureless Sahara lay a vast and ancient network of long-dry river beds. Moreover, further tracking showed that these "radar rivers," running contrary to the present course of the Nile and its tributaries, must have had their beginnings in long-vanished highlands in the northeast corner of the continent, from whence they flowed southwestward in a gradually converging fashion. Meandering across the once-fertile plains of the vast Sahara, this grandfather of the Nile at last emptied itself into the far Atlantic.[1]

Following up on the radar images, geologists with the U.S. Geological Survey have had no difficulty locating the ancient stream beds, complete with water-worn pebbles, at depths of a few inches to a few feet beneath the ever-shifting sands. As their work progresses, assisted by archaeologists who have joined them, the researchers are coming across many well-known types of stone tools, attesting to a once-thriving culture in the Sahara. The newest of the implements uncovered, thus far, are hand axes believed to date from about 100,000 years ago, though no remains of the ax-makers have yet turned up. Further digging may unearth more data as to their probable origins and species, as well as yielding more conclusive knowledge as to the nature of the earth changes that must have gradually—or perhaps abruptly?—altered the river's course, causing it to be abandoned.

Meanwhile, we may promulgate our own theories, of course. But inasmuch as the ones proposed here hinge primarily on psychic evidence, the only weight they may be said to bear is the element of coincidence they carry in relation to the latest scientific clues.

In 1932, almost a full half century before those radar images in 1981, Edgar Cayce had given the last in a series of thirteen psychic readings on the Atlantean era. He took the occasion to outline some of the major global features during the pre-Adamic, formative period of the five racial groupings, which preceded man's fullscale emergence as a distinctive multiracial species now technically known as *Homo sapiens sapiens*, or modern man. ("Homo sapiens," in lay terminology.) That was perhaps as much as 50,000 years ago, following closely on the heels of a cataclysmic shifting of the poles in the days of Asapha, in Egypt.

Earth's present polar regions, he explained, were then turned, or occupied respective positions some degrees away from the north-south axis of rotation, placing those areas more in a subtropical zone. Moreover, the geomagnetic polarity was just the reverse of what it is now, so that what we would regard as "the extreme northern portions were then the southern portion," and vice versa, viewed in terms of earth's polar alignment today. (Mariners, for a star to guide them, would have looked to the pole's precessional path in our *southern* sky.) The oceans were also turned about, as it were. In short, it was a very different-looking world than the one we know today. For one thing, its topography included two now-sunken continents, Lemuria and Atlantis, whereas much of the American continent—particularly the region of the Mississippi—was then totally under water. In Asia, the Gobi Desert was a fertile land. The Urals fell into a tropical zone. Meanwhile, in what is now North Africa (that portion of earth's ancient landscape with which this chapter is primarily concerned), the vast and empty Sahara was then an inhabited land, and very fertile. And what made it so? An ample supply of water, of course, which probably came principally from its still-famous river. For, explaining its altered route in those days, as it slithered like a lazy serpent across the verdant plains of the Sahara, Cayce concluded: "The Nile entered into the Atlantic Ocean."[2]

Fifty years ago, when he spoke those words in a trance state, it is doubtful that Edgar Cayce could have found a single geologist to agree with him, theoretically or otherwise, about the Nile's ancient course or anything else. (Some time after his death, however, one lone geologist did come forward to lend his anonymous support to much of what the now-famous seer had had to say about both past and future earth changes.) Today, with the truth of Cayce's 1932 vision of the prehistoric Nile confirmed by the geological record, how many scientists will be fair-minded enough to grant the late psychic proper credit for his remarkable clairvoyance, decades ahead of the scientifically proclaimed fact? And if true in the one instance, what of testing his "psychic geology" in other areas open to verification, as well? In this manner, it may be possible to determine by empirical means the existence in specially proven cases of a genuine occult or psychic science at work, which may be presumed to operate in accord with certain universal principles and laws beyond the present limits of natural science.

In fact, the subject of pole shifts—a phenomenon derided in Cayce's day, and still subject to a lot of scientific skepticism—may provide the ideal litmus test. Not only did the Virginia Beach seer look back in time, and "see" at least one prehistoric pole shift, as already noted, but he looked ahead to the end of our present century and "saw" another scheduled to occur.[3] It will mark our official transit from the Piscean into the Aquarian Age, and the fullscale commencement of a new root race, if Cayce was right. At the same time, it will be accompanied by the final phase in a series of catastrophic earth changes, which will leave few areas of the planet unaffected.

Psychic geology or psychic bunkum? In another decade, we shall know the answer to that.

The scientific notion of pole shifts is necessarily a controversial one. Whereas it offers a logical explanation of many of the planet's most puzzling geological mysteries, it is assumed by its critics to be too extreme and totally cataclysmic, if one analyzes the probable implications of such a devastating event, to pose as a valid hypothesis. Its supporters, however, while acknowledging widespread havoc, do not foresee total extinction as the inevitable outcome of a pole change.

What it really comes down to, perhaps, is the old antagonism beween Catastrophism and Uniformitarianism, with science showing a natural prejudice in favor of the latter, which supports a gradual and evolutionary approach to all planetary changes. But those who would debunk any theory linked to Catastrophism need to be reminded of the words of the noted 19th-century scientist, T. H. Huxley, who once observed that "catastrophes may be part and parcel of uniformity."[4]

We shall pursue that more liberal view of the matter.

In 1958, following tentative approaches to the subject by a number of scientific minds unwilling or perhaps not qualified to commit themselves to a simple, straight-forward theory on pole shift unencumbered by technical question marks, along came Charles H. Hapgood. A bold theorist, Hapgood with his somewhat limited scientific credentials which were more than compensated for, it became obvious, by a highly intuitive mind and a fresh perspective, also possessed excellent powers of observation, research, and analysis. The results were bound to be impressive. Thus, when Hapgood's theory of pole shift was first published, under the title *Earth's Shifting Crust* (later changed, in a revised 1970 edition, to *The Path of the Pole*), it bore the generous endorsement of no less a scientific luminary than Albert Einstein, who said of it, in part, in his Foreword: "His [Hapgood's] idea is original, of great simplicity, and—if it continues to prove itself—

of great importance to everything that is related to the history of the earth's surface."[5]

The mechanics of Hapgood's theory may be found in his book, along with the fundamental physics and geological evidence on which he has based his conclusions. Unlike certain of his predecessors, who had envisioned a periodic flipflop in space of the planet itself, or else a shift in the earth's axis of spin, to rectify the imbalance created by an overloaded polar cap, Hapgood took a more logical approach: he looked to the movement of earth's outer shell, rather than any rolling of the planetary body itself, to explain the theory of pole shift. In fact, it was the very simplicity and common sense of Hapgood's hypothesis, which did not in any way violate the well-established theory of isostasy or call into question other laws of physics, which had appealed to Einstein.

Moreover, Hapgood's meticulously compiled geological evidence from all parts of the globe did not conform to the doomsday notion of a full 180° crustal slippage, from pole to pole, or even a 90° slide as far as the equatorial bulge. (Granted, there is ample geological evidence of periodic reversals in earth's *geomagnetic* poles—a phenomenon recorded by Cayce also—but this is a separate subject, to which we shall return in due time.)

Hapgood, after carefully analyzing the impressive body of geological evidence he had gathered from every part of the globe, saw his theory begin to take shape. He concluded that periodic displacements of the earth's crust over its viscous underlayer, or mantle, have been natural planetary events occurring at well-spaced intervals ever since polar temperatures were cold enough to create large, cumulative ice-caps. The crustal wanderings apparently begin as the result of a slightly off-center buildup of ice at one or both of the polar caps, over a space of many millennia. (As an aside: the off-centeredness of the cap may conceivably be due to the well-known "wobble" effect in the earth's rotating axis. That same wobble enables us to experience the rather important precession of the equinoxes, which leads one to speculate that it may be a "programmed" anomaly, like the other planetary events we are considering here. It need not particularly matter to us that modern science is still obliged by its rules to reject the role of a divine Choreographer in human and planetary affairs, thus leading it to label the same events as the arbitrary flukes and flaws of Nature.)

However, let us get back to Hapgood, as his theory builds. The spinning planet, reacting to its off-center overload much in the manner of a gyroscope, seeks to rectify the imbalance and restore its equilibrium. The process of crustal slippage begins. As the displaced ice-caps from both polar extremities are carried into warmer latitudes on the sliding crust, two things happen. First, the glide-effect of the traveling lithosphere as it moves over the rapidly heating mantle is interrupted by increasing friction. It is as if a wedge has been inserted in its path. And this, in essence, is what has taken place. (At this juncture, Hapgood introduces us to the "wedge effect" theory developed by his late friend and co-theorist, James H. Campbell.)

The "wedge," in reality, is the gradually widening girth of the planet's diameter the nearer one approaches the equatorial bulge and retreats from the proportionately narrower girth at the flattened poles. For our earth, of course, is not a true sphere, but has an oblate shape. To be exact, its equatorial diameter accounts for an extra 6.7 miles across. Thus, to appreciate Hapgood and Campbell's "wedge effect," consider what would happen if you were to pull a net stocking over a football. Although the analogy is not altogether accurate, you get the picture: it would stretch quite easily over either end of the ball, but the nearer you pulled it toward the widening midriff the more likely the resistance factor would slow your progress, gradually bringing it to a halt as the stocking began to develop runs and splits. Similarly, the earth's outer shell, as it slipped equatorwards, could be expected to slow to a creeping halt after a certain interval of initial momentum. Meanwhile, frictional heat generated in the mantle, along with strains and cracks in the widening crust, would account for the violent earthquakes and volcanoes that Hapgood found to have been contributing elements in the devastating effects he had noted in relation to the geological record left behind by the last three polar shifts, or crustal displacements. (The earliest of these, dating between 80,000 and 75,000 B.P., marks the outward limits of all presently accessible geological evidence on the subject.) Finally, the stretching, tightening effect on those portions of the crust moving away from the polar areas and toward the equatorial bulge could account for the breaking up of continents and the formation and movement of tectonic plates. Contrariwise, portions of the crust moving polewards would experience a loosening effect, leading to a "doubling up" of the planetary skin, as it were, creating new mountain chains and other surface features. And so, with these observations, we can begin to appreciate the importance of Hapgood's theory. If it continues to hold up (as Einstein seems to have expected it to do), it will contribute much toward a proper understanding of earth changes—past, present, and future.

An unresolved aspect of the theory is the time frame of such a cataclysmic event as a pole shift. It becomes a crucial question. Hapgood seemed to incline toward a fairly rapid displacement period, creating catastrophic winds in some areas of the planet and rapid temperature shifts—confirmed, in fact, by the geological evidence, some of which is rather frightening, with countless thousands of large animals trapped in suddenly forming ice sheets, even as they grazed on grasses found only in temperate zones. (The Cayce readings, as we shall see shortly, appear to substantiate this notion of a fairly swift realignment, rather than one taking several centuries or millennia, as some scientists have proposed.) In any case, Hapgood concludes that new ice sheets will commence forming at once in the polar regions, following any crustal realignment, whereas the former ice-caps will dissipate rapidly, aided by the strong winds and warmer temperatures to which they will become exposed.

In tracing the last three polar shifts, Hapgood estimated that the earliest for which there was any reliable evidence occurred between 80,000 and 75,000 B.P., as previously mentioned. On that occasion, the North Pole shifted from what is now the Yukon District of Alaska to the Greenland Sea, at a point within the Arctic Circle. Next, it shifted to Hudson Bay, in a zigzag effect, sometime between 55,000 to 50,000 B.P.—the very time- frame, in fact, in which the coming events of this chapter fall, as they tell Cayce's story of a prehistoric council held in ancient Egypt, even as the Atlanteans were using the death-ray to rid their continent of the large animals then overrunning the planet. Finally, in keeping with the familiar zigzag motion confirmed by the geological evidence, Hapgood found that the last polar shift occurred at the end of the Pleistocene epoch, sometime between 17,000 and 12,000 B.P. It was marked by a 30° shift of the crust, relocating the polar cap from Hudson Bay to its present position (our familiar North Pole).

And the next crustal displacement, at the end of this century? We can only speculate that it will take the customary zigzag course, which may be Nature's means of distributing the polar pressure to different zones of the lithosphere, or crust. But it is somewhat alarming to note Cayce's prediction of another polar shift falling due so soon again, whereas previous shifts appear to have occurred some twenty-five to thirty-five millennia apart, rather than a mere twelve or so. Could it possibly have something to do with underground nuclear tests by the major powers over the past several decades, combined with various ecological abuses, which are adversely affecting global temperatures and the ice-caps, leading to a planetary imbalance far ahead of the normal "programming" for such a major change? Whatever the answer, or its karmic implications, we can at least take heart from the fact that this "planetary cleansing," as we might regard it, will not be without its survivors. For, emerging from the "safety lands," as Cayce referred to protected portions of the stricken planet, the fifth root race shall arise.[6]

Before getting on with our journey into prehistoric Egypt, in the days of Asapha, we must touch briefly upon geomagnetic reversals. (For the time-frame of our story is in a period when the north-south polarization was suddenly reversed.)

On the surface of the Sun, astronomers are able to observe a periodic 11-year reversal in the polarization of the sunspots, with the negatively charged spots becoming positively charged, and vice versa—though no one knows why. Moreover, current studies show that the moon, now a dead body, once had its own magnetic field—and a remarkably strong one at that—which apparently shifted periodically in respect to its spin axis.[7] As to our own earth, geomagnetic realignments are believed to have been frequent, with actual reversals of the geomagnetic field having occurred no fewer than nine times in the past 3.6 million years, and another probably imminent, based on an observed weakening in the present strength of the field.[8] Meanwhile, Robert D. Ballard, author of *Exploring Our Living Planet*,[9] tells of realigned iron particles recovered from a 30,000-year-old aboriginal campsite in Australia that yield evidence of earth's magnetic field having pointed south at that time—an interesting fact, which appears to confirm Cayce's account of earth's south-north geomagnetic orientation during the formative era of the five racial groupings, between the second and third pole shifts. Thus, it may be reasonable to conclude that another geomagnetic reversal accompanied the pole shift at the end of the Pleistocene epoch, bringing the planet back to its present north-south orientation. But whether a geomagnetic reversal is automatically an aspect of any crustal shift, rather than a simple magnetic adjustment to coincide with the degree of shift in the sliding lithosphere, is a moot question. No one really knows. At any rate, it is necessary to bear in mind that the earth's geomagnetic axis, whether its positive pole faces north or south, is always in fairly close proximity to the planet's axis of rotation. And however much earth's crust may shift at the poles from one zigzagging position to another, we are assured that the spin axis does not change. It remains always the same. It is one of the accepted laws behind the theory of isostasy, which concerns the condition of gravitational or hydrostatic balance with respect to the surface of our pleasant little planet.

"Pleasant little planet"?

In the days of Asapha, it was somewhat otherwise. In fact, it was a planet in crisis. None of its beleaguered occupants could possibly have thought of it any longer as a "pleasant" place to live. The problem? The green and innocent earth had suddenly become a nightmarish landscape, more akin to a vast hunting-ground—and it was the humans, not the animals, who were being hunted.

What had led to such an alarming proliferation of large, ravenous beasts? In part, it was an agreeable world climate, abetted by plenty of space in which to hide and roam. (For the population of the earth at that time, we are told, totalled only 133,000,000 souls, and these were widely dispersed about the surface of the planet, often in isolated tribes.) But also, the problem related to something more ominous: changing appetites. Much of the blame, it was said, fell to the Atlanteans. The animals in the earth at the time of their arrival had had their own hierarchy. They preyed upon one another, or they succumbed to other natural forces that tended to keep their numbers in proper balance. But even the fiercest of them kept their distance from gods and men, recognizing them as their masters. That is, until the "mixtures" began . . .

Ah, yes. Those strange mixtures, by means of which many of the Atlanteans began degrading themselves, thus descending to the level of the beasts, as it were, to gratify their lusts. For there was not yet the prevention of such abominations through genetic controls, as were later to be imposed upon all evolving species by the Creative Forces. And since the androgynous sons and daughters could create as they willed, the results of their willfulness began to abound, evidenced through the progeneration of the "things," which were often more animal-like in appearance than human. Moreover, since many of the early Atlanteans were themselves of giant stature, some of the more monstrous thought-forms they brought forth were of similarly oversized proportions. Many of these, often transported in chains to alien lands for labor in Atlantean-controlled mines and the like, managed to escape from their creators. Soon roaming the planet in growing numbers, they began producing fearsome mutations through crossbreeding with one another or with the animals of the fields and forests, as well as mating on occasion with the large birds of prey and flying mammals that terrorized the skies by day and night.

Thus, not surprisingly, the gradual overrunning of the entire planet by the uncontrollable predatory forces of the animal kingdom had begun. No longer submissive to gods or men as their natural masters, the animal element sought to gain physical ascendancy. And so the need had now arisen, in Cayce's words, for the people to come together to save themselves from "that of their own making in the physical."[10]

It was Asapha, an androgynous young ruler projected into the Egyptian land as one of the very early forerunners sent to prepare the way for the gradual emergence of a new, flesh-form race, who took command of the situation. For he was a natural leader, who had already gained renown for his wisdom among the broadly scattered tribal groupings in those many parts of the planet beyond Atlantean control.

Whereas Esai, the weak Atlantean ruler during that period of the first disturbances, was in the process of succumbing to mounting pressure from Belial and his followers to use one form of evil to combat another, in further disobedience to the Law of One, Asapha believed that the indiscriminate destruction of the beasts by deadly weapons would serve only to compound the karmic consequences already building. Instead, he sought a spiritual solution to the dilemma. Departing from the ways of further abuse and disobedience, the peoples of the planet must be persuaded to turn back to the Universal Forces, or God, for their salvation.

It was to this end that Asapha called for the convening of a world council of some forty-four tribal elders and wise men from

the furthest reaches of the earth. They met in the relative safety
of Asapha's seat of rule, in the heart of the Sahara land, where the
marauding animals had never intruded upon his peaceful
reign—a sign, many felt, of the protective nature of the spiritual
powers he now proposed that all of the tribal leaders invoke, in
unison.

It was in the first moon of the year 52,722 B.P. that the forty-
four chosen delegates assembled in tents set up for the occasion.
They arrived, for the most part, in primitive airships made from
the skins of pachyderms and propelled by gas, for the Atlanteans
had not chosen to share with the other peoples of the planet their
greatly advanced technology, employing the use of the crystals
and the nightside forces. Never before had there been such an
occasion as this one, bringing together in one place the divisive
forces of mankind for a common cause which served to unite
them. No doubt each of the forty-four delegates must have
sensed the uniqueness of the situation and the awesome responsibility resting upon his shoulders.

For nine moons their meetings continued, as Asapha reasoned with the more warlike members concerning the need for
man's return to full reliance on the divine laws established in the
beginning for his evolutionary development in the earth plane.[11]

Meanwhile, word was reaching them almost daily concerning actions already well under way in Atlantis to destroy the
predators with explosives. This approach was covertly approved by many of the delegates, who were growing increasingly restive. They wanted more visible measures taken than
Asapha's group prayers to the Unseen Forces. Also, it became
known that a charismatic rebel leader in Poseidia, named Belial,
was pushing hard for use of the dreaded death-ray, which went
against the original dictates of Esai and the other governing
forces among the children of the Law of One, in Atlantis.

At last, it was learned that Belial and his followers had won
out: the death-ray was to be used, after all. This ultimate weapon,
turned against the remaining predators on Atlantean soil, would
be able to penetrate their most remote hiding-places in the deep

pits and caverns. Many among the council members in Egypt now argued openly with Asapha that urgent appeals should be made to the Atlanteans without further delay to come to their assistance. Some of them were even willing to submit to Atlantean rule, if necessary, to rid their land of what they deemed to be a worse fate posed by the rapidly proliferating beasts of prey.

Yet Asapha urged further patience. He insisted, as one who seemed to know whereof he spoke, that help would soon come from a higher source. And so it did, quite unexpectedly.

Even as the earth began to quake and tremble under the whole of the stricken Atlantean continent, breaking it up into five separate islands of diminished greatness, other earth changes were being set into motion. For the Higher Forces had brought about a sudden shifting of the poles.[12] This catastrophe of nature reversed the climate in all of the lands most seriously threatened by the large animals, wiping out their numbers virtually overnight. Yet the people, more resilient and resourceful than the animals, managed to survive.

Asapha's fame as a prophet spread far and wide, as the forty-four council members gratefully returned to their purged lands. Meanwhile, many of the chastened Atlanteans, seeing the error of their ways at least temporarily, decided to rehabilitate great numbers of the more humanlike "things" still under their control, and set them free. In time, this resulted in a mass exodus of these formerly abused and pathetic beings to Egypt, where Asapha had let it be known they would be welcomed as freemen and full-fledged citizens among his people.

In their new homeland, they built themselves a city and erected temples, wherein Asapha was honored during the remainder of his long lifetime as God's representative on earth. After his death, the revered ruler came to be worshipped as the Sun-god. Certain of his teachings, contained in the Egyptian "Book of the Dead," were fortunately preserved for posterity. They exist to this day.

This same Asapha was to reincarnate many millennia later in

a somewhat similar role as Ra Ta, or Ra, as he came to be known. From his origins in the Caucasus, he was to migrate with others to Egypt, under divine impulsion, some 10,500 years before the Prince of Peace, as the planet was facing yet another period of crisis. We shall meet him in his later role in a future chapter. Yet let us take but a brief look ahead; for one of the early activities of the high priest Ra Ta, as the reincarnation of Asapha, may be seen to bear some special significance here.

Psychically drawn to the site of the long-buried city built in a portion of Upper Egypt by that large egress of "things" from out of Atlantis in the rule of Esai, the high priest Ra Ta began conducting archaeological excavations. As expected, he not only unearthed relics of the ancient city but came across the skeletal remains of many of his former sun-worshiping subjects. As further evidence of their Atlantean origins as "things," and not then fully human in appearance, the psychic priest drew the attention of his fellow excavators to their prehensile protuberances. For, as Cayce explained it in one of his readings, most of the immigrating "things" had tails![13]

No one, as it turned out, was better qualified than Mr. Cayce to know. For it was he himself who had been both Asapha and Ra Ta, in those two Egyptian incarnations.[14] Both appearances played a critical role in the evolution of the human race.

Meanwhile, let Darwinian evolutionists draw their own conclusions if contemporary digs in those old Saharan river-beds should yield further bone specimens with the same prehensile protuberances. Probably, as has too often been the case in the past, overeager anthropologists will rush to premature judgment, proclaiming that they have at last uncovered the true "missing link." Indeed, we can already hear rival groups scrambling to give the findings an appropriate designation. Will it be *Homo habilis nilus*? or *Homo erectus sahara*? No matter. The truth lies in the akashic records.

On the other hand, future digs may uncover a burial mound[15] in the vicinity of the Valley of the Tombs, or what was once called the Valley of the Shadow. Therein lie the remains of the androgynous ruler, Asapha. A study of his bisexual bones, if they are at all intact, should prove to be rather upsetting to the whole vast panoply of conflicting anthropological evidence concerning our evolutionary origins.

Accompanying the prehistoric Asapha's bones, we are told, will be found tablets of stone in a corner of the tomb. On these are inscribed in ancient hieroglyphs the first laws given to the sons and daughters of men relating to the Higher Forces. If they can be interpreted by modern scholars, may they not convey some deepening awareness of our celestial connections?

ADAM'S APPLE

Let us look at a mystery.

In all esoteric teachings, we find the ancient symbol of the pentagram depicting man the microcosm. What is its significance? It has been graphically illustrated in Leonardo da Vinci's famous drawing of a spread-eagled human figure encompassed by a circle: the outstretched arms and legs make contact with the circle's circumference, as does the head, thus taking on a configuration roughly parallel to the five directions of the pentagram, or five-pointed star.

The enclosing circle itself may be said to represent the inner world, or microcosm, in which corporeal man finds himself at present. Therein he is made a prisoner of his five physical senses, of the five elements of which he is visibly composed, and of the five races in which he may choose to materialize for any given cycle of earthly development as a flesh-form being.

First, let us consider the five races.[1]

In their formative period, we are told, they had their origins in five general areas of tribal gatherings with common goals, which gradually took on national characteristics. The antecedents of the white race occupied the region of Mt. Ararat and part of what is now Iran, as well as the Carpathian Mountains and the Caucasus, later embracing a portion of India. The red race had its primitive origins in Atlantis, and later, with the final evacuations, completed its development in America. The yellow race emerged in what was then called the Gobi Land, an Asiatic remnant of the largely sunken Lemuria; it incorporated much of Indo-China at the time, northward to what is now the Gobi Desert. And the brown race? It took form principally in the Andes, among the prehistoric peoples known as the Ohums, with a strong Lemurian infusion of separately evolved tribal elements from the central and southeasternmost portions of that lost continent. As for the black race, mistakenly regarded by many anthropologists as the oldest simply because of its relatively undisturbed skeletal remains throughout the periods of cataclysmic earth changes, its origins may be traced to the Sudan and what is now Upper Egypt and the Eastern Sahara.

Each of these five distinct racial groupings, it must be realized, began its development under a gradual evolutionary process requiring a relatively long "gestation period," as it were. Yet there was apparently a common genetic pattern in the making, established by Amilius, the Creator, in molding the form that would eventually emerge. The process was presumably being guided in the earth plane by early forerunners of the developing new root race of flesh-form man. (Asapha, it will be remembered, was one of those forerunners, who gave the first laws to the sons and daughters of men, more than 50,000 years ago, in prehistoric Egypt.)

The "official" entry of Adamic man may be computed to have occurred about 14,000 years ago, before the final demise of Atlantis and at the midpoint of the Virgoan Age. (Our evidence for this dating will be presented a bit further along.) It took place, we are told, with five simultaneous projections by Amilius of prototypes in each of the five evolving racial groupings that were now nearing their perfection as the ideal flesh-form man. It had been necessary for Amilius to create the proper physical vehicle, cleansed of its many former genetic weaknesses that had arisen through crossbreeding, before what was termed the "second influx" of souls could take place. And now that that time had arrived, Amilius Himself chose to enter in one of the five prototypes of what was to be the fourth root race, but the first fully human appearance of that now known as the "race of man." He came as Adam, in a portion of Atlantis known from ancient times as Eden, a sacred city in Poseidia.[2] In that fateful incarnation, He represented the red race.

Meanwhile, in their initial projection, each of the five racial types of the new root race was assigned a specific correlation with one of the five senses. This marked the particular attribute of the racial consciousness to be emphasized in its physical development, as a distinctive phase of evolutionary experience. To the white race was given sight, or vision; to the red, touch and sensitivity, or feeling; to the yellow, hearing; to the brown, the sense of smell; to the black, the sense of taste, or the gratifying of the appetites.

Additionally, we find Adamic man (ourselves) composed of the four principal elements, plus a fifth. (In fact, our psychic source informs us that every sub-element of earth is to be found represented in the human body.[3]) Water, of course, is the major element of man's physical composition. Fire, too, or electricity, informs every bodily cell. Nor do we need to be reminded of the role of air, or oxygen, in sustaining mortal life. But beyond these four basic elements lies a fifth: it is *spirit*, by means of which a man becomes a living being with his first indrawn breath.

Five elements, in all. And yet, without consideration of a sixth, man the microcosm would be forever caged within the circle of his mortal limitations. But by means of this sixth element, he is capable of transforming and transcending himself, through soul growth, into a celestial being at one with the Divine Macrocosm, or God. The soul-entity, or higher self, is that "sixth element" for which the house of clay was fashioned in the beginning as a temporal dwelling-place, even as a seed must lie in the earth awaiting the germination process that will enable it to break free at last and greet the Sun.

The symbol of this transformation process is the six-pointed hexagram, or "seal of Solomon." It consists of two intersecting equilateral triangles—one in inverted position—representing the descending Spirit of the Creator uniting with the ascending spirit of man, to form a perfect union, as in the beginning. This sacred symbol, which has its parallel in the esoteric symbology of the Tree of Life and the ten holy Sephiroth of the Cabala, is said to represent the synthesis of all the elements and the union of the opposites. In Hindu mysticism, the process of transformation is equated with the practice of Kundalini Yoga; but in Christian terms, it is viewed as the awakening of the Christ within, or what some have experienced as cosmic consciousness. The great Swiss psychologist, C. G. Jung, reverting to the language of the medieval alchemists, who sought to convert the base lead of the human condition into gold, labeled this same transformation process the *Mysterium coniunctionis*—a marriage, or synthesis, of radical opposites.

Other belief systems, other symbols. But by whatever name we call it, pursued under whatever religious or philosophic guise, the process remains the same for each of us as it did for our Wayshower and Maker, whose "individual selves" we are:[4] *God became man, man must become God.* Or, to put it another way for non-Christian thinkers: The One became many, the many must again become One.

And that, in an egg-cup, is the whole secret of evolution.

Cayce was quite explicit about it: Man did *not* descend from the monkey, nor did he in fact evolve from any of the lower forms in the earth plane.[5] But when the evolving planet Earth was finally made ready for his entry and experience here, he appeared as ruler over all that had preceded him in the animal, vegetable, and mineral kingdoms.

In the beginning, he came as a celestial being. Those early titans of Lemuria and Atlantis were truly the sons and daughters of God, fully conscious of their divine heritage and spiritual selfhood. Yet, in time, they began to lose touch with the Universal Consciousness as the separation became more complete, and we have seen how fleshly entanglements, commingling the divine with the bestial, led to the soul's permanent entrapment in the material plane of fleshly desires, with no visible exit.

It was for this reason that Amilius, the Maker, saw the need to provide the trapped souls with a way out of their self-created dilemma. No longer in the earth plane Himself, He nevertheless recognized the need to introduce a new racial form, genetically incapable of crossbreeding with the animal population as in the past, and containing within itself the seed, as it were, for its own spiritual regeneration through an evolutionary process of soul growth.

It has been said that man's spiritual journey is from the soles of his feet to the top of his head. This implies that the God we are seeking really lies *within* us. But where? And how to get there? The pathway, provided by the Maker, is well known in esoteric tradition; it has also been traveled by Christian mystics from the days of St. John, whose "Revelation," we are told, is actually a symbolic depiction of the soul's inward journey along this same path, leading to union with God.[6] The path, spiraling upward along the spine from its base to the brain-center, is linked by tributaries to the entire endocrine gland system, with its seven glands and associated spiritual centers, referred to in esoteric literature as *chakras*. The four lower centers, identified as the gonads, the Leydig cells, the adrenals or solar plexus, and the thymus (also referred to as the "heart center"), comprise the lower self, or the earthly man of physical desires and temptations. Before reaching the two highest endocrine centers, which are the pineal and pituitary glands, spiritually equated with the higher consciousness and the "kingdom of heaven" residing within us, the pathway of ascent leads through that gland situated in the throat area, known as the thyroid. This crucial glandular center, lying midway between "heaven and earth," so to speak, the Cayce readings identify as the seat of the will.

The soul, with its companion, the will, must gradually master the four lower centers before it is ready to regenerate the "earthly man" and move into attunement with the higher self, which, as Cayce termed it, ever stands in the presence of the

Infinite.[7] Opening the higher centers, represented by the pineal and pituitary glands, involves entering what some refer to as "higher dimensions," but which may more aptly be defined as raising consciousness to a higher, more spiritual, rate of vibration. This is best achieved through self-abnegation, God-centeredness, and loving service to others, as demonstrated by the Great Exemplar. It may take many lifetimes—at least some thirty or more, we are told—to replicate His final victory over the flesh, and regain the body celestial. For, not until the human will has voluntarily brought itself into full alignment with the Divine Will ("Not my will, O Lord, but Thine be done!") can the cells of the physical body so regenerate themselves as to reappear as the resurrected and luminous atoms of the celestial body, as in the beginning.

In the East, where the practice of daily meditation has been refined to an art form, many of the great sages and yogis have chosen this route exclusively as the path to self-enlightenment, eschewing the Way of the Christ, which is defined in Eastern terms as Karma Yoga. But whereas deep meditation has indeed been known to raise the current of creative energy along the spinal column, opening the spiritual centers along the way, Cayce frequently cautioned against "forcing open" these centers—an action to be equated with the biblical warning against trying to force open the gates of heaven, in the manner of a thief or a robber. Rather, meditation is recommended only as an adjunct to righteous living, in selfless and prayerful service to God and man. Moreover, premature opening of the higher centers can prove to be physically harmful: the sudden arousal of high-level currents of positive and negative energy, improperly balanced through lack of spiritual preparation, has often brought suffering to those seeking knowledge without the necessary wisdom. (Gopi Krishna, in his illuminating autobiographical book, *Kundalini*, vividly describes the dangers.[8])

In fact, it was knowledge of quite another sort, but equally uninformed by wisdom, that led, we are told, to Adam's fall.

In the fifth chapter of Genesis, unlike the second, we are presented at the outset with an androgynous being, created male and female, and named Adam.

No "deep sleep" is mentioned, no rib removal to make the woman. Already existent as Adam's "other self," or twin soul, Eve apparently made her appearance through the same gradual separation process as had begun in Amilius' day, among the androgynous sons of God. Interestingly enough, this amoeba-like act of self-division into masculine-feminine polarities at the physical level may be found indirectly confirmed in words attributed to no less an authority than Jesus, in one of the *logia* from the recently discovered *Gospel According to Thomas*: "Jesus said: On the day when you were one, you became two."[9]

At the time of Adam's appearance, the androgynous form had already become a rarity among the late Atlantean race. So much so, in fact, that it might be logical to assume that his Oversoul's chosen projection in that form marked its termination. However, in 12,800 B.C., some 800 years before the estimated date for Adam's arrival (to be explained a bit further along), we are told that an androgynous soul-entity named Aczine, or Asule, was projected by Amilius to become a ruler in Poseidia.[10] Taking the feminine form, as Asule, rather than the male projection, Aczine, she ruled wisely and well, until giving way to the temptation posed by the innate ability to create living "things" for her pleasure, through the ancient practice of progeneration. It proved to be her undoing. But before her untimely death, described as "karma exercised in coma," the entity Asule had become the envy of many of those about her because of her androgynous state, which had once been commonplace, of course, among the early sons and daughters of the Law of One. (The androgynous soul-entity in question, it might be appropriate to add here, was none other than Edgar Cayce's twin soul, Gladys Davis, with Edgar then in unmanifest form.)

Esoteric sources, in explaining the dual nature of Adam, identify the Archetypal Man, or Upper Adam (whom we know as "Amilius"), with the Macrocosm, from which comes the microcosm—the latter being simply a diminution of the former, as the inevitable consequence of a "fallen" state of consciousness, marked by the earthly Adam's separation from his spiritual identity. Adamic man's evolutionary journey, then, involves a spiritual pilgrimage to shed his dualism and become one with the Macrocosm. "All creatures that have flowed out from God," Meister Eckhart tells us, "must become united into one Man, who comes again into the unity Adam was in before he fell."[11]

He then identifies the "one Man" plainly as the Christ, who was both the first Adam and the last Adam, or Jesus.

But how—and why—the fall?

Let me make bold to suggest that it was a matter of inevitability. Amilius, or the Logos, was committing a voluntary act of sacrifice when He chose to re-enter the earth in flesh-form as Adam, thus intentionally limiting His divine nature to the confines of matter. An aspect of the human condition, which He had voluntarily taken unto Himself, is its proneness to sin. Without yielding sooner or later to that weakness, and thereby presenting Himself with the same set of conditions faced by the rest of mankind, Amilius (or Adam, as He now was) could hardly have become a suitable Wayshower to others, mounting the cyclical wheel of mortal death and rebirth through some thirty incarnations until He had at last perfected Himself in the flesh as the "last Adam," or Jesus. Indeed, if Adam's "fall" had not been an integral part of the Divine Plan for mankind's eventual salvation, how else is one to explain that reference in Revelation to "the Lamb slain from the foundation of the world"?

In this respect, there is an enlightening exchange in one of the Cayce readings. Asked when Jesus first became aware that He was to be the Savior of the world, the stunning answer was given: "When He fell in Eden."[12]

As Amilius, or the Upper Adam, He presumably knew from the beginning of time. But in His fleshly selfhood, it took the commission of a sin before Adam's eyes were opened to his world role.

And the nature of the sin? "Consorting with others," was the somewhat enigmatic and surprising explanation offered by Mr. Cayce, without any reference at all to poor, maligned Eve or the allegorical apple.[13]

What "others" did Cayce mean?

One can only speculate, of course. But to suppose that Adam and Eve and the serpent were the only inhabitants of that earthly paradise called the Garden of Eden would be misleading. In fact, in a psychic reading on her past lives, a lovely young 20th-century housewife must have been startled to learn from the entranced Cayce that she had been present many millennia ago in "the garden called Eden," and "was among 'the things'" inhabiting that place, when Adam—and, later, Eve—first appeared.[14] Though of a relatively undeveloped nature at the time, she was told that she had been touched in spirit by what she saw, as those two innocent souls dwelt together, and Adam assigned names and meanings to the trees, the birds, and all about them.

In their full-sprung innocence, how easily might they have been beguiled? Remember: Atlantis, in Adam's day, was in the period of its final decline, as the corrupt sons of Belial contested anew with the children of the Law of One for control of the governing councils. Civil war was close upon the Poseidians. Even in the sacred groves outside the bustling city of Eden, where the Lord had placed Adam for his initial safety, there probably lurked abundant evil in angelic disguise. How tempting may some of the "things" have appeared to both Adam and Eve, as they saw them cohabiting in sportive pleasure in the grasses nearby? "Thou shalt surely die," Adam had reportedly been warned by his own Oversoul at the time of his initial projection, "if you yield to any of the forbidden pleasures around you. For all flesh is *not* one flesh!" But the same Cayce reading that had identified the sin of Adam as "consorting with others," also alluded to rebelliousness and selfish motives, which were responsible for bringing Satan, or the serpent, into Eden. "Thou shalt surely *not* die," the cooing voice of the Tempter reassured him, within. And so Adam yielded, at last, to the carnal temptation all around him—perhaps at Eve's urging, yes, though she could hardly be held accountable for his actions. In the apocryphal writings, in fact, it is intimated that Eve, too, may have "consorted with others," and that Cain, her murderous firstborn, was the offspring of such an illicit relationship, possibly with one of the sons of Belial. Then, later, after Adam first "knew" his wife, she gave birth to the upright Abel, whom Cain slew. (According to this account, Abel would have been the "legitimate" heir, thus explaining why Cain killed him. It would also clear up the mystery of God's rejection of Cain's offering.) After Cain's exile, Seth was born. And it was through Seth, of course, that the proper generational line was established.

Meanwhile, Adam's proverbial "fall" was to produce some notable changes.

No, indeed, he did not "surely die"—not yet. But we are told that Adam's mortal span was shortened as the result of his disobedience. However long he might otherwise have lived was not mentioned; but the Cayce reading in question added that he was only able to put off the inevitable consequences of his sinful behavior for another six hundred years.[15] Inasmuch as Adam's total life span, as given in Genesis, was nine hundred and thirty years, this means, of course, that he must have been three hundred and thirty when he fell from grace.

To fall from grace would seem to be punishment enough; but the author of Genesis adds that he was evicted from Eden, as well.

Perhaps. Yet, looking at the Cayce data, one might consider a somewhat different version. Whatever Adam's sin, he was not unrepentant. In fact, we have learned that his sin had caused Adam's eyes to be opened to the higher purpose for which he had come into a fleshly existence in the earth. Surely, then, if the Garden of Eden, in Atlantis, on the island of Poseidia, was still the place where he could best fulfill that mission, particularly now that he was awake to his predestined role, the Universal Forces would not have caused him to be driven out by vengeful angels and cherubim. May we not assume, instead, that it was the approaching destruction of Poseidia that caused Adam to be resituated in a new and safer environment—a "relocated Eden," so to speak—where he could fulfill the parenting phase of his destiny? For it was vital to the appearance and subsequent survival of the new root race that each of its five chosen progenitors be placed in an auspicious environment. And whereas Poseidia may indeed have been such an environment initially, its sins were soon due to find it out, as it were, and cause it to perish. Whether or not Adam might have saved it, had he not sinned, must remain a lingering question. Yet, probably not. For, paradoxically, we have already noted that it was only as the result of his sin that Adam at last awoke to his divine mission.

In Hindu lore, there is a fitting story of a man called *Adi-ma* (*Adi*, in Sanskrit, meaning "first") and his wife Heva, who once dwelt on an island—localized, as is typical of most folk tales, and identified with Ceylon—which they left one day. Having reached the mainland, they were cut off by a mighty convulsion and could not return. This account bears a curious relationship to the Chaldean story of a dark race, called *Ad-mi*, or *Ad-ami*, who were identified as the race "who had fallen." (As for the prefix *Ad*, suggesting the biblical "Adam," it is also associated in many ancient texts with *Ad*lantis, or Atlantis.[16] Yet again, a more orthodox source traces the name of the first man to *adama*, meaning "the red earth."[17] However, it may also be interpreted as further confirmation of Adam's Atlantean origins, inasmuch as the red race, born of the "red earth," is linked by a number of persistent legends to Plato's lost continent.)

But what became of Adam and Eve, we must ask, when they departed from Poseidia, and how did this affect the fate of the developing red race of flesh-form man?

Interesting questions.

Whereas all of Atlantis was at one time referred to as "the Eden of the world," and the original city of Eden was in Poseidia, on whose outskirts the fabled Garden of Eden was presumably located, Cayce surprises us by telling of yet another, later Eden.[18]

Since it is located far from Atlantis, in the region of the rolling foothills of the Caucasus and the Carpathian mountains—an area of the planet actually associated with the emerging white race, in the days of Adamic man—this sets one to wondering. Did the descendants of Adam and Eve merge with the peoples of the white race, leaving the red-skinned Atlanteans to their own evolutionary resources? It is a highly valid hypothesis.

In the first place, the scattering Atlanteans who survived the final cataclysm were absorbed, for the most part, by other racial groups and lost their own identity. The exception was in the Americas, where the Maya and the Incas, with their copper-colored skin, jet-black hair and haughty features, carried on certain of the Atlantean traits, as did the proliferating descendants of the sons of Belial who fled to the northern continent and became the American Indians. And although the Atlantean influx into ancient Egypt, to the Atlas Mountains of what is now Morocco, as well as to other parts of Africa, and the Basque region of Spain, may have left its racial imprint temporarily, today it is scarcely in evidence in any of these places. Similarly, the desert-wandering Semitic tribes descended from Adam and Eve, though genetically darkened by generations of gradual adaptation to the burning Sun, show a marked affinity today, as do most European Jews, to the white race, with little or no visible infusion of the red pigmentation of their legendary "parents."

Come, now, let us go a-sleuthing.

Adam, if we accept Cayce's account of things, was 330 years old when he and Eve left Poseidia for the general region of the Caucasus. As Atlanteans, living in an age of highly advanced technology, they presumably traveled by air, though their new environment would have been considerably more primitive than that which they left behind them.

The ill-conceived Cain, whether or not he was fathered by Adam, as the Bible states, was presumably born in the "new

Eden," as was Abel also. The fourth chapter of Genesis recounts the generations of Cain, who had been exiled to the "land of Nod," somewhere east of the Caucasian Eden, after murdering Abel. Seven generations, leading up to the birth of Tubal-cain, are given, before the author of Genesis tells us that Adam again knew his wife, and the result was a son "in his own likeness," named Seth. We are told, in Genesis 5, that Adam was then 130 years old, though we must assume that this reckoning inadvertently excludes the 330 years of his previous Atlantean existence. If we add the two figures together, this puts Adam's actual age at 460 at the time of Seth's birth. (All of this arithmetic, as we shall shortly discover, is of genuine importance in correlating the Cayce data with biblical history.)

Seven generations of Adam pass, until the birth of Enoch, 952 years after Adam's original Atlantean projection (using the preceding calculations, plus the generational intervals cited in Genesis 5). This places Enoch's birth 22 years after Adam's death, which is recorded in Genesis at age 930. This is significant. For, without taking into account the 330 years spent in Atlantis, Enoch's birth would have occurred during Adam's lifetime, thus presenting us with a dilemma. Why so? Because it is believed that Adam and Enoch were the same soul-entity, in successive incarnations. Not only do we find this view expressed in the *Clementine Homilies* and other apocryphal writings, but it was psychically corroborated by Edgar Cayce.[19]

Very well, then. If we accept the approximate dating of Adam's appearance at about 12,000 B.C., or the midpoint of the Age of the Virgin, this means that Enoch's arrival some 952 years later must have occurred circa 11,000 B.C. From Enoch to Noah was another three generations; but in those long-lived days, we find that they totalled 434 years. And it was in Noah's 600th year, the Bible informs us, that the Flood occurred. So we have accounted for yet another millennium, bringing us to 10,000 B.C. (give or take a century or so, depending upon Adam's precise date of arrival).

We are now getting down to the nitty-gritty, so pay close

attention.

The Edgar Cayce readings place the construction of the Great Pyramid of Gizeh in a one-hundred-year time frame, from 10,490 to 10,390 B.C., *before* the days of the Flood.[20] And the master architect, surprisingly, was none other than the patriarch Enoch. Having departed from the sight of his own kinsmen in his 365th Year, the apocryphal tradition says of Enoch that he traveled to the four corners of the earth to warn the people of an impending cataclysm. This was to be the final sinking of Atlantis, later followed by the Flood. In Egypt, however, Enoch was known to the people by another name: Thoth-Hermes.[21] By my reckoning, the patriarch would then have been perhaps 500 years old—still in his prime, one might say, compared to his son, Methuselah, who lived to be 969.

And the date of the Flood? The Cayce readings are imprecise. However, modern science can come to our aid on this point. In the September 22, 1975 issue of *Science*, a professor of marine geology, Cesare Emiliani, reported the discovery of seashell evidence of an ancient flood, which had apparently occurred as rapidly melting glaciers from the last Ice Age had caused the seas to rise with dramatic suddenness. Emiliani estimated a time frame in the general vicinity of 9,600 B.C., or 11,600 years ago. Confirmation of this general dating was obtainable from marine sedimentation in the Gulf of Mexico which clearly showed an episode of very low salinity and unusually cold water temperatures—factors clearly pointing to rapid glacial melting, along with rising ocean levels. Two further factors, not mentioned by Emiliani but obviously contributing to the flood phenomenon, would have been the simultaneous sinking of the last island remnant of the former Atlantean continent and the shifting of the poles as the Pleistocene epoch ended.

In any case, Emiliani's data not only lends credibility to Plato's legend of the lost Atlantis, but to the biblical account of Noah's primitive ark, which ultimately beached itself upon the heights of Mt. Ararat, in what is today a portion of Turkey, near the Iranian border. One would be inclined to guess that Noah had launched his rather cumbersome and overloaded vessel from a point not too far distant from where it was ultimately grounded, some seven months later. In short, if we may assume that Cayce was right as to the location of the "second Eden," we might be talking about a region of the Caucasus, where it borders the Caspian Sea.

Based on Emiliani's 9,600 B.C. timing, and this author's approximate dating of 10,000 B.C. for the Flood, it will be noted that the disparity is a mere four centuries (allowing for a modest discrepancy of two hundred years or so). Surely, in terms of millennia, that is amazingly close. Furthermore, Emiliani's dating, however scientifically arrived at, is undoubtedly subject to some fine-tuning, which could bring the psychic and the scientific evidence into nearly perfect synchronicity.

To contradict the notion common among Judeo-Christian fundamentalists that Noah and his immediate family were the only descendants of Adam and Eve to escape from the Great Deluge, we come to a rather astonishing life reading Cayce gave for a little seven-year-old girl.[22]

This child was told that she had been one of the female companions of Tubal-cain. The latter, of course, was a seventh-generation descendant of Eve's firstborn, Cain, who had been exiled to "the land of Nod." And where was that? East of Eden, says the Bible, in rather vague terms. Cayce, however, appears to place Cain's early descendants in the area of the great Euphrates River, probably down near its entrance into the Persian Gulf, where in ancient times it joined with the Tigris, creating a vast alluvial plain noted for its fertility. But the area was also noted for something else: it was on "the other side of the Flood." This, in fact, was where the city of Ur was located, from whence Abraham received a call from the Lord many centuries later. (Here the Chaldeans, famous soothsayers and worshipers of idols, dwelt in Abraham's day.)

In that same reading for Tubal-cain's companion there were some further surprises. For one thing, we are told that Tubal-cain, born to Lamech's second wife, Zilah, was "the first of the sons [in Cain's lineage] that had been made perfect," which is certainly a redemptive note of sorts. At the same time, Lamech's introduction of polygamy into his branch of the Adamic tribe brought discord and tribulation. And here we are suddenly confronted with a major surprise: Tubal-cain's new bride, dismayed and unhappy over her status as only one of a multiple number of wives, seeks out the great matriarch, Eve, who apparently resides nearby with her daughters, for solace and comfort. We are told that the entity Eve was then "in the tenth generation," or the generation of Noah, which meant, of course, that she had outlived Adam by several centuries. On his passage into the Interbetween, had she chosen to relocate nearer to the offspring of her firstborn? Despite Cain's grievous sin, no doubt the "mother of mankind," like any other mother, had long since forgiven him in her secret heart, and had sought out his children's children in her latter days. In fact, it may have been a way of atoning for her own wrongdoing. Moreover, however slight her good influence may have been upon Lamech, it is conceivable that she had played a part in Tubal-cain's upbringing, which led to Cayce's designation of him as "the first of the sons that had been made perfect" in those days. Whether she was able to turn him away from his father Lamech's polygamous path, however, is doubtful, inasmuch as it was to become a traditional way of life in that part of the world. (A clarification needs to be made at this juncture: Genesis presents us with not one, but *two* Lamechs. The one in reference here, in the line of Cain's descendants, should not be confused with the Lamech among Seth's more righteous offspring, whose famous son was Noah, not Tubal-cain.)

Meanwhile, some years before Noah's appearance, mankind's evolutionary march was being helped forward by another great matriarch in the Adamic line besides Eve.

In 1932, a 23-year-old Jewish girl learned from Mr. Cayce that she was indeed an "old soul," in terms of earthly experiences, and one who had taken bodily form for a designated purpose in the days after Adam's passing.[23] She was used, she was told, "rather as the experiment" for the expression of spiritual forces. In short, she became the chosen channel—as Jared's companion, presumably—for the return of Adam to the earth plane, in what was to be his very first fleshly appearance as a man-child born of woman. He came, in that specially prepared incarnation, as Enoch, bringing with him great wisdom in the furtherance of his world role, far exceeding his accomplishments as Adam.

That particular life reading must have represented a very special experience, at least for Edgar Cayce. When it was over, and just as Gertrude Cayce was about to give her reclining husband the customary suggestion to wake up from his self-induced psychic trance, he suddenly spoke of himself in the third person, telling those assembled to watch closely, and they would be able to see the returning soul-entity, which had traveled far this time in its out-of-body seeking, hover and re-enter "as the light of the body." (His secretary, Gladys Davis, when I once asked her what, if anything, she might have seen on that occasion, said a sudden bead of light was briefly visible.)

Whether or not the authentic remains of Noah's ark still lie somewhere atop Mt. Ararat, as various expeditions have sought unsuccessfully to prove, there is little reason to doubt the legend of the Flood. It persists in almost every language and culture, while the unfolding new discoveries of modern science, as we have already noted, tend increasingly to reinforce its reality rather than otherwise.

The oldest of Noah's sons was Shem, and one of his descendants was Peleg, whose name meant "division," referring to those postdiluvian days when the earth was divided and most of its remaining peoples were cut off from one another—or, as one of the Cayce readings put it, "when the waters were divided, and the earth's sphere was changed,"[24] thus linking the Deluge to the shifting of the poles.

It is small wonder, then, in the centuries and millennia following such catastrophic events, that much of the evolutionary record of mankind became obscured or permanently lost.

This refers, as well, to much of the antediluvian evidence, which was erased or buried by the earth changes. Meanwhile, it is not hard to imagine the generally chaotic conditions that must have prevailed in the immediate postdiluvian era, as the widely scattered pockets of surviving populations around the vastly altered planet were forced, in many instances, into the most primitive of circumstances just to maintain a marginal existence.

Thus, when today's archaeologists and paleoanthropologists look at the available evidence confronting them, they are almost bound to come up with some badly flawed and contradictory conclusions. On the one hand, there are such architectural marvels as the Egyptian pyramids, while on the other, one looks at the primitive stone tools and weapons of the early American Indians and concludes that they were a race of slowly evolving savages—rather than the reverse, perhaps. Those suddenly transplanted Atlanteans, leaving behind them all of the amenities of a highly evolved civilization, were now obliged to become hunters and gatherers, often even attacking and killing one another to protect their territories, much in the manner of animals. Similarly, in caves throughout Europe, there are baffling signs of highly artistic and emotionally sensitive cave-residents from the unknown past, along with the more primitive remains of the Neanderthals. And whereas it was once assumed that the Sumerian culture, dating back to 5,000 B.P., was the world's oldest, the recent unearthing of a 10,000-year-old town in southern Turkey, at a site identified as Cayonu, has upset all former assumptions.[25] Its sophisticated architectural remains offer dramatic testimony in support of the long-held esoteric view that our civilization has far more ancient roots than most of us ever imagined. (And how great was Cayonu, one wonders, compared to the sunken marvels of an infinitely more ancient and splendid Atlantis?)

Classical Darwinism has long been out of date. Indeed, a number of Darwin's most cherished views have subsequently been challenged and overturned by his successors, which, after all, is in the nature of scientific progress. Even his pivotal theory of natural selection has not escaped a critical reassessment, with many scientists willing to concede that it is more speculation than fact. On one stubborn point, however, and despite the continuing lack of any reliable evidence to support them after more than a century of searching, evolutionists seem to be universally agreed that Darwin was right about the simian connection. Belief in a "missing link" between man and ape (or, more precisely, the chimpanzee) has become an article of faith, as firm and unshakable as the religionist's faith in man's higher, more spiritual origins.

The earliest hope of the anthropologists was the discovery of Neanderthal man, back in 1856. His skeletal remains suggested a stooped and beetle-browed figure, brawny but rather brainless. Later, however, as other Neanderthal bones showed up—not only in Europe, but elsewhere—it was determined that the "stooped" posture of the first find was apparently due to arthritis, since the others walked upright. But despite the look of promise on his simian-like brow, Neanderthal was dropped as a prospect only recently. In truth, his candidacy fell by the wayside some 35,000 years ago, when, as we now know, his breed suddenly vanished from the earth without leaving a trace. Neanderthal disappeared as mysteriously as he had come, some forty millennia earlier. (An Atlantean subrace, perhaps, resulting from the mixtures with the "things," which either played itself out or underwent regeneration?) Meanwhile, since it has now been determined that modern man, known as *Homo sapiens*, has at least been around for 200,000 years, it is intriguing to note the correlation of that general dating with Cayce's psychic input on the origins of the Atlantean culture and first coming of the third root race.

Let us run through the roster of ancestral candidates dug up by the anthropologists, from the Piltdown hoax of 1912 and, later, *Hesperopithecus* (who turned out to be an extinct pig), to such relatively respectable findings as *Homo erectus* and *Homo habilis* (though the ancestral status of each of these two is still indeterminate), or the 3.2 million-year-old fossil hominid dubbed "Lucy," whose 1979 discovery in Ethiopia is still beset by many problems, we are told, before her identification as an ancestral species can be positively confirmed.[26] We have skipped more than a few; but the complete list tends to be rather unproductive, offering us no truly convincing evidence as to our purported simian origins.

Meanwhile, man's scientific search for his evolutionary roots has taken a turn down an altogether different path than that of the "bone peddlers." The geneticists, working in lab coats rather than carrying pick-axes, hope to find Adam and Eve and Bonzo by tracking down the clues in the human DNA coding. Let us wish them luck. In one sense, at least, they are on the right track: rather than sifting through the external evidence, they have begun to look within.

Yet it is mind, not matter, that holds the clues to our origins. Mind, said Cayce, is ever the builder; the body is merely the result. And the origin of mind? The Maker.

EGYPT'S DAY IN THE SUN

History repeats itself. It moves in cycles. These cycles, in turn, are linked to the cyclical journey through time and space of the stars, the Sun, and our own spinning earth, as they carry us inexorably forward in our evolution. For, indeed, each entity, each soul, as it returns again and again to this plane of activity, is in the process of evolving toward the First Cause. Yet each, in patience, must repeat its lessons until they are properly learned; and thus we take note of the repetitive nature of things as we slowly advance, though sometimes with seemingly backward steps, from one stage to the next, from one age to another . . .

Angelic hosts attend us here. And from time to time, God's messengers appear among us. They come at propitious moments in the earth's history, in answer to a higher call, fulfilling that role which is suited to our particular development and need at the time. Born in the flesh, with the same earthly burdens and mortal frailties as the rest of us, all that sets these fellow souls apart is their awareness of a spiritual mission. Their purpose is always to point the way that will lead us back to the center of our being, beyond the web of time and space or the dark dream of separation from our Creator, whose divine spark lies dormant within us, a potential god in the making.

Such a chosen messenger concerns us now, for his is the central role in the unfolding story that lies ahead.

Into ancient Egypt, as the Adamic Age was still in its infancy, there came an unusual figure. Tall and priestly looking, with kindly but penetrating eyes the color of azurite, a noble brow and vaguely sensual mouth, he had a tumbling mane of flaxen hair that framed a beardless face whose patrician profile was as exquisitely carved and pale as if sculpted from alabaster. Though obviously youthful yet, he with his grey-blue robe and cowl had an air of unmistakable spiritual authority, which was matched by the compelling power of his speech. All stood in awe of him, marveling at his strange appearance and charismatic manner. But the one aspect of the newcomer's physical makeup that most impressed the worshipful Egyptians was the startling whiteness of his skin: its likes had never been seen before.

Nor was this surprising. For this was the legendary Ra—although Ra Ta, we are told, was his original name. Symbolically, it was a name said to represent a joining of the hieroglyphs for "Sun" and "earth," and in the superstitious minds of the sun-worshiping inhabitants of early Egypt meant "Sun [brought to] earth." Our psychic source, however, in a more literal interpretation of the matter, tells us that the name really signified "the first *pure* white" in the earth.[1] In short, the priestly Ra Ta marked the emergence of the developing white race in its final, purified form, among the chosen five racial groupings initiated by Amilius in the days of Adam, somewhat earlier.

A spiritual guide to his own adopted tribal group, which had journeyed into prehistoric Egypt from the distant slopes of Mt. Ararat, in what is now Turkey, Ra Ta had come in response to a psychic prompting. He had been here before, as the ancient ruler Asapha, and so it could be said in a sense that he was now returning to his own. Yet the former time was in the days of man's first faint beginnings as man, and many millennia ahead of the Adamic ideal now in the process of establishing itself as the fourth root race.

Between earthly appearances, we are told that each soul-entity undertakes planetary sojourns within the present solar system as a kind of schooling process. These "sojourns" are akin to spheres of consciousness wherein the soul may review and assimilate its recent experience gained in the earth, and then prepare itself for further soul development in the next earthly round. In this respect, Asapha's re-entry into the flesh as Ra Ta had been "from the infinity forces, or from the Sun,"[2] which was sufficiently unusual to suggest an earth-being visibly in tune with the Creative Energy itself, thus contributing to the Sun-god legend that was later to surround his name. Additionally, Ra Ta's arrival in Egypt had occurred during the Age of Leo, whose astrological ruler is the Sun. Inasmuch as the ruler of any zodiacal sign is known to wield its influence throughout its reign, it was one more reason for a sun-worshiping people to attach a symbolic significance to the shining appearance in their midst of a flaxen-haired, pale-bodied stranger, whose priestly garb convinced them of his higher origins.

In truth, Ra Ta's origins were sufficiently "different" to set him apart in other respects, as well. A Cayce reading on that formative era in mankind's history tells us that his birth was influenced by heavenly forces, referred to somewhat cryptically as "the gods in the Caspian and the Caucasian mountains," and that he was "the son of a daughter of Zu that was *not* begotten of man."[3]

An immaculate conception? So it would seem, from the wording given. And our first impulse might be to reject such a notion as either myth or sacrilege—perhaps both. Yet, logically considered, such spiritually guided conceptions may have been occurring at that time within each of the five branches of the new root race. Enoch's conception and birth through some unexplained mode of "experimentation," as mentioned in the preceding chapter, may have been of a similar nature, thus giving us a clue as to what was taking place. For, in that crucial stage of its unfoldment, it may have been essential to the survival of the new race to introduce a mode of higher intervention which would ensure the genetic purity of a certain number of chosen prototypes. These, like Ra and Enoch, were destined to play key roles in carrying forward the Divine Plan for the eventual salvation and return of the souls trapped in the earthly cycle.

Furthermore, we are told that the individual of that period in human history was not so closely knit in matter, being still within the orbit of its spiritual origins.[4] It is an important distinction to make: it places into proper perspective the near-miraculous accomplishments by Ra Ta and his priestly associates later on, working in the Temple of Sacrifice and the Temple Beautiful, which were established for the physical, mental, and spiritual regeneration of the thousands of Egyptians still trapped as "things" on a lower rung of the evolutionary ladder.

Ra Ta's personal history can be briefly told. It has been recounted in detail elsewhere;[5] but here we are concerned primarily with his evolutionary role.

Rejected in childhood by his own kinsmen because of disputes among the elders as to his odd appearance and his contested origins, Ra Ta found his way to Ararat's tribe, on the flanks of the great mountain that was later to bear the leader's name, as it does to this day. There he was warmly received by the wise shepherd-king, and grew up in company with the king's son, Arart. Given to dreams and visions, Ra Ta one day received a command from the Spirit to go into the land now known as Egypt, which lay far to the south, where the gods would further instruct him what to do. He went, unhesitatingly. Joining him were some nine hundred hardy pioneers from among Ararat's people, led by the king's son, Arart, who was to become the first of Egypt's legendary "shepherd-kings from the north," with Ra Ta assuming the role of high priest over Arart's forces and the peacefully conquered Egyptians.

All went well, at first. Harmony reigned among the invaders and the native population for a number of decades, as Ra Ta established the Temple of Sacrifice and the Temple Beautiful to carry out his revealed work of cleansing the lower beings among the local population and fitting them mentally and spiritually for full participation in the new root race. But some of the restrictive measures being instituted by both Ra Ta and Arart were eventually resented by a portion of the population, particularly among the former ruling class and the increasing numbers of Atlantean immigrants, including a troublemaking handful of sons of Belial allowed in by the king.[6] The Atlanteans, escaping from a prophesied worldwide cataclysm that would totally devastate the remaining islands of their once-mighty continent, sought as usual to impose their will upon all around them. Their limited numbers, however, prevented any actual takeover, whereas members of their priesthood, working closely with Ra Ta, actually contributed much to the temple activities through their superior technical knowledge and spiritual training.

Nevertheless, in an astute move to quell the growing friction throughout the land, Arart stepped down and let his 16-year-old son Araaraart, who had been born in Egypt, succeed him. He also placed a locally popular young scribe in the role of chief councilor to his son, which placated the dissidents for a while. And thus things bumbled along until the young king's thirtieth year, when subversive elements set about hatching a plot to undo both king and high priest. Ra Ta, in his overeagerness to advance and expand the development of the white race he himself epitomized, was easily trapped by the plotters. Using the king's favorite dancer, Isris (or Isis), as their bait, they persuaded her to convince the priest that she would be the ideal companion with whom he might produce the perfect offspring. When Ra Ta yielded to Isis' suggestion, not only did he violate his own ruling regarding monogamous relationships (for by now he already had a wife and several children), but he unthinkingly invited the wrath of the young king. The dismal and not unexpected outcome, much to the glee of the plotters, was the priest's exile, along with Isis and a retinue of faithful followers, to a high mount in the Nubian hills. Meanwhile, the child who had been born to Isis was kept hostage by the king; she was destined to die of desolation in her sixth year.

Now the plotters set about trying to topple the isolated king, but their cunning machinations were foiled in the end. Yet the stubborn ruler, inwardly aware of his foolishness in alienating himself from the priest and his many supporters, continued to keep Ra Ta in exile for nine turbulent years before he was finally persuaded by wise advisers that bringing him back would be the only way to restore peace, order, and prosperity to the badly divided land.

Yet, Ra Ta's exile was not wholly unproductive: joining him in the mount was that great Teacher referred to by Cayce as Hermes,[7] who came to be known to the Egyptians as Thoth, or Thoth-Hermes, and who was to be identified much later by the Greeks as Hermes *Trismegistos*, or "Thrice-Great." As previously disclosed, however, the wise stranger's proper identity, if we accept as true the long-held legendary synonymity, was the patriarch Enoch, a reincarnation of Adam. And he had come to warn Ra Ta of the need to preserve the records of things past and things to come, as a testimonial to a future new age.

Meanwhile, during the long years of exile among the Nubians, Ra Ta and his followers, aided by that great Initiate, or Teacher, who had one day appeared so mysteriously in their midst, kept busy. There was much work to do. Ra Ta, with help from the cooperative Nubians, was conducting what would be termed archaeological research through psychic guidance; also, digging deep into the surrounding hills, he began the first studies of latitude and longitude, and engaged in astronomical studies of the planets and the constellations, observing and charting their movements through the heavens. As for Hermes, he ever remained in close communion with the Creative Forces. For he was formulating his master-plan for the construction of the basic features of what was to become known as the famous "Gizeh complex" in a latter-day Egypt (when its major edifice would be mistaken as a tomb for the Pharaoh Cheops). To be built upon Ra Ta's anticipated repatriation, and involving a full century for its elaborate construction, the massive layout would begin with a hidden Pyramid of Records to be buried under the sand, where it would await discovery by appointed initiates in the dayspring of the next root race. Next there would be that most visible of earthly monuments and marvels, the Great Pyramid itself, dominating the Gizeh plain. This dazzling monolith of incredibly precise inner and outer dimensions, with its various puzzling passageways and chambers, including the mysterious empty sarcophagus meant to symbolize victory over death, was to be a temple of initiation, first and foremost. Yet, simultaneously, it was planned by Hermes as a virtually indestructible record in stone (interpretable only by initiates) of coming events leading up to his own Second Coming as the resurrected Savior of mankind, many millennia hence. Finally, on Ra Ta's advice, there was to be included in the plan a memorial actually begun before his exile. Known today as the Sphinx, it would commemorate the regeneration of the "things," through the activities in the Temple of Sacrifice and the Temple Beautiful—a half-human, half-animal figure, crouching in the sands like a beast, but gazing, godlike, into Infinity: the ultimate paradox. (To its inspired builders, and to successive generations of Egyptians for some time to come, the great symbolic statue must have constituted a powerful evolutionary statement; but to the uncomprehending eyes of future ages, it was destined to become—what? The ultimate enigma!)

Ra Ta's attunement with those solar forces which rule our lives in the material realm undoubtedly indicated a close vibratory kinship with the Divine Son, who is also identified with celestial Fire and Light, and whose visible symbol in the earth is the Sun. (One of the Cayce readings, in a metaphorical reference to "thy own little solar system" within, which draws its pattern from without, alludes to the varied spheres of consciousness represented by the Sun and the planets, and asks: "Have you— love, the circle, the Son [Sun]?"[8]) It should not surprise us, then, to find that the Son himself, in His role as Hermes, ultimately joined forces with the exiled high priest and apparently worked in close collaboration with him for the 100-year span during which the Great Pyramid and its related structures were going up, from 10,490 to 10,390 B.C. Hermes, in fact, is specifically identified in ancient legendary accounts, as well as in the Cayce readings on the Egyptian epoch, as the pyramid's master architect.[9]

Meanwhile, there are some scholarly notes this author has pulled together. They are relatively brief, so let us have a look at them, for they are very instructive at this juncture of our story. More than that, they lend some respectable reinforcement to the psychic view being presented herein of not only Hermes, but Ra as well.

The eminent Egyptologist, E. A. Wallis Budge, in *The Gods of the Egyptians*, tells us that Ra was the visible emblem of God. Embodiment of the Light, come down to man, he had his home both in heaven and on earth. Of all the gods known to the ancient Egyptians, only one was greater than Ra: this was Thoth, or Thoth-Hermes, who epitomized the Word. Thoth, called "lord of divine words," and "thrice great," was the scribe of the gods, and regarded as "the heart and the tongue of Ra." Identified as Ra's "vicar on earth," he was sometimes symbolically depicted with the head of a black and white ibis (emblematic of the union of the opposites), wearing a crown.

Continuing in this vein, the anonymous authors of *The Kybalion* claim that this same scribe of the gods was also called "the Master of masters," and that savants journeyed to Egypt from all parts of the ancient world to learn the Hermetic teachings from his lips. That legendary bit of information has its curious corollary in the Cayce readings, where we learn that Egypt, after Ra's return in company with Hermes from the mount of exile, became a great center of spiritual learning, where savants from all of the developing races of man gathered, and later sent forth emissaries to share their new-found knowledge of the universal laws with others.

In a reaffirmation of Hermes' earthly identification with Enoch, as well as with the original Word, or Logos, we go to several sources. First, Manly P. Hall: "Investigators believe that it was Hermes who was known to the Jews as 'Enoch.' Hermes of all creatures was nearest to God."[10] Next, citing a teaching of the Naassenes, an early Gnostic sect, C. G. Jung relates: "For they say Hermes is the Logos, the interpreter and fashioner of what has been, is, and will be."[11] Similarly, Jean Doresse cites this line attributed to Hermes from an untitled Gnostic treatise in the Chenoboskion library: "I have told thee, my son, that I am the Nous [the Word]."[12]

In the apocryphal *Book of Enoch* not only are the patriarch's journeys to the four quarters of the earth and the upper heavens recounted, but Enoch is credited with all manner of revelations and prophecies supposedly divulged to him by the angel Uriel. This included foreknowledge of the Universal Deluge, an event apparently attributed to a shift in the poles, for our source adds that "the earth became inclined."[13] History, as we have already noted, repeats itself . . .

We have also observed, at the outset of this chapter in our journey, that angelic hosts attend us here. (That biblical assurance, "He hath given His angels charge over thee," may presumably be taken quite literally. In fact, our psychic source tells us it is true that there is a guide or guard for each and every soul in the earth.[14]) Which brings us back to that angel Uriel, who aided and instructed Enoch in his earthly rounds. In our modern age, we are inclined to mock such notions. Superstitions, we call them, with that knowing wink of the worldly-wise. Yet the educated skepticism of our modern age in the face of unseen forces in our midst may not be so much a sign of our intellectual advancement as a symptom of our waning spiritual awareness under the rapid onslaught of materialism—a trend that needs to be reversed, of course, but will probably require another major cataclysm, even as Cayce foresaw happening at the close of our present century, as the necessary prelude to a new age and a new root race ... and a new awakening.

Uriel is identified in noncanonical lore as the archangel of salvation, and the messenger sent by God to Noah to warn him of the impending Deluge.[15] Quite appropriately, then, this same angelic force may have been watching over Enoch, even as Uriel's counterpart, the dark angel Ariel, is said to have caused the same entity to stumble in his prior incarnation as Adam. "Where is Ariel," Cayce once asked rhetorically, "and who was he?" He then proceeded to answer his own question: "A companion of Lucifer or Satan, and one that made for the disputing of the influences in the experience of Adam in the garden."[16]

As we can see, there are angelic voices to be heeded, and others to be shunned. But the lures of the latter, which are always linked to some subtle form of self-aggrandizement (even as Ra Ta listened to Isis, Adam to Eve), can only take hold when the lower self, or human will, is allowed to do all the listening ...

The Temple of Sacrifice, the Temple Beautiful: how to define and differentiate those two temples of service in ancient Egypt during the time of Ra? For, between them, they embodied the larger, but now forgotten, part of the priest's earthly mission, and along with the Great Pyramid and other more visibly enduring memorials, marked Egypt's most glorious hour in history—her everlasting day in the Light.

As for the Temple of Sacrifice, it might find its modern

equivalent in any well-staffed hospital employing the most up-to-date facilities for the specific diagnosis and treatment of physical disorders—up to a point. For there were vast differences involved, partly of a genetic nature, and partly technological and psychological, which placed those medical services in the Temple of Sacrifice far beyond the scope of our present-day understanding. The successful evolution of the unfolding new root race required the elimination of any remaining impediments to the total regeneration of those unfortunate beings who still remained in the lower evolutionary stages. Therefore, the first step, or stage, was a sacrificial one, in the sense that the *physical* hindrances must be removed. The animal-like characteristics or appendages were too varied and grotesque to enumerate in detail, but required in many instances massive surgery and modes of electro-therapy unknown to us today. The major contributors in these areas, particularly following the resumption of the healing activities in the priest's post-exile phase, were experienced teams of Atlantean surgeons and technicians among the children of the Law of One. For Atlanteans were arriving in Egypt in ever-increasing numbers in those days, as underground rumblings in their stricken homeland became more ominous than ever, signaling the inevitable approach of the final cataclysm.

As for the Temple Beautiful, even as its name implied, it entailed a quite different set of activities than the Temple of Sacrifice.

Over the entrance were these words: PARCO SO SUNO CUM. In translation, they meant, "Lord, lead Thou the way."[17] The novice, upon passing through those sacred doors, was committing himself (or herself) physically, mentally, and spiritually to an elaborate process of inner and outer purification, as he undertook the several stages of initiation. Upon completion, he would be expected to dedicate himself to service in accord with the teachings received, which were based upon the Law of One.

Externally in the form of a pyramid, the temple's colorful interior, decorated with linens and silks and precious gems and metals from every known land, was in the shape of a globe, symbolizing to all who passed through, or served there, a service to the world. Apparently somewhat open-structured, not only for visual effect, but to permit a weblike crossing of ascending and descending passageways through the middle portion, leading from one station or stage to another, there was a total of seven stations. Representing the seven stages of man's development, each had its seal and symbol. They were given by Mr. Cayce as follows, without further explanation: the world, the beetle; birth, the cockrel; mind, the serpent; wisdom, the hawk; the cross; the crown; the door or gate, the way.[18]

As for the first-named, we may assume that the "beetle" was the scarab, a well-known Egyptian symbol of the divine nature, which enters the lower, from which it afterwards emerges. Epiphanius, we learn, spoke of Christ as "the scarab of God." One is tempted to speculate whether it was perhaps the Great Initiate himself, as Hermes, who introduced that symbol to the Egyptians, through Ra, who thereafter incorporated it as the introductory stage of the initiation process?

Colors and auras, music, dance, vibrations—all played important parts in the temple services, along with chants and prayers and meditation. Quite obviously, it was a consciousness-raising experience, with the innate potential of liberating any trapped being from its material bonds and fetters.

The purified fourth root race was well along its way.

Besides the scarab, another ancient symbol with esoteric connotations has come down to us from the days of Hermes. It is the Egyptian *ankh*. Originally a heavenly circle atop an earthbound *tau* cross, it was meant to depict the temporarily suspended union between God and His crucified Son, or the Word, then known as Hermes, who was destined to dwell in the earth until raised up again. With the passage of time, however, the Egyptian *ankh* degenerated into a sexual symbol, representative of the life-force in the earth. It is a perversion of its spiritual origins and its higher meaning, which must re-emerge as the New Age consciousness is further awakened. For the *ankh*, properly understood, portrays the present human condition and the necessary purification process confronting each and every soul that has separated itself from its Maker. But if the cross is a symbol of earthly suffering, it is also a joyful sign; it points the way to the resurrective experience, and the soul's reunion with its Source.

THE CITY OF GOLD

It could be said in truth that the City of Gold, like the fabled phoenix bird, arose out of the ashes of a dying Lemuria. For, without Lemuria's demise, it could not have had its beginning.

As internal fires caused that ancient continent to erupt in volcanic fury, at last sinking into the Pacific in what must have seemed to many of its horrified inhabitants like divine retribution for their ungodly ways, those who managed to escape fled either to the east or the west.

To the east lay the primitive Americas. Largely ice-bound in the northern hemisphere, the high and arid plateau region of the Southwest became an area of choice for some, as did the connecting central belt and portions of the southern hemisphere for others. Meanwhile, to the west of the lost Lemuria lay the vast Asian landmass, much of which was still largely unsettled. It was in this direction that scattered Lemurian tribes of what were to become the united peoples of the extensive Gobi Land—also known, to some, as the Land of Mu—decided to go. Many wandered southward, settling in what is now Indo-China and Thailand, while others moved up through China to the then-fertile area known to us today as the Gobi Desert and Mongolia. Though great distances separated them, they were to remain as one people for many generations to come.

The leadership, however, found its focus in a place called the City of Gold, built on the fertile Gobi plains. For it was here that the great leader Mu made his appearance in the flesh, in those days when the five Adamic projections were entering into the experience of the children of men.

We are told that those relocated tribes, stretching from Indo-China to Mongolia, were separate clans of evolving "things," now gathered together for a common purpose. Described as "separate entities or souls disentangling themselves" from the animal associations, they were projections that "had come from those influences that were termed Lemure, or Lemurian"; and they now chose to establish themselves as a free and classless society under Mu, their wise ruler and lawgiver, who was equally revered by them as a prophet.[1]

In their ongoing evolution, the united tribes under Mu and his early successors, though tending to differ considerably in stature and appearance at the start, gradually took on those fairly uniform physical characteristics that have come to be commonly associated with the yellow race. These included, in addition to the distinguishing pigmentation, a certain roundness of face; small, flat nose; black hair; and a relatively modest height, compared to the other races. Such typical features, in fact, we find mentioned by the sleeping Cayce in describing an Indo-Chinese descendant of the original immigrants, in 9,026 B.C.;[2] whereas Muzuen, the son and successor of Mu, who lived in the preceding millennium during the days of Ra and Hermes, is described as being nearly six feet tall, blue-eyed, hair dark gold, hands *six*-fingered![3] This last-named genetic trait may originally have been common among certain of the Lemurians, though later genetically modified to conform to the five-fingered Adamic pattern. (Eugenics, we are told, was regularly practiced among the people of the Gobi Land throughout the formative period of the new race.)

The Gobi region, in the early days of Mu's long reign, was a timbered wilderness. We must place Mu's arrival there simultaneous with that of Adam, in Eden, judging by the synchronicity Cayce assigned to the initial five projections of the ideal flesh-form prototype, of whom Mu appears to have been one. But if Adam's days were to be cut short by his willful disobedience, we may assume that such was not altogether the case with Mu. Mu must have walked somewhat more closely with God. At any rate, his days on earth would seem to have extended several hundred years beyond Adam's 930-year total.

The basis for this conclusion lies in the given dating for

Muzuen's rule, which began in his sixteenth summer, we are told, on the eve of the Ra Ta era in Egypt. He was later destined to participate in that era in its latter days as one of the visiting dignitaries and savants who joined with Saneid from India, Yak from Carpathia, Ajax from the doomed Atlantis, and numerous others from the various lands of the children of men who assembled in Egypt's City of Bethel to exchange knowledge and to hear the higher teachings directly from the lips of that great Teacher of teachers, Hermes, in association with the high priest Ra.

Mu, as one of the five prototypes in the days of Adam, must have been well past the millennium mark when Muzuen was born, toward the end of his long rule. Meanwhile, it is indeed quite fortunate for us that this former "prince of the Gobi Land" found his way to Edgar Cayce in a modern-day incarnation, and obtained a number of life readings dealing with his ancient life as Muzuen. For it is from those readings[†] that we are now able to construct a fairly accurate and detailed picture of what life in that early evolutionary epoch must have been like for one of the five developing branches of Adamic man. Added to what we already know of the same era, as it existed in both Egypt and Atlantis, it provides us with a useful comparison of separately evolving cultures and adds many fresh insights into the early origins of *Homo sapiens*—ourselves, in brief, a little earlier bound.

From the very beginning, one of the secrets of Mu's successful rule over a broadly scattered population lay in the principle of harmonizing the needs of man with the laws of nature, which he taught to all the people. In effect, he saw man as the husbandman of the land around him, responsible for maintaining its productivity through intelligent use and conservation. As a consequence, the people remained respectful of their resources, never exhausting them out of thoughtlessness or greed, or going hungry through waste. If a tree was cut down to provide one with timber, a seedling of its kind was planted nearby; one hunted to obtain needed leathers or furs for winter garments, but not to the threatened extinction of any species, and never in excess of one's actual needs; and so forth, with all things.

This may explain why bodily adornment, with precious stones or metals, was never popular in the Gobi Land, as it was elsewhere. At the same time, any visitor to the famed "City of Gold" during the rule of Muzuen, in marveling at the glittering splendor of its architectural masterpiece, the Temple of Gold, might have wondered at this ostentatious exception to the general rule. No doubt the explanation lay in the fact that this gilded structure was intended to honor and glorify the Maker, not man. Even so, in keeping with the conservative principles instilled in him by his wise father, Muzuen turned to vari-colored, polished woods for the interior walls and paneling, eschewing an excess of gold. (Cayce indicated, incidentally, that this magnificient showpiece of prehistoric Oriental architecture, long since buried by earthquake or other natural disaster of a bygone age, is still intact and may one day be uncovered— including electric elevators!)

Gold, which may have been in relative abundance in the many high mountain streams that watered the Gobi plains, and thus easy to come by, was adopted by Muzuen as the coin of the realm. At first minted in a smooth, almost square shape, with a hole in the center so that the coins might be strung together and worn about the waist or neck, the design was later modified slightly when Muzuen learned that it was almost identical with its Atlantean counterpart: a raised edge was thus added as a distinguishing mark. Payment for a day's labor, regardless of the nature of the work or the age or sex of the laborer, was the same for everyone: a single gold coin. As a consequence, the price of any commodity tended to be held within the reach of all.

Monogamy was the rule of the land. Another rule, strictly enforced, was this: "He that labors not, eats not." There were, of course, exceptions in the case of the very young and the very old or infirm. With respect to the latter, however, euthanasia was commonly practiced, though in a very humane and painless manner, and only after ascertaining that a return to health or further usefulness to the community was not possible.

As to the spiritual philosophy, it was founded on an early version of the Golden Rule: "As ye would that thy neighbor do unto you, do unto him." In the temple services, there were no priests as in other lands. Instead, the services were in the manner of an open forum, much in the present-day manner of the Quakers, where any member might speak up when moved by the spirit of thoughtfulness.

Equality between the sexes was another admirable aspect of life in the Gobi Land. Nor was there any taxation: all labored, and it was truly a government of the people, by the people, and for the people. A common storehouse was maintained, as well as a common bank. In summary, it was a very utopian form of communism.

But like all utopias, it could only survive in isolation. When it came to defense, Muzuen was "a *prepared* pacifist." A system of warning drums, and the setting of explosives, kept any potential enemies at bay. Only in a much later era, with the gradual disintegration of the ideal society built up by Mu and Muzuen, did armor and the training of warriors become a necessity. For it was the intrusion of aliens, and alien ideas, that gradually brought about divisions in the land in a later age.

The inevitable cycle of change and dissolution, which is also the harbinger of renewal, had ended one era so that another might be born, with its own set of lessons for an evolving mankind.

13

A PERSIAN PALIMPSEST

It was an unusual way to begin a life reading. "Yes," said the unconscious Cayce, "the book is opened here."[1] (What he was referring to, of course, was the entity's akashic record, also called the "book of remembrance.")

As the reading unfolded, it was like a Persian palimpsest. A palimpsest, of course, is an old scroll or parchment on which the former words have been rubbed out to make room for a more modern transcript. In this case, however, just the opposite was happening: the modern record of Persia's origins was being replaced by an extremely ancient version of events—one quite unknown to our history books.

Of particular interest in this reading, which was set in a time-frame approximately 12,500 years ago (simultaneous with the Ra Ta era in Egypt), was its apparent linkage of the 900-mile arc of the Carpathian hills, in what is now Eastern Europe and a part of the Soviet Union, with a prehistoric Persia. The entity was told that she had then been a princess in "the Persian or Carpathian experience." It was at a time when "the Persian or Aryan land," as Cayce termed it, was in its primitive beginnings as one of the five nations of Adamic man, and the seat of the emerging white race. Composed, one suspects, of loosely feder- ated tribes joined by common interests, its vast domain and influence apparently extended for a time into upper India, forming the great Indo-Aryan empire. (By way of confirmation, our source tells us in a separate reading that "a portion" of the white race found its expression in upper India, although that country was not an original site for any of the five racial projections.[2])

In looking at a map, one will see that the Carpathian region does not connect directly with modern-day Iran, or Persia, but rather with that portion of Asia Minor identified today with the Caucasus and eastern Turkey, which lies between them. Thus, if Persia and Carpathia were indeed joined as one, they must have embraced this midsectional land as well. In fact, we are reminded that Ra Ta, described in a previous chapter as "the first *pure* white" in the earth, had his origins in the Caspian region and the Caucasus, later joining with the people of Ararat, in what is now the northeasternmost tip of Turkey, all within the speculative boundaries of the unified Aryan land.

But let us return to our "palimpsest."

In those days, India was known as the Land of Said, where the wise Saneid ruled. It then shared a common border with Persia (which Iran today shares with Pakistan, in the changing order of history). And across this border infiltrating tribes from Said had begun pushing into Persia. This created turmoils. Help was therefore sought from the stronger Carpathian forces to stem the unwanted invasion. In relating this point, Cayce told the entity for whom the reading was being given that she had personally assumed control of the situation; for, though a female, she was a figure of authority in the ruling household. Things went poorly at first. Then, in an odd turnabout, the reading implies that she found a "helpmate" among the invading tribesmen, and peace with Said was thus established. We might logically assume, as a sequel, that the union of these two was a factor in later introducing the influence of the emerging white race into a portion of India, as well as establishing the relatively short-lived and historically obscure Indo-Aryan unification. In any case, the offspring of the entity's marriage were among "the first of the pure white race in the Carpathian land," she was told. (Apparently the happy couple had returned to the bride's native region, rather than the groom's.) Later, the royal entity, and presumably her spouse as well, were among those invited to journey to Egypt to receive directly the teachings of the Law of One, for this was in the days of Ra and Hermes. On their return, after a period of service in the Temple Beautiful, they became emissaries to other lands. There, like Peace Corps volunteers in the present, they put their higher knowledge and services to work for those evolving children of men still in the lower stages of development and opportunity.

That term "Aryan": Whence its origins? What its significance?

If we turn to our psychic source, the answers are fairly easy to come by. First, the reader is reminded that the period of the second upheavals in Atlantis, some 30,000 years ago, reduced its five major islands to only three: Poseidia, Aryan, and Og. It was an alarming catastrophe that triggered the first wave of evacuations, well ahead of the final cataclysm. Some went to the Pyrenees at that time, we are told, others colonized the American Southwest, and still others (from Og, one may logically guess) set up a colony by that name in what is now Peru. In all likelihood, a similar group fleeing to Asia Minor from Aryan may have formed the nucleus of what was to become a new state with the old "Aryan" name. ("Iran," in all probability, is a corruption of the original term, "Aryan.") As for the significance of the word, philologists are of a divided opinion, one group maintaining that it carries clear ethnological associations with the white race (meaning, in the narrow view of some, the Indo-Germanic), another group insisting that "Aryan" is merely a term for the whole body of languages more commonly known as Indo-European, whose speakers should be called "Aryas," whether they be Hindus, Persians, Greeks, Germans, Celts, or whatever. The chief proponent of this latter group in the last century was the authoritative Max Mueller, who convincingly pointed out to racist-motivated spokesmen of the former group that even the blackest Hindus represent an earlier stage of Aryan speech and thought. His was a cogent point, but not a total answer. What Mueller had no way of knowing, of course, and might very well have rejected in any case, although it would certainly have tended to bolster one part of his argument, was Cayce's psychic revelation about the "original" Aryan peoples who, as Atlanteans, were neither black nor white, but of the early red race in its formative stages. In any event, Teutonic claims to pure Aryan blood might seem less valid, in light of the Cayce data, than the claims of other, more likely candidates; and if one is to consider the almost ceaseless migrations that have taken place around the globe from prehistoric times to the present, there are probably no "pure" lines of descent remaining . . .

Finally, one useful aspect of Mueller's research was to un-cover clear Indo-Aryan connections, thus indirectly corroborating our psychic source on the matter. He brought to light the little-known fact that "Aryan" was used as a national name not only in Persia (the Zend *airya*, or Old Persian *ariya*), but also in India (where the Sanskrit term was *arya*).[3]

Hats off to Herr Mueller! Philology may not be one's subject of choice, but one is nevertheless grateful to him.

Upon completion of the Great Pyramid, in 10,390 B.C., Ra's Egyptian cycle came to an end. He had served well. In what was apparently a conscious exit from the flesh, we are told that the ageing high priest "ascended into the mount and was borne away."[4] The next stage in his ongoing soul development brought the entity we know as Edgar Cayce back to the earth plane in ancient Persia, where he incarnated as the nomadic ruler Uhjltd (pronounced *Yew-ult*). This appearance is believed to have oc-curred in the year 8,058 B.C.[5]

His personal story in that incarnation, though it is full of high drama and great accomplishments, requires no special elabora-tion here. I shall recount it very briefly. From an evolutionary perspective, which is of primary importance to this narrative, it will be better to concentrate upon his famous progeny. For the nomad Uhjltd, who rose to be king of all the Aryan land, was also the father of Zend. And it was Zend who gave to the children of men the first complete religious philosophy, embodied in the Zend-Avesta. Moreover, Zend's own illustrious son was the first of the Zoroasters. And Zend himself? Our source informs us that he was none other than a further incarnation of Adam, or Enoch-Hermes.[6]

Uhjltd's ancestry, interestingly enough, was said to include Egyptian and Indian bloodlines, in addition to those of his native Persia. His historic and evolutionary role, after putting an end to the repressive reign of Persia's Croesus II, was to set up his own enlightened rulership at Is-Shlan-doen, called the "city of the hills and plains." It came to be known far and wide not only as a great trading capital open to all, but as a center for spiritual learning. Uhjltd himself attained personal fame as a healer, teacher, and prophet, even as his youthful son Zend, though little more than a boy, exhibited strong religious inclinations and spiritual powers. But at the height of Uhjltd's career, he was betrayed and assassinated, and Is-Shlan-doen was sacked by Greek infiltrators who had posed as friends. Zend, and Uhjltd's second son, were snatched from death by loyal supporters and spirited off separately to safer parts of the land, where each eventually rose to positions of leadership and power, though of an opposite nature and purpose. It was probably at about this time in Persia's strife-torn history, as warring factions divided power among themselves, that the old Indo-Aryan empire began to crumble and disintegrate. Carpathia, as well as the Caucasus region, in all probability retreated into separate boundaries, and India may also have closed its borders at this time, leaving the Persians to their own developing destiny.

If one consults an encyclopedia, it will be discovered that the terms "Avesta" and "Zend" are alike obscure; and a similar obscurity surrounds the historicity of Zoroaster.[7] He lived, yes. But no one seems to know when.

Moreover, inasmuch as there is no historical record whatsoever of an entity named Zend, it is assumed by some researchers that the term Zend simply refers to the ancient language in which the Avesta was written, though others dispute this and have their own theories. At any rate, the Zend-Avesta is significant today as the only remaining document, and a partial one at that, of the religion taught by the original Zoroaster—for there have been as many as six different Zoroasters reported, some several millennia apart. Moreover, we find this plurality supported in the Cayce readings themselves, where reading 507-1 refers to "the first Zoroaster," while there is a reference in reading 1219-1 to "the earlier portion of the Zoroasters" (plural). Turning to Greek sources for help, one is only further confounded. Hermodorus and Hermippus of Smyrna place the original Zoroaster 5,000 years before the Trojan war, which is itself of an uncertain dating. Xanthus suggests a date 6,000 years before Xerxes, while Eudoxus and Aristotle say the great Magus appeared 6,000 years before the death of Plato. Agathias, however, concludes with perfect truth that it is not possible to determine with any certainty when Zoroaster lived and legislated, but only that he *was*. (So recounts the Greek historian Plutarch.)

All the same, those several Greek datings all appear to validate the antiquity of the first, and original, Zoroaster. A tentative dating, based on the Cayce data, would be about 7,950 B.C.

What remains of the Zend-Avesta is a collection of mere fragments. It consists of five small books, or parts, out of fifty or more attributed to the original collection of sacred writings, which was said to have been destroyed by Alexander the Great when he invaded Iran and ordered the palace and archives at Persepolis to be burned.

In the first book, the *Yasna*, we have the hymns of Zoroaster. The second, the *Vispered*, is a minor liturgical work. The most important book, in gaining an understanding of the Zoroastrian teachings (and, simultaneously, the teachings of Zend, we may presume), is the third text, called the *Venidad*. Its opening pages contain the priestly code, involving elaborate ceremonies of purification and atonement. It then proceeds with a dualistic account of the creation, reminiscent of Genesis (though the Bible, of course, had not yet come into being). Its major theme is the war against Satan and unlawful lust. The fourth book, the *Yashts*, consists of songs of praise and closes with a prophetic present-ment of the end of the world. Finally, the fifth book, known as the *Khordah Avesta*, or "Little Avesta," comprises a collection of short prayers.

Zoroaster, as the founder of the doctrine of the Magi, taught a dualism that is only temporary, destined to terminate in time as the Evil Spirit, represented by the dark twin Ahriman, is over-come by his counterpart, Ormazd—the Good Spirit, whose symbol is the Light. It is not unlike the underlying theme in most of the world's major religions, right up to the teachings of the Christ.

Until rather recently, it was the prevalent opinion among archaeologists and historians that the 5,000-year-old Sumerian culture, in what is now Iraq, represented the very earliest begin-nings of our modern civilization. Yet, throughout the pages of this book, we have been pointing time and again to evidence of far more ancient roots.

Now it is science itself, however, that has stumbled upon dramatic evidence at last of a large urban culture that existed some 5,000 years ahead of the Sumer civilization. Twice its age, in other words, dating back to 8,000 B.C. I had alluded to that surprising discovery (first widely publicized in 1985) in an earlier chapter, but it deserves more detailed mention here. Those 10,000-year-old ruins unearthed at Cayonu, in what is now southern Turkey, offer startling testimony of an advanced civili-zation that was not only contemporaneous with the great Indo-Aryan empire in the days of Uhjltd, but probably a part of that empire. In brief, what was unearthed at Cayonu may be consid-ered typical of similar civilized communities all over the Aryan land at that time. Lying near the headwaters of the Euphrates

River, Cayonu is the site of a former town of some magnitude and evident prosperity. There are the impressive remains of dozens of rectangular stone houses, some with terrazzo floors and decorative pilasters, not unreminiscent of the much later architecture of early Greece, and perhaps for good reason: we are reminded that Greek influence, though of a less desirable sort, existed at Is-Shlan-doen and proved to be Uhjltd's undoing . . .

The ongoing archaeological research at the Cayonu dig, incidentally, is a project under the joint control of the Prehistoric Section of the University of Istanbul and the University of Chicago's Oriental Institute. This is intriguing; let me explain why. In 1936, in one of his psychic readings, Edgar Cayce referred to "researches in the Persian land in the present." And he urged the recipient of the reading, who wanted more information, to "seek it out through the University of Chicago."[8] (This author followed the same course, fifty years later, to learn about Cayonu!)

It is conceivable that someday in the future, if peaceful relations with Iran can be satisfactorily restored, further researches in the Persian land may uncover Cayce's own bones in a cave not far from Shushtar, near the Iraqi border. For that is where the remains of the assassinated Uhjltd, his former self, were said to be buried . . . even as he also lies in state, as Asapha, somewhere in the Valley of the Tombs!

14 ————————

YESTERDAY IN YUCATAN

Crank literature? Lunatic ravings?

The language is a tad intemperate. Not what one would expect, surely, of someone trained by his profession to be objective. Yet they are the words of a scientific writer of some renown, whose specialty is popular archaeology.[1] Wary of anyone whose realm of research overlaps his own, and openly hostile if another's mode of investigation fails to fulfill his definition of legitimacy, he is unfortunately not too unlike many other professionals in the fields of archaeology and anthropology. In this particular case, he has aimed his verbal broadside at all those who would promulgate the crackpot notion that the survivors of legendary sunken continents, such as Atlantis or Lemuria, somehow played a role in the ancient peopling of the Americas.

One should consider oneself properly chastised, perhaps. Except that the critic in question inadvertently blunts his attack by alluding, a bit further along, to "academic shouting matches" which result from competing hypotheses by rival scientists. Now, if the scientists hold such widely divergent views on the populous origins of the Americas, can they really expect to command our respectful and exclusive attention? This self-admitted lack of unanimity among those who sift and dig in the earth for their only evidence, unmindful of the rich resources to be found in myth and legend which might help them along, not to mention psychic guidance, is sobering and instructive. Let us take heart from it. It inures us to further attack from such quarrelsome quarters. At the same time, it should inspire us to continue unperturbed our highly fruitful research at the mythic and psychic levels.

Come, then. Let us go back by our familiar route to yesterday in Yucatan.

"This is the account of how all was in suspense, all calm, in silence, all motionless, still, and the expanse of the sky was empty. . . Then came the Word."

So begins the *Popol Vuh*, one of the few remaining writings of the ancient Maya. It is a work of unknown antiquity.

The Maya cosmology tells of other worlds before the present one, each destroyed by water. Those of the first world, they say, built the great ruined cities. This world, however, was ended by a universal deluge, known as the *haiyococab*, or "water over the earth." The second world, inhabited by people called the *dzolob*, or "offenders," was ended by the second flood. (Offenders of whom, we wonder? The gods, perhaps? And if so, in what way?) Next came the third world. This world was occupied by the Maya themselves; but it, too, was eventually devastated by water, in a lesser flood called the "immersing." This apparently led to the abandonment of existing sites and a beginning anew elsewhere—relocations that continue to puzzle the archaeologists, who apparently ignore local legends. After this third flood, so goes the story, the present world of the Maya became inhabited by a mixture of peoples from all of the Mesoamerican peninsula. Yet this world, too, they believe, will ultimately be destroyed by flood, like the others.[2]

Maya archaeology is just now coming of age. Although Spanish conquerors first arrived in Yucatan in the 1530s, with the explorer Montejo, they promptly set about erasing rather than preserving all records of the Maya culture and history. It was not until 1839, some three hundred years later, that the travels of John L. Stephens and Frederick Catherwood into the area first aroused public interest in this long-overlooked site. Even then, archaeological studies moved slowly and revealed very little because no one could decipher the hieroglyphs remaining on many of the temple ruins—the only reliable clue, it was felt, to the original builders of these elaborate complexes of pyramids and palaces that had been mysteriously abandoned at some unknown date, and for some unknown reason, leaving them to the slow encroachment of the jungle.

Then, in the 1970s, along came two American cipher experts, Floyd Lounsbury and Linda Schele, who have succeeded in deciphering many of the inscriptions. They are still at work on a complex series of 620 hieroglyphs (the longest in Maya culture) at the Temple of Inscriptions. But at the Temple of the Cross, Lounsbury came upon an interesting dating in the hieroglyphs he decoded there: the temple, read the legend, had been dedicated to the son of Lord Pacal on exactly the same day as an ancestral mother figure had been born 1,359,540 days (3,724 years) previously. Lord Pacal, it was determined, had been a 7th-century Maya ruler of Palenque. His abandoned palace is in the tall rain forests of the Yucatan peninsula, in what is today the Mexican state of Chiapas. From its tower the ancient Maya once studied the stars, for they appear to have been well-versed in astronomy. The religious buildings at Palenque consist of three similar temple-pyramids, of which the best known is the Temple of the Sun. Apparently built over a former temple site of the same name, as was an occasional practice among the Maya, probably for ritualistic reasons, the original is associated in the Edgar Cayce readings with the first Atlantean settlers in the Yucatan land (then called Yuk), under the leadership of Iltar, of the house of Atlan, on the island of Poseidia.

The date of Iltar's arrival is given as 10,600 B.C., possibly as much as a full millennium before the "universal deluge" that the Maya cosmology says destroyed the "first world," the world of those who built "the great ruined cities." In this author's interpretation of the matter, this does *not* allude to the present structures, which are relatively intact, but to those only

partially revealed ruins which still lie beneath them. The original pyramid housing the records of Atlantis, which Iltar
erected in Yucatan, is in fact synonymous with that first Temple
of the Sun, or Temple of Light, as it was alternately called. Like
the Great Pyramid in Egypt, as well as the long-sunken Pyramid of Records left behind in Poseidia, it was built, we are told,
by "the lifting forces of those gases that are being used gradually in the present civilization," and by the spiritual activities of
those familiar with "the Source from which all power comes."[3]

The temple built by Iltar, we are assured, will rise again.
Then the records placed there will be revealed. We are told that
this will take place as the time draws near "when changes are
to come about"—a reference, almost certainly, to the prophesied shifting of the poles at the turn of the present century, and
the accompanying upheavals as the crust of the earth is displaced once more.

No doubt it was due to similar convulsions in the earth,
effective with the last pole shift which ended the glacial age and
brought on the Great Deluge, that the ill-fated temple was
initially entombed along with the rest of the transplanted
Atlantean culture in pre-Mayan Yucatan. In fact, the whole
topography of Mesoamerica was considerably altered, taking
on its presently recognizable features and changing from a
temperate clime to a subtropical.

Meanwhile, at some time during the several centuries that
elapsed between the days of Iltar and the coming of the Flood,
Poseidia had sunk into the sea, followed by Aryan, leaving only
the island of Og, presumably, to be destroyed at the time of the
worldwide cataclysm brought on by the shifting of the poles.
Our source tells us that Yucatan had been experiencing a
substantial influx of Atlanteans from both Poseidia and Aryan;
and although mention is made of survivors from Lemuria, who
had crossed over from what is now lower California, as well as
from Indo-China, pushing into Yucatan, along with those from
colonial Og, or Peru, little is said concerning a "native" popula-

tion. The logical conclusion, therefore, is that Yucatan may have been a relatively unsettled land at the time of Iltar's arrival, or perhaps sparsely inhabited by wandering tribes of primitive hunters and gatherers who later became an agrarian population and a "mixture" people. From their loins arose the early Maya of the Preclassic era. Whether they also absorbed the Olmecs into their culture and bloodlines is uncertain, but Cayce tells of a definite infusion of Hebrew blood, which occurred about 3,000 B.C., as a remnant of the lost tribes crossed over from Asia, escaping Persian domination. They brought with them, however, a regrettable legacy of the Canaanites: blood sacrifice.

An aside: in the many Atlantean colonies scattered across the stricken planet, including those in Yucatan and elsewhere in the Americas, it is not difficult to comprehend why their once-flourishing culture was never revived. Faced with constant hardships, there may simply have been no opportunity. But also, in the area of global transportation and communications, which would have been a necessary prelude to serious reconstruction efforts, the sinking of Poseidia had simultaneously deprived the Atlanteans of the Firestone, or central powerhouse. This crystal energy-accumulator had fueled their air fleet and major naval forces, as well as providing the energizing element of their vast communications network. No doubt, in the decades or centuries that may have intervened between the sinking of Poseidia and the disappearance of the remainder of Atlantis, a makeshift air and naval fleet were put into hasty operation, using long-abandoned propulsion mechanisms that were far less sophisticated. But these, too, must have become useless to the migrating Atlanteans as they relocated in primitive areas where gases or other fuels were no longer readily available to them. For a while, of course, they may have had fuel storage facilities to rely upon, until those backup supplies also ran out. (This is suggested in a reading Cayce gave for a former Atlantean aviator and navigator, who busied himself after the exodus by scouting those areas in Yucatan and Peru, and also in North America, where displaced Atlanteans were already settling or might, in time, choose to go by overland routes afoot.[4])

Indeed, in the period after the shifting of the poles, which brought major earth changes to Mesoamerica, as well as an influx of transplanted Lemurians and other tribal groups displaced from their West Coast encampments, a group of Atlanteans who were the descendants of Iltar's people chose to migrate northward, perhaps relying on information supplied many decades earlier by that Atlantean air scout. They were to become the forerunners of the American mound builders.

As for the Lemurians who displaced them in Yucatan, they built other temples and worshiped other gods. Were these perhaps the "offenders," whose efforts ended with the second flood? If so, they were to be followed by the Maya...and then the "mixtures."

We now confront a mystery.

In the 1930s, a survey party was sent out by one of the large banana growers in Central America to find suitable new planting areas in the Costa Rican interior. What they found instead, as they were hacking their way through a thick tangle of vines, was a small clearing in which a large, smooth, perfectly round stone about six feet in diameter was resting like a votive object upon a slightly raised platform. The platform itself was paved with flat river-pebbles. Looking further, the baffled crew found many more of the curious stone spheres—some large, some small, but all amazingly smooth and round, and resting like the first on altar-like foundations. Digging underneath some of these, in the suspicion that they might mark grave sites, they found nothing at all. Nearby, however, archaeological experts called to the scene came upon shards of crude pottery estimated to be several hundred years old. It was incongruously assumed, by mere geographic association, that the crafters of the crude pottery of relatively recent vintage must also have made the incredibly perfect, polished stone spheres. (Rather like assuming that modern-day picnic litter found at the foot of the Sphinx might be an acceptable means of dating that venerable object or identifying its builders!)

For our part, our psychic source leaves no doubt as to the spheres' ancient origins or purpose. (That is not the mystery confronting us; we shall deal with that momentarily.) We know, of course, that the stones were first used in early Atlantean religious ceremonies to contact "the sources of light" through their magnetized influence. Later they were adapted to more mundane usage in connection with propelling the crystal-powered air fleet and surface vessels. Finally, large numbers of them were apparently transported to Mesoamerica by fleeing Atlanteans, including Iltar, prior to the demise of their island empire. Made of highly polished granite, a substance containing crystalline elements, Cayce had explained that the Atlantean initiates "listened to the oracles that came through the stones, the crystals, that were prepared for communications in what ye now know as radio."[5] (For anyone who lived in the 1930s and remembers the sales boom in crystal-operated radio sets, that particular Cayce reference should strike a cord of familiarity. But the Atlantean listeners were tuned to a quite different "waveband," as it were, set at much higher frequencies than any earthly radio could handle. . .)

Ah, but now to the mystery alluded to earlier. Simply put, when—and why—did the Atlanteans make a decision to remove the spheres from Yucatan and transport them to the interior of Costa Rica? Although we do not find present-day Costa Rica mentioned anywhere in the Cayce readings, we must conclude that a considerable number of Atlanteans, in a second move that probably coincided with the pole shift and subsequent disruptions, chose to relocate in that southwesterly direction rather than follow the northward route of other exiting Atlanteans. A sizable number of the stone spheres were apparently taken along for mainly religious reasons. This is deduced from the altar-like beds on which they were found by their 20th-century discoverers. Similar objects in isolated numbers have turned up in Guatemala and Mexico, as well. Meanwhile, one large sphere from the Costa Rican site is now on permanent display in the courtyard of the National Museum in San Jose, Costa Rica.[6]

Some archaeologists, for lack of contrary evidence, have tended to place the so-called "Early Formative" Period of Maya civilization at a time-span from 2500 B.C. to 300 A.D., during which time they believe that a hunting and gathering lifestyle was practiced. They estimate that this gave way at last to a settled village existence only after 300 A.D. Supposedly this date marks the beginnning of what has been termed the time of the greatest cultural achievements, and has therefore been designated the "Classic Period." We need hardly mention that this dating sequence totally ignores a far earlier culture, in the days of the Atlantean and Lemurian occupations, respectively, with their much more remarkable achievements that have yet to be unearthed.

However, in coastal Belize nearby, surveys conducted by an adventuresome archaeologist named Richard S. MacNeish have disclosed existing sites attesting to a settled civilization on the Yucatan Peninsula as far back as 9,000 B.C., a period not too long after the Universal Deluge.

It is the first bit of scientific evidence to turn up in Yucatan which corroborates our psychic source. In time, hopefully, we can expect more.

The Maya, in their late-blossoming culture, undoubtedly owed an enormous debt to their Atlantean predecessors. Not only the architectural skills reflected in the temples and palaces of the Maya in their so-called Classic Period, but their impressive knowledge of numbers and the stars, as well as their exquisitely wrought hieroglyphs just now being deciphered, attest to an inherited Atlantean influence. Whatever the Maya may later have acquired culturally from other occupying groups, such as the Lemurians, the Toltecs and Olmecs, the wandering Canaanites with their Baal worship, or occasional independent bands of invading Aztecs, it could hardly have matched the initial impact made by the highly civilized Atlanteans upon a primitive and isolated people.

Upon their arrival in Yucatan, said Cayce, most of the first pioneers from Atlantis were males, not only in Iltar's group but in several successive waves of early arrivals who came to prepare the way for later evacuees. Consequently, they sought out female companions for themselves among the relatively backward native population. To demonstrate the impact of this blood infusion upon the evolution of the Maya, we can turn to a reading Cayce gave for one of those who had been "among the firstborn from the combination." Upon maturity, she became a priestess, "making for the use of symbols and signs . . . drawing upon the activities in the heavens as well as the growth of vegetation."[7]

It was thus, in all probability, that the first religion came to be introduced to the forerunners of the Maya, well ahead of the corrupting Lemurian influence, or that of the later Olmecs and Toltecs; and certainly many millennia before the Spaniards and Christianity appeared on the scene with their paradoxical mixture of plundering and piety . . .

FROM THE PYRENEES TO PERU

I have in front of me a 1970 publicity shot of Hugh Lynn Cayce, caught in a contemplative pose. It is little wonder that the son of the late psychic, Edgar Cayce, was thus engaged in ponderous thought. For the past several minutes, he had been quietly gazing at an utterly improbable object which now rested on a table at his right.

The object was a lifesized skull of pure rock crystal brought back from British Honduras by the British explorer, F. A. Mitchell-Hedges. An ancient masterpiece, the skull was so exquisitely sculpted in every detail, without trace of a traditional sculpting tool of any known type, that its likes would be well-nigh impossible to replicate today. Its creation suggests some unfamiliar form of laser art, or other exotic technique.

Momentarily unaware of the camera, Hugh Lynn may well have been pondering the likelihood of the object's Atlantean origins.

You may logically ask, "Why Atlantis?" Let me respond with equal logic. Back in the 1930s, in a series of readings on Atlantis, Mr. Cayce had said that evidence of that lost civilization might be found "in the Pyrenees and Morocco on the one hand, British Honduras, Yucatan and America upon the other."[1]

Here, then, was an otherwise inexplicable piece of crystal artistry from British Honduras that seemed to fulfill at least a part of that prophecy. Moreover, its estimated age—set at about 12,000 years, according to scientists at the California labs of Hewlitt-Packard, who reportedly examined it—coincides eerily with both Plato's and Cayce's dating for the last days of the legendary Atlantis. Certainly the Atlanteans, like none before or since their day, had demonstrated in many ways their superb mastery of crystals.

In Yucatan, on the other hand, we may look for our evidence in the eventual resurfacing of Iltar's original "Temple of the Sun," with its buried records of the rise and fall of Atlantis. Elsewhere in the Americas, aside from the stone spheres of Costa Rica, we have the mysterious mound builders and others to the north, the Incas and Ohums to the south. We shall be examining all of these possible Atlantean connections as our journey proceeds. As for Morocco, we suspect that it, too, may hold some long-concealed evidence of the great Atlantean migration, awaiting discovery in the little-explored Atlas Mountains (though our psychic source has left us with no traceable clues). But in the case of the Pyrenees, it may well be the people themselves—the present-day Basques, an enigmatic and inbred population of proud sheepherders and fishermen—who constitute the Atlantean "evidence" we are seeking, what with their unique customs and incomprehensible language.

Meanwhile, a moment's regression. It's about that crystal skull. In the interests of psychic research, one would hope that its current owner, the daughter of the late F. A. Mitchell-Hedges, if she has not already done so, will one day seek out a qualified psychometrist to examine this ancient treasure and try to unlock the secrets of its origin, purpose, and history. (The fascinating story of that skull, and the many hands through which it has passed, could undoubtedly fill a book!)

Actually, the first exodus of Atlanteans to other lands occurred as early as 28,000 B.C., following the second of the upheavals. Colonies were initially established in what is now Peru, but was then called Og by the colonizing Atlanteans (some of whom must have come from the Atlantean island of that transferred name), and also in the Pyrenees Mountains that today mark the rugged border between Spain and France.[2]

Over the passing millennia before the final upheavals, there is evidence in the readings, if not presently recognizable in the archaeological record, that other hardy pioneers from Atlantis journeyed by air to the high plateau region of what is now the American Southwest. There they probably encountered Lemurians entering from the opposite direction. In fact, as their vast Pacific continent had begun to experience increasingly alarming volcanic upheavals, even preceding the Atlantean disturbances, Lemurian evacuees appear to have found their way to many coastal regions of the Americas, notably in the area of lower California and further south, gradually working their way inland. In all probability, they formed the first human populations wherever they went, a brown race of evolving *mixtures*—the hominid offshoots of long-fallen gods.

Until quite recently, the oldest scientifically accepted date for human occupation in the New World was the 11,500-year-old "Clovis" site, so named for the town in New Mexico where the modern-day unearthing of flint artifacts attested to the presence of a hominid population of hunters in an era believed to coincide with the ending of the glacial age. However, not only have other flint finds pushed the earliest-known North American date back to around 14,000 years ago, but bits of charcoal found in artwork scratched on the wall of a cave in northeastern Brazil have been determined to be about 17,000 years old, according to the respected British journal *Nature*, while further finds still being uncovered suggest that humans may have inhabited the South American continent as much as 32,000 years ago.[3]

Very interesting, to say the least. And right in line with our psychic source. But actually, based on the Cayce records, the earliest Atlantean arrivals would have descended from the Peruvian skies no more than 30,000 years ago. Any earlier arrivals, whether they had crossed overland into Brazil or remained nearer the coastal areas, would presumably have originated in Lemuria, not Atlantis.

As for that Clovis flint on the North American continent, *Science News* has reported an exciting new find (or, rather, a series of finds) in its April 23, 1988 issue. In an apple orchard near Wenatchee, Washington, an undisturbed collection of beautifully executed spear points has turned up, of the same approximate vintage as the 11,500-year-old Clovis flint. Artifacts left behind by ancient Mongolian hunters in their southerly migration? So say the archaeologists. But just as likely, they mark the northward movement of Lemurian or Atlantean colonists from the Southwest, seeking out new hunting preserves as the ice sheet receded.

Meanwhile, back to those Basques.

To understand the Basques, however, it may be necessary for us to know something about the much later Carthaginians. Phoenicians originally, who had settled on the North African coast at what is now Tunis, in the 9th century B.C., they eventually founded a powerful empire that included much of western North Africa, Spain, Sardinia, Corsica, and the western half of Sicily. A Semitic people, the Phoenicians who settled at Carthage, or the "New City," could trace their ancestral roots to Tyre and Sidon primarily, and their original leader was Dido, a daughter of the king of Tyre. Through much intermarriage with the dark-skinned Libyans, however, the Carthaginians gradually became a "mixture" people. It was under their famous leader Hannibal, in the third century B.C., that the campaign into Spain was undertaken, presumably in a search for copper and silver in the Pyrenees. There they encountered fierce resistance from the brave but hopelessly outnumbered Basques, the apparent descendants of the original Atlanteans. Most of the surviving male population that didn't manage to escape into the hills was probably sold into slavery, which was a Carthaginian custom. But the Basques, as an independent and deeply religious people, somehow salvaged their heritage and survived—not, though, in all likelihood, without an unwanted infusion of alien blood from the Carthaginian conquerors, whose stay was fortunately a limited one. Indeed, no newcomers had ever chosen to stay for long among the Pyreneans, whether in their harsh and isolated mountain villages or the simple coastal shacks where their fisherfolk dwelt apart from others.

If all of this relatively modern history may appear to be a needless digression, its pertinence will soon become apparent as we pick up the thread of our story.

The readings suggest that those original emigrants to both the Peruvian land, or Og, and the Pyrenees, back in 28,000 B.C., were not only motivated by a concern for personal safety after the second period of upheavals. Of equal importance, there was a felt urgency to build more peaceful lives for themselves in a place apart from the growing degeneracy of Atlantean society, which they believed had been responsible for the earthly turmoils and destruction.

In Peru, the settlers founded the peaceful empire of the Ohums, a tribal designation possibly derived from the name of the ruling Atlantean family among their numbers. On the other hand, the name may have signified "God," inasmuch as we find an odd Cayce reference to God as "the Father, the Spirit, the Ohm."[4] (Similarly, the successors to the Ohums were the Incas, or Incals—an Atlantean synonym for God, as well as the Sun, says Phylos.)

It was the Ohums, in their dual desire for an isolated as well as a secure existence, who "builded the walls across the mountains in this period," we are told[5]—monolithic barriers of stone and adobe, some fifteen feet wide and high, and running as far as fifty miles in length, which have mystified researchers to this day.

Meanwhile, reverting again to the Basques, those Atlanteans who fled to the Pyrenees may have depended upon the natural barriers of the rugged hills all around them for their defense. It was a defense that probably remained effective until the time of Hannibal's brutal Spanish campaign, many millennia later. Up until then, however, it had enabled the inhabitants to evolve a lifestyle of their own, rooted in religion and their pastoral pursuits, without brooking any outside interference. In 1938, during the Spanish Civil War, German planes from Hitler's Condor Legion tried in vain to shatter the independence of the Basques by the dreadful bombing of their town of Guernica, an event whose sheer horror and brutality was captured on canvas to prick the conscience of all mankind in Picasso's famous mural of that title.

This long heritage of fierce "separatism," which has always

marked the Basques, may explain why, in several of Cayce's readings referring to later incursions into the Pyrenees region by fleeing Atlanteans during the final upheavals, few if any of the groups or individuals appear to have remained there for long. Instead, that isolated Atlantean outpost seems to have been regarded mostly as a transfer point to Egypt and other safety lands.[6]

The origin of the Basques and of their language is still a vexing mystery to scholars. Some theorize that both can be traced to the Caucasus, but any solid proof of this is lacking. Certainly the language of the Basques, which they call *Eskuara*, has no apparent affinity with other European languages. And though the Basques have adopted the Catholic faith, they have always maintained freedom from ecclesiastical domination, whether in the appointment of their priests or the scheduling of their festivals.

Among the later Atlanteans, in the last of the evacuations, Cayce referred to one named Armath, who "remained in the Pyrenean areas." He helped to re-establish the half-forgotten truths and tenets of the original Atlantean teachings, apparently, as a member of the priesthood of the Law of One. He aided much. We are informed, however, that eventually "hordes from the African land brought destruction to those peoples."[7]

Was Cayce alluding to the invasion of Hannibal's troops in the third century B.C.? Presumably so. At any rate, we have no record, psychic or otherwise, of another, earlier intrusion from the African continent.

Finally, we cannot overlook an apparent *gaffe* in one of the Cayce readings, wherein the Pyreneans are referred to as "the Carthaginians as later were known—or the Carpathians."[8] Yet there is no historical confusion as to the Phoenician origin of the Carthaginians (quite unrelated to the Carpathians, of course); nor does it appear likely that the pastoral lifetsyle of the native Pyreneans would have appealed sufficiently to the warrior-nature of the adventuresome Carthaginians to convert them to permanent residency... What, then, did Mr. Cayce really mean to say? We shall never know, of course. But, hopefully, this narrative has managed to piece together with reasonable accuracy Cayce's interesting patchwork of references to the Pyrenees and the proud Pyreneans in their highly individualistic evolution.

The Peruvian rule of the Ohums, in its final days, extended north into what is now Ecuador, and south as far as the Chilean border, where there was "a breaking up of the deeps, and the lands disappeared and reappeared."[9]

This was at the time of the Universal Deluge, when the fate of Atlantis was not so fortunate: its disappearance was total and irrevocable. (Most of it, in fact, had already vanished beneath the sea long before the Flood.)

As for the fate of the Ohums, our psychic data suggests a dividing of the rule between two stronger forces that emerged.

First, we learn of a male survivor in the troubled southern sector of the land. It was "in the days of the peoples coming from the waters in the submerged areas of the southern portion as is now Peru, when the earth was divided, and the people began to inhabit the earth again. The entity among those who succeeded in gaining the higher grounds, and then in the name Omrui." Destined for a position of leadership, in the changing order of things, his name was changed to Mosases, we are told. It was a name that must have signified "leader," or its equivalent; "for the entity became the ruler and the guide, or the patriarch of that age. . ."[10]

Meanwhile, among the Atlanteans who had fled to the Land of Og, or Peru, in the period of the final upheavals, was a leading member of the Poseidian aristocracy, of probable allegiance to the Law of One. In her life reading on that incarnation, she was informed that she "went into what later became known as the [land of the] Inca."[11] Then, in a surprising personal tie-in with the "Inca" name, she was told: "For the entity then was in the line of the house of Inca." The inference to be drawn from that statement is that the original Incas were a royal Atlantean household—revered as gods, perhaps, which would explain the "Sun/God" equivalency of "Inca/Incal," mentioned earlier —which eventually took over the rule from the weaker Ohums. In fact, confirming the Atlantean roots of the new royal lineage in the land, the woman's reading added that she became "the mother of an Inca" in the Peruvian country.

Indications of the dual rulership that seemed to be emerging, at least initially, turned up in a number of life readings touching on the period. Let me recount a few. In one, we learn that "the Ohums were being besieged by the people from the Poseidian land" through the period of the final upheavals, and that the entity in question "was then in the rule, and was overthrown."[12] Yet again, we encounter a reading for one who was related to that ruler who "was dethroned on account of conditions brought in from the Atlantean land," and came into a position of power herself "through the dethroning of that king."[13] Did the Atlanteans, then, before openly establishing the house of Inca as the ruling force, work through the local peoples to set up an interim rule? Such would appear to have been the case. It is a conclusion reinforced by a reading that apparently alludes to that "ruler and guide" from the south, named Mosases. The reading was actually given for one who had been a scribe to the Ohums' last ruler, but based in the southern region, where the Ohums are described as "an unwarlike peoples subdued by the peoples coming in from the place of many waters in the south country," a region that possibly bore the designation of Oz or On.[14] (We encounter both of those tribal names, at any rate, in relation to the Peruvian land in those days, in addition to the dominant name, Og.)

Whatever their outward rulership role at first, there is little doubt that the Atlanteans—consisting, apparently, of opposing groups from the children of the Law of One and the children of Belial—played a significant part in all future developments. This was for weal or woe, as usual. It is likely that the local populace, though themselves largely descendants from former Atlanteans of a much earlier era, had devolved into a relatively primitive society over the passing millennia, affected by a much harsher environment and other factors. But now the Atlanteans began giving them instructions in such matters as ritualistic procedures, the worship of the Sun and solar forces, and, alas, "even to that of the offering of human sacrifice," we are told.[15] This bloody obsession, as we know, was to take fearful root later on, reaching uncontrollable proportions. It was not only practiced among the Incas, but the Maya as well, and eventually, in the most ghastly excess of them all, among the Aztecs in the Valley of Mexico, where the Spanish conquistadors led by Cortez in the 16th century finally put a stop to the appalling slaughter with their own grizzly form of bloodletting. It was time for Quetzalcoatl, the god represented by a plumed serpent, to be replaced by the Christian God.

To look at the copper-skinned descendants of the Incas today in the high Andes, or the typical Maya still living in Yucatan, along with those startlingly Aztec-type faces occasionally spotted in the streets of Mexico City, is as physically close as one will ever get, probably, to meeting an Atlantean. The cheekbones are high, the noses long and aquiline, eyes dark and almond-shaped, hair glossy-black, the bearing innately proud and dignified.

Peru is the site of two of the world's most ancient marvels and mysteries. One is located high in the Andes, near Cuzco, the other close to the coast, near Nasca, on a flat and grassless mesa that is one of the driest desert landscapes on the whole earth. What has preserved the first site from destruction has been its extreme remoteness and inaccessibility, while the latter avoids the erosion of time by a relative absence of rainfall that is believed to have persisted for almost 10,000 years.

The fabulous Inca citadel of Machu Picchu, lost to the world until it was rediscovered in 1911 by Hiram Bingham of Yale University, is a walled city of white granite buildings and temples precariously perched on a 7,000-foot high mountain shoulder in the picturesque Andes, reached by steep stairways among the towering rocks. When it was built, or why it was abandoned, remain unanswered questions to this day. Particularly puzzling to scholars and scientists alike is how the Incas, presumed to have been so technologically backward that they had neither wheel nor beast to aid them, somehow managed to construct these magnificent walls and edifices. They are fitted together with large blocks of granite so cleverly hewn and adroitly joined with interlocking angles that not even a pen-knife can be wedged between their mortarless seams. The explanation, of course, is that it had to have been a highly sophisticated technology at work in the construction of Machu Picchu—namely, the Atlantean. No other civilization in that era, or even in ours, could have done it. Such is the unavoidable truth of the matter.

It took a technology that was not only well-acquainted with laser-beam principles for cutting through the hardest stone like so much butter, but that was also capable of lifting and transporting vast weights (even as in Atlantis originally, and later in Egypt and Yucatan) through the use of anti-gravity methods still unknown to us, but then as common to the Atlanteans as the Sun riding effortlessly over their heads. Ah, yes, that Sun! An object of perpetual worship. Here in Og, as formerly in Atlantis, it was the keystone of their life and religion. And so, at Machu Picchu, there was not only the familiar Tower of the Sun, but the unique and exquisitely sculpted *Intihuatana*, as well. A sacred stone observatory cut from a single outcropping of rock, it was used by the Incas for marking the solstices, equinoxes, and lunar movements. But its vertical marker doubled as a "hitching-post" to tether the wandering Sun and ensure its return. (Among the native peoples, the Sun was known as "Inti," rather than "Incal," its superimposed Atlantean name. Thus, the "*Inti*huatana," or Sun-tether.)

As for that ancient marvel on the desert plateau near Nasca, it was of a quite different sort, yet equally impressive.

To the airborne viewer looking down upon the perfectly straight lines and giant art-forms drawn from the world of nature, made by removing literally tons of dark surface shale to expose the light-colored earth of the mesa in the desired patterns, it might at first appear to be an ancient "astronomy book" of some sort. So some say; and so it was, perhaps. But I have another notion. For one thing, the lines appear to have been superimposed, with a number of them leading off pur-posefully into the hills like skyline markers. Indeed, looking at a map, they would seem to point any alert aviator precisely in the direction of Machu Picchu, dead ahead. Was this, then, the whole purpose of those giant lines and symbols—aerial markers that only the knowledgeable airman could properly interpret and use? It is a logical speculation. Two arrow-like figures at the northern approach to the mesa reinforce my theory.

Then, another matter. It has been pointed out that the wide, straight lines could not have been used for take-offs and landings, which would have left countless tracks in the soft mesa floor (yet there are none). All the same, it is the consensus of most of those "experts" who have applied themselves to the problem that some sort of aerial guidance had to have been employed in laying out the meticulously straight lines and the large, stylized symbols, some of the latter as large as two football fields. At the same time, it has been noted that there are circular "burn pits" at the ends of some of the straight lines. It has been theorized, therefore, that the primitive Nascan Indians, who are believed to have laid out this ancient masterwork, went aloft in hot-air balloons, ingeniously fashioned, to supervise the workers on the ground. (One can only greet such archtheorizing with an indulgent smile. Scientists are sometimes like children: lacking answers, they will not hesitate to resort to the ridiculous to explain the sublime. Balloon-flying surveyors bucking the wind? or riding the stillness on a straight-line course? Indeed!)

Let us take a more rational approach. Rational, at least, from the perspective of anyone who is willing to accept the premise that unseen or unexplained phenomena are not necessarily non-existent for that reason.

We turn to our psychic source. There we read of "the visitation of those from the outer spheres," in the period of the great Atlantean exodus to other lands, including the land of Og.[16] As for the type of aircraft used by the Atlanteans themselves (at least, before the loss of the Firestone, or powersource), we are told that "the airships of that period were such as Ezekiel described of a much later date."[17] To locate that description, one has only to turn to the opening chapter of the Book of Ezekiel and read about the fiery "rings," or "wheels," not dissimilar to the numerous UFO sightings in our own century, be they fact or fiction. Says the prophet, following a visitation from the sky: "When the living creatures were lifted up from the earth, the wheels were lifted up. The wheels went with them."

Then, finally, in yet another reading there is an intriguing reference to "those that were visiting from other worlds or planets" during the latter-day Maya experience in Yucatan, shortly before the arrival of the Spaniards in the early 16th century.[18] A bit curious, that. For, by an odd coincidence, the eminent Swiss psychologist, C. G. Jung, writes of strange aerial objects sighted in vast numbers a few decades later in that same century in the skies over Basel and Nuremburg.[19] (In that respect, it appears to have been a century very similar to our own, with cyclical sightings of so-called "flying saucers" cropping up all around the planet at targeted intervals some decades apart, as if in response to available windows of entry in the earth's magnetic field perhaps.)

Now, by all of this speculative data it is not my intention to propose that the aerial visitors who may have used the lines and pictorial symbols on the Nasca desert to guide them to the hidden Inca sanctuary of Machu Picchu in the high Andes were extraterrestrials. No. Rather, I opt for an Atlantean explanation of the matter. But my point is simply this: the aircraft used by the Atlanteans, if Cayce was right about them, were startlingly similar in appearance, and probably in flight pattern, to the unidentified flying objects reported so frequently in the world news, both past and present. Flying "wheels," so it seems. Eerily weightless-behaving vehicles that are capable of sudden suspension in space or the most rapid acceleration. Also capable of vertical landing or lift-off, according to the sworn testimony of those who claim to have seen them performing such operations. Moreover, the sites where they are said to have rested, however momentarily, are reportedly marked afterwards with circular patches of scorched earth that give off lingering radiation signals.

True or false? I press no claims here. But one is bound to be reminded of those curious "burn pits" in the Nascan sands, where the straight lines terminate. All of which leaves one up in the air, quite literally. No ground-based, rock-clearing workers at all. Everything handled by computerized flight patterns from above, lifting and clearing the rubble in swift, meticulous swaths. Anti-gravity forces, you see. The Atlanteans knew all about such things. Or, so we are told by our psychic source. And we find him more credible in these matters than the perplexed, and perplexing, scientific opinion-shapers, with their ill-formed hypotheses . . .

Let them take note of psychic wisdom before they set aloft their hot-air balloons!

FROM ABRAHAM TO THE CHRIST

Our long journey has now brought us to the feet of Abraham.

Abraham means "call," we are told.[1] Thus his role is a symbolic one. We may look upon the ancient patriarch as a universal "father figure" in the unfolding story of mankind's evolution, transcending any particular racial or religious connotations.

Let us turn to him for a metaphor.

The evolution of Adamic man, up to the time of Abraham, may be said to have comprised the embryonic or rudimentary stages of development, comparable to the physical growth of a child. Yet that period from Abraham to the Christ marked the gradual unfoldment of the *mental* body. "For, that which leads to the Christ is the mind," said the sleeping Cayce. "And the mind's unfoldment may be that indicated from Abraham to the Christ."[2]

The promise of the Lord to Abraham was that his seed (meaning all who are called) would multiply and be as numberless as the stars. But those who are called do not always answer at the first calling. The present stage in which a continually evolving mankind now finds itself, then, may be likened to the spiritual. It is the age of the seeker, as the answering soul responds to its Maker. Today, said Cayce, all who seek that inner awakening to their true selfhood are the spiritual heirs of Abraham, and their collective name is Israel.[3] They are not confined to any single race, any separate nation. Nor are they even confined to this planet. For they are truly as numberless as the stars.

The soul's journey ends where it began, in the Body of God. Caught up in the Eternal Now, there is no longer any mystery to the Master's words: "Before Abraham was, *I am*."

The call came to Abraham at Ur.[4]

Ur of the Chaldees, as it was to become known in a somewhat later era, was situated "on the other side of the Flood." Already a proud and prosperous city in Abraham's day, its strategic location on the fertile delta of the great Euphrates River near the entrance to the Persian Gulf meant that it was destined to be a major hub of trade and commerce throughout the ancient world. Under the rule of Sumerian kings, it would reach its pinnacle of fame and power. It was an era epitomized by the mighty ziggurat erected by the ruler Ur-Nammu as a shrine to the moon-god. For the Sumerians worshiped many strange gods. Yet today the multi-tiered tower is nothing more than a heap of rubble lying on the baking sands. It lies amid the other ruins of a vanished city and a forgotten culture. Gone, too, are all of Ur's fabled riches and its many gods, its highly vaunted sorcerers and soothsayers, all left behind as the unpredictable river altered its course and the crops ceased to grow in that place.

Abraham's mother, we learn, had been brought to Ur as a captive from that land now known as India. A woman of great intelligence and talent, she rose in time to become what Cayce termed "the real business head" of that group later known as the Chaldeans.[5] One may suppose that she did her best to dissuade her foolish son from abandoning the obvious opportunities and security at hand to go chasing off in search of an unknown "land of promise."

As for Abraham's father, Terah, he was a maker of idols. A picturesque Arabian legend, recounted by C. G. Jung, ascribes to Terah a dual talent: he was considered a master craftsman who could "cut a shaft from any bit of wood," which had the additional meaning in Arabic usage that he was "a begetter of excellent sons."[6]

Abraham's search for God arose from within. It was not an ideal implanted in him by either of his parents, presumably, who worshiped other gods.

Meanwhile, what of that call from the Lord unto Abraham? For the Lord had sent him a very clear message: "Depart from your country, and from your kindred, and from your father's house; and come unto a land that I will show you."[7] But did the call actually originate within Abraham's heart, as a result of his strong spiritual yearning? or did that yearning serve merely to create a condition of psychic receptivity, and did the call itself come from without?

The latter, according to our psychic source.

The call, in fact, came from another city named Ur, which was the spiritual counterpart of the wordly Ur of the Chaldees, where Abraham was residing. This other Ur, it is my interpretation of the matter, was Ur of Salem, or "Uru-salim," as the holy city of Jerusalem was originially called.[8] It was a separate kingdom in those days. Its ruler, who had presumably sent forth the psychic call heard by a spiritually attuned Abraham, was none other than that prefiguration of the Christ, the priest-king Melchizedek.

In telling us that the call was from Ur, Cayce identifies Ur as "a land, a place, a city," from whence the entity we know today as Jesus (who was then in the earth as Melchizedek) was "able to impel or guide those thoughts in that period, or experience."[9]

In naming the more significant incarnations of the Christ throughout the world's history, Cayce confirmed the long-established aprocryphal tradition by listing Adam, Enoch, Melchizedek, and Jesus; he also added Zend, Joseph, Joshua, Asaph, and Jeshua.[10] Out of some thirty or more earthly lives attributed to the Christ, it is of interest to note that of the nine major ones just given, all but one (Zend) are traceable to the Bible, while the last five—including Jesus—follow the lineage of Abraham. This should tell us something of the profound importance of Abraham's role, not only in the evolution of the Judaic, Christian, and Islamic religions, but in the personal soul development of He who came as Amilius in the beginning, and took on the fleshly experience for Himself. This led to the need to work out His own salvation, as well as ours. To accomplish this objective, a Divine Plan became necessary. And Abraham fitted into the plan.

Based upon what the Edgar Cayce readings reveal about the repetitive nature of soul relationships from one incarnation to the next, and the use of planetary sojourns between earthly appearances as a means of preparing the soul for its next round of development, it may not be too presumptuous to proffer some tentative conclusions at this juncture. Jesus, for example, appeared to know in advance the "soul background" of each of the twelve chosen disciples (including Judas, His betrayer), probably as the result of prior associations in the earth as well as a pre-set plan that had its origins in the Interbetween. In like fashion, did the Lord in His much earlier role as Melchizedek choose Abraham as a result of a previously tested relationship in the earth, as well as in fulfillment of a plan worked out at the "soul level" preceding the earth-entry of each? Just as the twelve seemed to gravitate naturally toward Jesus, or to find themselves appearing as if by chance athwart His path as His earthly mission began in that fateful phase of the Divine Plan leading up to His crucifixion and resurrection, so too did Abraham find himself brought inevitably into physical contact with Melchizedek as if by some prior arrangement. Moreover, Abraham appeared to recognize the Lord instantly. Indeed, he paid obeisance to Him automatically at their first physical encounter at the vale of Siddim, following Abraham's victory in the battle of the kings and his subsequent blessing at the hands of Melchizedek.

No meeting, said Cayce, is by chance. The crucial test, however, lies in the nature of our free-will choices when the given opportunities occur, even as was the case with Abraham, whose actions often went contrary to the Will of God. Yet the Lord remained patient with him throughout, apparently knowing Abraham's heart well enough to trust to a favorable outcome.

And how did the Lord's plan relate to Abraham? This old and proven soul was to become the founder of a new nation, whose faith and tenets would be based on the higher teachings said to have been imparted to Abraham by Melchizedek, in what was the original Cabala[11]–an esoteric rendering of the Law of One. By keeping the faith alive through various vicissitudes and periodic lapses, and maintaining a pure lineage in accordance with the given laws, the descendants of Abraham were able to provide the necessary channels through countless generations for many a great king and prophet to enter the earth plane in the successful furtherance of the Divine Plan. This ensured mankind's eventual salvation, leading up at last to the entry of the King of kings.

In the days of Abraham, the Word dwelt in Melchizedek. This name, Melchi-Zedek, means "King of Righteousness"; and Melchizedek's kingdom was, of course, Ur of Salem (forerunner of Jerusalem). "Ur," from the Hebrew *aur*, signifies "fire" or "light," whereas "Salem" translates as "Peace." The appropriateness of the symbolism throughout scarcely needs to be remarked upon, other than to add that the future "Prince of Peace" was indeed fully prefigured in the priest-king Melchizedek.

In all of His incarnations, from the "first Adam" to the "last Adam," Jesus was an embodiment of the universal Christed Consciousness, carrying the Word of God to man. But in Melchizedek—"without father, without mother, without descent, having neither beginning of days, nor end of life, but made like unto the Son of God"[12]–there was the first *perfecting* of the lower self as it merged into, and became one with, the Higher Self. For this reason, no doubt, Cayce referred to "Melchizedek in the perfection."[13] Logically viewed, there was no apparent need for Him to undergo any further incarnations for His own sake, but only for ours did He keep returning.

Though depicted as a man of flesh and blood, Melchizedek, with neither beginning of days nor end of life, obviously transcended the normal human limitations. If we were to attempt to define His unique state, we would have to describe Him as a fourth-dimensional being who dwelt beyond the physical restrictions of time and space. This would readily explain His several appearances to Abraham, as if out of nowhere, as in that passage in Genesis describing the altar Abraham built in Canaan unto the Lord, "who appeared unto him."[14] (In what form? And from whence?)

All of which leads us, by an interesting and unexpected linkage, to the Book of Job.

To most biblical scholars, the Book of Job is viewed solely as an allegory, whose author remains unknown. Cayce dispels the common ignorance on both points. *Job lived*, we are told.[15] His period in history is somewhat vaguely placed "before Moses was." Before Moses, but some generations after Abraham, as will shortly be demonstrated. The real surprise, however, is to learn of the authorship of Job's tale of temptation and perseverance in the face of adversity. Said the sleeping Cayce: "Melchizedek wrote Job!"[16]

Yet that revelation should surprise us not at all, upon proper reflection. For who but a firsthand witness to the event—nay, who but the spiritual protagonist himself, let me suggest—could have written that marvelously moving account of the conflict between the Lord and Satan in a contest for the soul of man that is at once both real and symbolic? An allegory, of course, in one sense. But also more than an allegory.

For the story of Job was *true*.

We cannot speak of the days of Melchizedek, who was one "without days or years." Yet we can speak of the days of Job. Job dwelt in the land of Uz, which lay east of Palestine. Uz was a son of Aram, one of the sons of Shem, a son of Noah; and this was apparently the country in which Uz had settled with his kinsmen after the Flood. It was good pastureland, although it bordered the desert; and marauding bands of Sabeans and Chaldeans crossed over the desert from time to time and plundered the region. It was also here in the land of Uz that the sinful "daughter of Edom" dwelt—a designation for the descendants of Esau.

The time of Job may be judged, then, by examining these and certain other historical and genealogical trappings in the story—placed there by Melchizedek as clues, perhaps, to its authentication. The erstwhile friends of Job were Bildad the Shuhite, Zophar the Naamathite, and Eliphaz the Temanite. There was also Elihu, the son of Barachel the Buzite, of the kindred of Ram. Now, Ram was the second son of Hezron, born to Tamar's son, Pharez, the offspring of Judah's strange union with his daughter-in-law. This places Ram five generations after Abraham, and probably a space of some hundred years or more after the patriarch's death. Similarly, the Temanites can be traced to the same general period in Hebrew history, for Tema was the ninth son of Ishmael, who was born to Abraham and the Egyptian woman, Hagar, fourteen years before Sarah conceived Isaac in her old age.

Of the Naamathites we have no record, although these may actually have been the Naamites, a family descended from Naaman, the grandson of Benjamin, Israel's last son. We come at last to the records of Bildad the Shuhite; but nothing is known positively of this tribe, except that it was located near Uz, and may have come from Assyria.

Thus, based upon genealogical data the author carefully included in his tale, we have been able to establish with reasonable accuracy the days of Job.

As for Melchizedek's role as author and protagonist, there is a puzzling factor. We must go to work to resolve it. It will not prove too hard. First, the reader will have noted that the days of Job have been placed in a time-frame five generations after Abraham, whose spiritual mentor was the same as Job's: namely, that incarnation of the Lord identified as Melchizedek. This, of itself, poses no discernible problem in time or space: certainly a special being such as Melchizedek, said to have been "without days or years," could have appeared as readily in Abraham's day as in the following days of Job, a century or two hence. A conundrum of a more puzzling sort arises, however. For, if Cayce was right, one of the Lord's incarnations betweeen "the first Adam" and "the last Adam" was as Joseph, the beloved son of Jacob (or "Israel," as he was renamed). A great-grandson of Abraham, Joseph's appearance in the flesh preceded that of Job. How, then, in His role as Melchizedek, could the Lord have made a re-entry, so to speak, after His interim role in the flesh as Joseph, enabling Him to be present in the troubled days of Job? But remember: Melchizedek was "made like unto the Son of God," with a fourth-dimensional consciousness transcending time or space. Thus it was as easy for Melchizedek to step forward into the time-consciousness of Job as to appear in the time-consciousness of Abraham.

Job's tale of woe is also a tale of victory.

"If a man die," Job asks, "shall he live again?" He speaks symbolically of a tree: "For there is hope of a tree, if it be cut down, that it will sprout again, and that the tender branch thereof will not cease."

Job lives, in a sense, forever. He is immortalized in the imperishable Word of Melchizedek. But more than that, his earthly encounters and conversations with the Lord (who on one occasion appeared to him "out of the whirlwind"), not only comforted and strengthened Job in his sorrows but brought to him the lessons of eternal life. And if a man *live*, we might re-phrase Job's question, shall he ever die again?

The mortal Job died in time, of course, as will the rest of us. But as an enlightened soul, the experience of death would have been an illuminating transition.

Meanwhile, here's a novel notion. It may startle the mind at first, though its logic is impeccable. Indeed, the likelihood of its reality looms increasingly large, upon proper reflection. Consider, if you will, the possibility that Job may have been a reincarnation of Abraham; and that Melchizedek, in his concern and love for this chosen servant of the Lord, moved through time and space to be at hand when the patriarch came into the earth again to meet what he had sown, as every soul must do. In this way, Melchizedek was able to do personal battle in the earth with Satan and lend direct spiritual assistance to Job through the severe testing he was to endure as a karmic carry-over of his shortcomings as Abraham. (For Job, we are told, was born a perfect man, and it was not as Job that he had sinned.)

As Abraham, the patriarch had a high calling. Yet he not only jeopardized his sacred mission on several occasions through disobedience and wavering, but displayed impatience with the Lord when he felt that the latter's promises were too slow in being fulfilled.

Patience, as every reader of the tale knows, is what the story of Job is all about. That, and consistency. In the end, not only was Job's health restored to him, but all that had been deemed "lost" came back in abundance, so that the latter days of Job were better than the first.

We turn now to our psychic source and his favorite text, the Bible, to close this chapter of our journey with some brief insights and observations. They concern those several incarnations of the Christ between His mystical appearance as Melchizedek and His triumphal entry as the humble Nazarene.

Of Joseph, first.

Sold into bondage by his own brothers, he later used his high position in Pharaoh's court not to wreak vengeance upon them in their hour of dire need and humble supplication, but to extend salvation—not only to his starving brethren, but to all of Israel. It was the way of the Christ, as opposed to base human instinct. Selfless love, turning aside all negative responses, enabled Joseph to fulfill his probable purpose in that incarnation. Finally, we learn that the tender bond of affection betweeen Jacob and his favorite young son found repayment in kind in the life of Jesus. For Jacob reincarnated as the beloved disciple, John, youngest of the twelve, who leaned on Jesus' breast at the Last Supper.[17]

And Joshua? Cayce describes him as prophet, mystic, and leader, as well as "the mouthpiece of Moses," thus playing a far more crucial role than is generally accorded him—a role intentionally muted perhaps, as was ever typical of the Christ in His earthly sojourns. On the other hand, the spiritual might Joshua was capable of invoking on the side of righteousness was fearful. It is most powerfully exemplified in the biblical account of the day the Sun stood still upon Gibeon, and the moon stayed its course in the valley of Ajalon, even as Joshua commanded of them until the battle against his enemies was won.[18] Those inclined to look upon such a biblical incident as a mere metaphor are reminded of a later, somewhat similar, incident recorded in Isaiah. As a sign from the Lord, the shadow of the degrees on the sundial of Ahaz regressed ten degrees, and then returned by the same degrees it had gone down.[19] In both instances, let me suggest, there may have taken place a correlating shift in the crust of the earth, which would provide a scientific explanation of the phenomenon. Yet such an explanation in no way removes *divine intervention* as the propelling force. Moreover, Cayce refers in several of his psychic readings[20] to a related instance of divine intervention controlling the activity of the Sun and the elements during Jesus' time. It was at the period of the crucifixion, described as a day when the Sun was darkened by an eclipse and the earth shook, as "the Son of Man, the Son of God, was suspended between earth and sky."

Of Asaph, there is much that might be said of an esoteric character. Yet it would require a fuller exposition than is appropriate here.* Instead, let it merely be noted that Asaph, dear to the heart of David as a trusted seer and adviser, as well as a leading musician in his court, was the known composer of a number of the more prophetic psalms. He probably authored, as well, that mystical trio of psalms, the 117th, 118th, and 119th. The first of these is the shortest chapter in the Bible, the last-named is the longest. The latter consists of 22 sections, based on the 22 letters of the Old Hebrew alphabet, supposedly given to Abraham by Melchizedek. Each of the 22 sections is comprised of 8 verses. If we look back at Psalm 118, lying by some curious juxtaposition between its long-and-short neighbors, our attention may be expected to focus on verses 8 and 22. The former tells us, very simply, that it is better to trust in the Lord than to put confidence in man. The 22nd, however, would appear to carry the prophetic imprint of the Master Himself, in that incarnation as Asaph. It is often quoted as a reference to the Christ: "The stone which the builders refused is become the head stone of the corner."[21]

Finally, we come to Jeshua the scribe. Cayce says of him that he "reasoned" with those disenchanted Israelites who returned from captivity after Cyrus of Persia conquered Babylon in 539 B.C. He sought to restore their shattered faith. In his role as a scribe, Jeshua busied himself in translating those books of the Bible that had been written, up to that particular time.[22]

One Christ, many lives. But ever serving others, teaching and practicing the precepts of the Law of One. An Exemplar to all.

---

* See chapter note 21, in Appendix, for additional data.

THE MYSTERIOUS
MOUND BUILDERS

Among the many effigy mounds discovered in North America, none has surpassed in sheer size, spectacular beauty, or potent symbolism the Great Serpent Mound of Ohio.

Discovered in 1848 by American archaeologists Ephraim Squier and Edwin Davis, it has stirred the minds and imaginations of millions ever since. Students of Amerindian culture, in particular, have pondered over this ancient puzzle in search of a logical explanation. It has closer ties, certainly, to Egyptian, Hebrew, or Gnostic tradition than to any known Indian legend. Even the Plumed Serpent of the Aztecs, in Mexico, does not come close enough, in symbolic terms, to link it to this gigantic, writhing snake that stretches in a series of whiplike curves along a creek embankment for almost a quarter of a mile. (Surely it was meant to be viewed from above! But by whom? And why?)

Clasped in its open jaws is an oblate sphere reminiscent of the Egg of Seb, from whence the world issued forth, in Egyptian mythology.[1] In Hebrew literature, of course, the serpent has been an ambivalent symbol of wisdom, from the days of Adam and Moses, whereas to the Alexandrian mystics and the Gnostics, it became an emblem of the Christos, the Logos. And it was out of the body of the Christos, through the spoken Word, that the visible universe came into being.

Another factor contributing to the special mystery surrounding the Great Serpent Mound has been the absence of any artifacts. At most other mounds, a rich yield of burial objects or other relics has made it possible to determine the approximate date of their construction. The mounds of the Adena culture, for example, which are among the most famous if not the most prolific, appear to date from 1,000 B.C. to A.D. 500 or thereabouts, while the equally famed mounds from the Hopewell culture probably got a somewhat later start, outlasting the Adenas by a small margin. Yet these dates remain somewhat speculative at best. To give an idea of the typical uncertainty surrounding carbon-14 dating methods, which have provided us with the tentative datings for the Adena and Hopewell cultures, the estimated antiquity of the Drake Mound, in Kentucky, has recently been pushed back by a thousand years. This could happen elsewhere as dating methods are continually improved and former determinations re-examined.

Because an Adena burial site not far from the Great Serpent Mound has yielded a carbon-14 dating in the first century B.C., this has led some archaeologists to conclude that the Great Serpent Mound itself dates from the same era and was a product of the Adena culture. But as that old tune wisely tells us, it ain't necessarily so. In any event, it is only among the Hopewell relics that we find the serpent sometimes depicted, carved in stone in a fully coiled form, *sans* "world-egg" or any other apparent symbolism. So our wonderment is bound to grow . . .

Nevertheless, the once-popular belief, even held by some of the first archaeologists to arrive on the scene, that many of the thousands of tumuli scattered across much of North America east of the Mississippi might eventually yield evidence of truly ancient origins has long been put to rest. Meticulous archaeological research over a span of many decades has definitely ascertained that the mound builders, though apparently of a higher and more complex social order than the other tribal occupants on the Northern Continent, were nonetheless "Johnnies-come-lately," relatively speaking.

In certain of their physical characteristics, the Adena and Hopewell peoples (so-named in honor of their 19th century discoverers) not only differed markedly from the Indian tribes already inhabiting North America at the time of their arrival, but differed from each other. The Adena type were unusually tall, with the men often approaching seven feet, and the skeletons large throughout. Equally distinctive were their skulls, which were large and round, with a prominent forehead, heavy brow ridges, a jutting chin. They must have been quite majestic to gaze upon. As for the Hopewells, who rivaled and even surpassed them in certain artistic and creative respects, we are told that they had the agile bodies and narrow-headed skulls more typical of the existing Indian population of the eastern woodlands; yet there was a distinguishing hauteur and mystique about them, adorned as they were with copper and pearls, which set them apart from their more savage brethren who had preceded them in those parts.[2]

Yet another group of mound builders, believed by some to have arrived much later on the scene from Mexico, are identified as the Mississippians. Not so distinctive as either the Hopewells or the Adenas, they nevertheless built their temple mounds on a grand scale, in probable imitation of the Aztecs. But like all of the mound builders, whether constructing effigy mounds, burial mounds, or the later temple variety, they substituted earth for stone.

All of the mound builders exhibited an exquisite appreciation of geometric form. The layout of their mound complexes, and the variations in the construction of the mounds themselves, display a keen devotion to form, ritual, and a diverse symbolism. Yet, with the probable exception of the Mississippians, we are left with two unanswered questions: Where did they come from? And what caused their demise? As to the Mississippians, the coming of the white man probably led them to abandon their temple complexes and adjoining farms. We can surmise that they were readily absorbed into existing tribal populations. But both the Adena and Hopewell peoples appear to have dropped out of sight far ahead of the white man's arrival.

The tall, powerfully built Adena population, with their large, round skulls, seem to have been totally obliterated, whether by plague or warfare. They have left no genetic traces. As for the Hopewells, who had ceased to build their ceremonial centers by A.D. 550 or earlier, they too may have fallen victims to disease or tribal warfare, with any remnant population being absorbed into humbler tribes. One clue pointing to the "war-fare" theory is an earthen-walled, ancient fort built atop a long, narrow plateau several hundred feet above the Little Miami River in Warren County, Ohio. A few burial mounds inside the fort attest to casualties from skirmishes. Meanwhile, evidence that unrest of some kind was afoot at this time throughout eastern North American Indian tribes is seen in the stockades that began to appear for the first time, encircling many villages in more northerly areas.

But let us turn from those barricades for a moment. We have some construction work of our own to do. As we start fitting together odd pieces of the puzzle picked up from the psychic readings of Edgar Cayce, here and there adding a beam or a brick from other sources, we shall build our case. On completion, it will at least partially vindicate the long-ridiculed mythmakers. They intuitively sensed in the work of the mound builders an ancient heritage, traceable perhaps to the lost Atlantis, and they were right. Half-right, at any rate; for they appear to have been wrong as to the antiquity of the mounds themselves. The reconstructed picture that emerges, as the pieces of our puzzle come together, is a complex one: it involves the uneventful passage of several millennia, followed in time by the entry of some unexpected actors on the scene.

The peopling of the Americas, if one accepts the modern-day consensus of science (which generally rejects the late Louis Leakey's controversial claim of hominid occupation at Calico Hills, in California, some 100,000 or 200,000 years ago), was in a southeasterly flow that had its origins in Siberia 11,500 years ago. This migratory movement was supposedly a result of the melting of the great Wisconsin glaciation, which made the North American continent habitable to roving bands of Mongoloid hunters. Within another millennium, the migratory wave had swept through all of Central and South America, as well.

Pointing to the vast expanses of ocean to east and west of

the Americas, which are believed to have posed an insur-
mountable barrier to any prehistoric navigators, the experts
argue with imperturbable logic and finality that a land-route
across "Beringia" (their name for the Siberia-Alaska link, which
was then presumably walkable) was the only plausible entry-
point to the previously uninhabited lands. Now that other
evidence than Leakey's rather tenuous Calico Hills findings is
turning up to suggest a much earlier human occupancy in parts
of the Americas, the unimaginative response is simply to revise
backward the date of the first Beringia crossings.

As for the origins of the mound builders, the scientific
opinion-shapers are split. Some contend that they evolved
naturally, as certain tribes moving down from the north into
the eastern woodlands began burying their rubbish under
earthen mounds, gradually leading to a highly ritualistic
"burial mound" cult to honor the dead—a practice that gave
way, in time, to temple-building. Others see a move up from the
south by Mesoamerican Indians with a pyramid-building tradition inherited from the Maya.

We come, now, to the Cayce record on the subject.

First, though, let's take another look at that Beringia land-
bridge of 11,500 years ago. That date closely coincides with two
cataclysmic events: the shifting of the poles and the worldwide
deluge. With rising ocean levels all around the globe, we are
inclined to wonder just how passable to boatless travelers that
so-called "land-bridge" really was! But let us move on, and
leave them to their foot-slogging ... (One can readily agree that
migrants from the Gobi Land may once have come that way,
packing portable boats. Their heirs are probably the Eskimos
and the Aleuts, with their Mongolian features. But clearly, one
does not see any of their broad, flat faces among the hawk-
nosed Iroquois, for example—"pure descendants of the Atlanteans," said Cayce—or the other red men of the prairies or the
eastern woodlands of North America, or yet among the brown-
skinned Mesoamerican mixtures, or the stately Peruvians and
their likes.)

Referring to a period 3,000 years B.C., when the Atlantean
descendants of Iltar, in Yucatan, "gradually lost in their activi-

ties," we learn of the introduction of "the Baal or Baalilal" influences among the people of the Maya civilization. This was brought about by an infusion of "those peoples that were of the lost tribes," coming first "among the peoples from Mu in the southernmost portion of that called America or United States," and then moving on to Yucatan, settling also in what is now Mexico City, where they centered their activities eventually—giving rise, we may speculate, to the later Aztec civilization. Meanwhile, it is stated of their entry into Yucatan that it brought about "a different civilization, a *mixture* again." As a result, Iltar's descendants migrated into North America, where they "came to be that people termed . . . the mound builders."[3]

Asked how the children of the "lost tribes," who were believed to be Canaanites fleeing from Persian domination, reached the shores of America, Cayce answered: "In boats."

The Canaanites (also known to history as the Phoenicians, who founded Carthage) were renowned for two traits, one of which was admirable and the other not. The admirable trait was their seamanship; for in this respect they were equaled only by the Vikings, far to the north of their Mediterranean shores. On the negative side, alas, they had gained notoriety among their fellow Israelites as practitioners of the dread cult of Baal. Yet this unsavory trait perhaps gave them spiritual kinship with those outlawed hordes among the sons of Belial who had "been banished from Atlantis"[4] in the latter days, forced to take refuge from the coming cataclysm on the primeval American shores. There they became the nucleus of the many American Indian tribes that first settled the northern continent, except for the Southwest portion, where much earlier colonies from among the children of the Law of One had joined with settlers arriving from Mu to found the peaceable tribes in that area.

Cayce's reference to seafaring Canaanites landing on American terrain some 5,000 years ago, or 3,000 B.C., finds its echo in more recent reports from scientific sources. In the July 18, 1970 issue of the *Saturday Review*, the science editor, John Lear, recounted evidence that the ancestors of one of America's surviving Indian tribes, the Yuchis, had come to the Western

Hemisphere from the Mediterranean area almost 3,500 years ago. Also, a Brazilian document uncovered by Professor Jules Piccus of the University of Massachusetts, and subsequently translated by Professor Cyrus H. Gordon, of Brandeis University, tells of another band of men from the land of Canaan who reached the shore of what is now Brazil in the year 531 B.C. Identifying themselves as Sidonian Canaanites, the document speaks of having "sacrificed a youth to the celestial gods and goddesses" as they "embarked from Eziongeber into the Red Sea." The account adds that they "were separated by the hand of Baal" from their companions, at last arriving —twelve men and three women—on the "New Shore."

Yet another bit of evidence to suggest Canaanite infusion into the bloodstream and psyche of the American Indian population came to light in 1885 at Bat Creek, Tennessee, where a stone tablet inscribed "For Judah" was found, along with an ancient Canaanite coin identified as being from the period A.D. 132-135. These treasures ended up in the hands of the Smithsonian Institute, untranslated and unidentified, until they recently came to the attention of that same Brandeis University professor, Cyrus H. Gordon.[5] Moreover, Gordon has stated that there exists in eastern Tennessee today a group of people known as the Melungeons, who may be the descendants of Canaanite settlers. They appear to be Caucasian, rather than Indian, but are probably a mixture.

In a psychic reading for a woman who had experienced an incarnation in what is now southern Florida "when there were the beginners of the mound builders," she was told that her name then had been Alta, which is plainly suggestive of Atlantean ancestry. She also learned that her sojourns at the time "were with those of a race of unusual height, unusual proportions," whom we can thereby identify with near certainty as the Adena mound builders. Were these unusual people the descendants of Iltar, then? For the reading goes on to identify them as having been "the lords of the land," although the entity herself was said to have been "among those that were the more lenient in that lording," seeking "that development where all under the Lord—as law—are *one*."[6]

Still another reading for one of the former mound builders tells of struggling northward from Yucatan, and settling in those lands that are now a portion of Kentucky, Indiana, and Ohio, "being among those of the earlier period known as mound builders." What is intriguing in that quoted excerpt, of course, is the word *earlier*. In fact, the entity had also been told that he was "among those of the second generation of Atlanteans."[7] Should we take that "second generation" reference in a literal or a figurative sense? If the former, it would mean that the mounds in North America have a far more ancient history than any of the presently existing tumuli would indicate, based upon carbon-14 datings of their remains. Yet such a conclusion, however exciting to contemplate, is highly speculative at best. It does not match the archaeological evidence, thus far. Neither does it coincide with the information given in other readings on the mound-building era.

All the same, evidence that a long-vanished people of migratory instincts, perhaps sailing up from Yucatan (who knows?), may once have landed amid the bog-filled shoals of Florida's eastern shore near Titusville, or were passing afoot through that hostile terrain in transit from other parts, has come to light in a peat bog in that area. Moreover, they must have encountered some resistance from rival tribes. Over the past five years, archaeologists at what is now known as the Windover site have carefully excavated more than 125 cloth-wrapped skeletons of men, women, and children who died under adverse conditions nearly 8,000 years ago. Quite astonishingly, the well-preserved, shriveled brains of as many as ninety-one of the bodies have been found to contain intact cells. This DNA discovery is enabling scientists to examine the genetic origins of these ancient people in ways that were never before possible in archaeological history. (If they are the direct descendants of the highly advanced Atlanteans, as one suspects, there may be some exciting genetic secrets locked in the DNA coding of those 8,000-year-old cells! We shall see.) Signs of ancient strife and warfare were observable, with an antler point from a primitive spear-tip found embedded in the hip bone of one of the bodies. Others had broken bones.[8] It is con-

ceivable, of course, that they may have been local residents—
North American descendants of the original children of Belial
who had come to those alien shores some 3,000 years earlier–
but the evidence more strongly suggests that they were newly
arrived immigrants, probably from Mesoamerica.

Not all of those Atlanteans who journeyed "north and west
from Yucatan" ended up among the mound builders. Some of
them, apparently, went as far as the ancient Atlantean and
Lemurian colonies in what is now Arizona. One in that group,
a priestess among the children of the Law of One, was told of
attempts to establish a unified activity "with those peoples that
had been a portion of the lost or strayed tribe" who had come
across from Lemurian island-settlements in the Pacific, apparently; also with "those that came from the lands of bondage by
the Persians," as well as Lemurian colonists from what is now
Indo-China. The entity must have succeeded in her harmonizing efforts, for it was said of her life in that experience that she
"aided in establishing a new unison."[9]

Not all, however, sought a "new unison." Elsewhere in the
new land, "there were activities in separating the peoples in the
southland from those coming in from the western lands or from
the isles of the sea."[10]

It takes us back to those forts and stockades. Indians
battling against Indians, in karmic encounters between ancient
adversaries—the children of Light versus the children of darkness, back in the dim corridors of a bygone history. Similarly,
when the white settlers arrived many centuries later, Cayce
spoke of "the children of the Law of One coming again into the
closer relationships" with "the children of Belial" who had
escaped to these same lands earlier.[11] It was undoubtedly an
opportunity for the meeting of self, in attempting to establish
a "new unison" and heal long-outlived antagonisms. Indeed,
many of the former "children of Belial" were now in the fore-
front among the peacemakers.

Unfortunately, the pipes of peace yielded little more than
smoke that time around. The karmic encounters between old
antagonists will have to be repeated again and again in future
lifetimes, until all concerned have learned to resolve their

ancient differences in a spirit of forgiveness and true brotherhood, under the Law of One.

THOSE VALIANT VIKINGS

In 1969, an intrepid explorer named Thor Heyerdahl set out in a 50-foot-long reed vessel from the port of Safi, in Morocco, with a crew of seven men. He hoped to prove that ancient seafarers, in similar boats, were indeed capable of crossing the Atlantic from the Mediterranean to the New World.

Because of design flaws, Heyerdahl's swan-shaped reed vessel—christened *Ra*, after the Egyptian Sun-god —had to be abandoned after traveling 1,700 miles and coming within just a week's sail of Barbados. But despite the valiant Heyerdahl's failure (which was really a partial success, in the eyes of many), this modern-day descendant of the Vikings remained convinced that his theory was sound.

Our psychic source confirms him, of course. The Americas were indeed within reach of Old World mariners in ancient times, even after the disappearance of the culturally advanced Atlanteans with their amazing fleets of solar-powered vessels. However, neither the Phoenicians nor the Vikings relied on such fragile building materials as Heyerdahl chose. Instead of reeds, the Canaanite shipbuilders selected choice cedars of Lebanon, and their Norse counterparts must have relied upon similarly sturdy timbers to carry them across the icy Atlantic waters to Greenland, on down to New Foundland and the St. Lawrence Waterway. The Vikings traveled inland as well, if Cayce was right, reaching as far as Montana. And they traveled down the North American shoreline to "that land known as the vineland, or coasts about Rhode Island and portions of the land lying north, or Massachusetts as called in the present."[1]

The excerpt just quoted is from a life reading for an entity who had journeyed with Eric the Red in the 10th century A.D., in a Norse incarnation as Osolo Din.

Nevertheless, there must have been much earlier arrivals from the Norse land than Eric the Red and his stalwart companions. In fact, on two separate occasions the sleeping Cayce made reference to the presence of Norsemen in the New World simultaneous with the early mound builders. That would mean 1,000 B.C., or perhaps considerably earlier, inasmuch as we don't have a reliable fix on the mound builders' actual beginnings.

In one life reading, for instance, we find a female member of the so-called "Adena" people arriving in Florida from Yucatan "during those periods when there were those settlings from the Yucatan, from the lands of On or the Inca, *from the Norse land*, when there were the *beginnings* of the mound builders. . ." (italics added).[2]

And here is another case:

"The entity came into the northeastern coast of this country, being among the *descendants* of the Norse people who *first landed and settled there*.

"Being strong, physically, the entity gave much aid in establishing forts and outposts of those who *later* joined with the people, in the country south from there, who were known as the *mound builders*" (italics added).[3]

A most interesting historicity! That reference to the "northeastern coast of this country" as the original entry-point for the entity's Norse ancestors, as the "first" who had landed and settled there, suggests one of two things. Either it was a point as far north as the Maine coastline, which would have been deep in the inhospitable grip of the Ice Age when the sons of Belial were first settling the New World some 11,600 or more years ago, thus allowing the more hardy Norse seafarers to claim it later on; or evacuees from the Norse land were seeking refuge along the American shore simultaneously with the arriving Atlanteans, but stayed to the frozen north to avoid territorial conflicts in those parlous times.

The latter is a distinct possibility. Their numbers were probably rather limited in comparison with the resettling Atlanteans. In all likelihood, however, they blended with the Atlantean population, in time, becoming as one people, though these gradually separated into many different tribes throughout the country, developing their own distinctive characteristics.

In support of this theory, we find a reference to "the Nordic from the upper portions of what is now Norway" in a reading relating to the time of "the first appearances of the Adamic influence,"[4] during the days of Ra Ta. This of course affirms the antiquity of the Nordic peoples, who were obviously present during the days of Atlantis' final demise and the accompanying earth changes. We may assume that they, too, were affected. As for their developing racial stock at the time, it is not clear. We are told that "it was a quite different-looking Norway then" (called "Auk," in fact, which is a rather primitive-sounding name!). Predecessors of the Goths, the Auks may have been a people closer in appearance to the red race than the white. In any case, their rugged ability to cope with nature in the raw would have given them a natural affinity with the hard-pressed Atlantean settlers of yore, as readily as with the later Indians in Viking times. Nor should it strike us in any way as unrealistic to suppose that evacuees from Auk, at the time when the poles changed and the waters of the earth were divided, found themselves seeking refuge on the North American continent, along with the sons of Belial.

In further testimony to the innate ability of the Norsemen to establish an affinity with the Indians, we had earlier noted that Cayce tells of their successful penetration into Indian territory as far west as Montana. One of those Vikings who had been with that group, led by Eric the Red, "remained to become a part of those peoples in that land." His name was Olsen-Olsen. His good influence among the Indians must have been considerable, for Cayce went on to explain that when Lewis and Clark made their expeditions through the Northwest territory some centuries later, they encountered no hostility or resistance from the Indian tribes in that area. This, said Cayce, was the result of Olsen-Olsen's legendary impact upon the tribal memory-patterns of the Indians as a peacemaker of some renown.[5]

It was one of those small, upward turns on the evolutionary screw-thread that carries us all forward a little further.

The Viking heritage is ethnically traceable to the Goths of Norway and Sweden. Eric the Red, one of their earlier leaders, was the father of the famous Leif Ericson, born in Iceland in A.D. 970. It is he, of course, who is credited by many historians as the true discoverer of America, back in the year 1003, several centuries ahead of Columbus. Sailing from Greenland, the exact location of his "accidental" landing after having been blown off-course by a storm is disputed. He called the new land "Vinland." It was probably Cape Cod, in Massachusetts.

Archaeological evidence of inland penetration by the Vikings has been found in both Ontario, Canada and in Minnesota. On the north shore of Lake Superior, in Canadian territory, the so-called Beardmore find consisted of a broken sword, an axe-blade, and the remnant of a Viking shield. Meanwhile, in Minnesota, back at the turn of the century, a farmer digging around the roots of his fruit trees struck a hard, stone object. Suspecting an ordinary rock, what he actually uncovered to his great surprise was a flat, oblong stone inscribed with many strange markings. It turned out to be ancient Gothic, and the tale it told was of an exploratory party of thirty men, some of whom had made camp by a lake one day's journey north from where the buried stone, or rune, was left as a memorial to their misfortune. Ten of the men had apparently gone out from camp on a fishing trip, another ten had remained at sea to look after their ships. When the fishing party returned to camp, they found the other ten of their number slaughtered. Apparently they had been ambushed by hostile Indians, in an experience sadly dissimilar to that of their peaceable fellow-Viking, Olsen-Olsen, who had succeeded in convincing a potential enemy that he was their brother and their friend.

The date inscribed on the rune was 1362. America's leading historian on Viking matters, Dr. O. G. Landsverk, in 1967 declared the Kensington Rune Stone, as it was called, to be authentic, as did the director of the Danish National Museum. Yet there remain the inevitable skeptics, as always; for skepticism runs deep, among scientists. They stolidly maintain that the stone is a fraud.

If the stone itself spoke to them, one supposes, they could not be induced to change their minds. But stones *do* speak, and heeding what they have to say to us is what archaeology is all about. From the Great Pyramid to Machu Picchu, from Stonehenge to the Acropolis, from a granite sphere in the jungles of Costa Rica to the hieroglyphs on a Maya temple, or to a rune stone found on a Minnesota farm, the past continues to speak to the present.

The whole story of our evolutionary journey has been writ in stone. It has been this author's task to interpret it, insofar as possible, aided, of course, by our psychic mentor. But now, even as we leave the stone-strewn rubble of prehistory behind us, bypassing the more familiar tracks of recorded time leading up to the present, we find ourselves approaching yet another uncharted stretch in the soul's long passage toward its ultimate destination.

For it is the unknown future that now confronts us. We stand on the threshold of a time as yet unmapped, unwritten. But is this truly so? How much of the soul's unguessed-at destiny may already be limned on the skein of time and space? For we are reminded that in the Universal Consciousness, wherein the soul-self has its true being, all time is one. Perhaps it is for this reason that the extra eye of the prophet, rather than being confined to the reading of past events, has more frequently and appropriately focused on things to come.

Not all events may be given, obviously, but only the barest outlines of the whole: the soul, imbued with the gift of free will and choice, may still rewrite its own individual script, and thereby alter the collective pattern to some degree, including the timetable.

But let us take a backstage look in our closing chapter at certain coming events, as previewed for us by Edgar Cayce half a century or more ago, so that we might know not only from whence we came but whither we must go . . .

THE RULERS OF THE UNIVERSE

A New Age awaits us. A new order of conditions, we are told, is about to arise.[1]

Some of us can already sense its unfolding presence. It makes itself felt in the current turmoil and disarray all around us. The old order of things is threatened by the approach of the new, and we should not be surprised that it puts up a clamorous, last-ditch resistance. Yet revolutionary change is in the air, and its arrival inevitable. When it comes, it will sweep overhead with the sudden swiftness of an eagle riding on the wings of the morning, swooping down on the enemies of spiritual hope and promise wherever they are hiding.

God, said Cayce, has been left out of the purposes of man. This has led to the present turmoils. The New Age ethic will be a worldwide spiritual awakening, marked by greater cooperation and equality between peoples and nations, and a mutually shared ideal: "The Lord thy God is *One!*"

Asked if a date could be given for the beginning of the New Age, identified as the Aquarian, Cayce referred to a certain overlapping of influence between the old age and the new, although he mentioned 1998 as the year when the Aquarian influence would apparently come into a recognizable ascendancy over the Piscean. At that time, he added, we will begin to "fully understand" its significance.[2]

At least two other major events were set for that same year: "the entry of the Messiah in this period" as a fulfillment of biblical prophecy, followed by a millennium of peace; and the reincarnation of Edgar Cayce as a New Age "liberator."[3] Finally,

1998 had been mentioned as a year marking the culmination of a series of major earth changes of a global nature, the last and most significant of which would be the shifting of the poles. But on a later occasion, when asked what great change, if any, might be scheduled for the year A.D. 2000-2001, the entranced psychic appeared to revise his earlier predictions on two counts, responding: "When there is a shifting of the poles. Or a new cycle [i.e., the Aquarian Age] begins."[4] On the other hand, that turn-of-the-century dating for both events, rather than the previously given 1998, may only have been intended in a general, rather than a specific, sense. Meanwhile, the emergence of the fifth root race may be viewed as an event commencing simultaneously with the new cycle, of course. Its forerunners are already among us, making the necessary preparations. It is a task Cayce enjoined *all* of us to undertake, whether or not we enjoy the privileges of a parenting role. The promising new race, which will mark a further stage in mankind's evolutionary development back to its Maker, must inherit a world where equal opportunity exists for all, and where self-interest is secondary to the common good. A more idealistic social order and educational system must supplant the existing ones, which extoll materialistic values that corrupt our young. Body, mind, and soul must be nurtured alike, in a manner that will promote the purity of each. Peace and universal brotherhood must be the aim of all nations. (Cayce, in fact, endorsed the "United Nations" concept long before it became a living reality.)

Concerning the biblically prophesied Armageddon that so many doomsayers envision taking place at the turn of the century, Cayce once remarked that it would actually be fought mainly at the spiritual level on the Other Side, between the souls entering and those leaving the earth plane. In this same context, he reported on one occasion an unusual psychic impression that had come to him while in trance-state during a reading. He was given a futuristic glimpse of "things happening up in the air" such as have never been experienced or seen before, with wars and rumors of wars—but the forces of Armageddon "stopped by the forces in the heavens."[5]

That should ease our fears, until we turn our attention to

another worrisome topic: the shifting of the poles.

Will the predicted pole shift at the turn of the century be of the same devastating magnitude as the last one, in Noah's day, when "the earth was divided"? Probably not. That was a 30-degree shift, following many, many millennia of crustal stability and inaction. Even so, it is significant to note that Edgar Cayce designated certain areas as "safety lands," including eastern Canada, parts of the Midwest, the Tidewater area of Virginia.[6] And he gave considerable emphasis in a number of his psychic readings to the need for self-sufficiency in years to come. The value of the small, home-operated farm was particularly stressed. Somewhat ominously, a life reading for a native of Montana included the statement that Saskatchewan, in Canada, and the Argentine Pampas and portions of South Africa, along with certain grain-growing areas in Montana and Nevada, must someday *feed the world.*[7] In still another reading, England, France, and Africa were mentioned as places that would one day mean much in the rehabilitation of man in connection with coming events having to do with "the reorganizing of man's purpose in the earth."[8]

Warning of the shift in America's values away from the nation's spiritual roots to material goals centered in self, Cayce spoke of grave dangers ahead. The enemy is not without, but *within.* A self-cleansing process is obviously needed. There must be a greater leveling of the wealth, for one thing, and many in high places who have abused their trust and power must be brought down. (Indeed, we already see this happening to some degree, both on Wall Street and in Washington.) Finally, our failure as a nation to fulfill America's original promise as a spiritual haven for the oppressed and a protector of human freedom in all of its forms could mean that the mantle of spiritual leadership may one day pass westward to China.[9]

For what, after all, is "freedom"? Cayce made it clear that we too often misconstrue its meaning. Freedom of speech, freedom of activity, must ever be bound within that which is constructive. Freedom that is licentious, freedom that is self-indulgent, freedom that is contemptuous of the law or does not consider the needs or legitimate desires of others, is a corruption of freedom's true meaning.[10] True freedom begins with the mastery of self, not letting self's untamed desires run loose in unlicensed liberty, such as we see all around us today and as was the sinful way of the lawless sons of Belial in the days of Atlantis' final undoing.

Stand aside, we are admonished, and watch self pass by. It is the only way to eventual liberation.

The earth, said Cayce, is God's footstool. Yet it has been given into man's keeping, with the command to "subdue" it— meaning, to gain mastery over the elements of matter. We may stand upon it to reach among the stars, in the fulfillment of our most ambitious dreams; or we may plow its soil and harvest its abundant crops to feed our physical hunger, just as we coax from its other elements our remaining needs. Or, we may so abuse this living planet of ours with our poor stewardship of its resources that it rebels. Not only does it begin to lose its productivity, as is happening at present, but it gradually loses its equilibrium in space. The only way the planet can purge and renew itself is through a periodic pole shift, reshaping much of its surface area, shifting the climates around, and cleansing its seas in the process.

Come, then, while we re-examine this important subject. We shall look at it more closely to see where we may have failed, and what we must do about it.

If a pole shift results from the sudden slippage of the earth's crust due to a top-heavy polar cap, let us bear in mind that man has in his power the ability to delay, halt, or at least minimize the effect of such a phenomenon through his control of the environment. The current "greenhouse effect" now very much in the world news, and so alarming to climatologists, demonstrates how we have done just the opposite. A gradual warming trend in earth's atmosphere, the greenhouse effect is produced by a rapidly increasing concentration of man-made pollutants—gases produced through burning fossil fuels, leveling forests indiscriminately, fertilizing fields with chemicals, mishandling industrial wastes, and mass-producing a

vast multitude of products that contain ozone-destroying chlo-
rofluorocarbons. As these escaping gas molecules concentrate
in the upper atmosphere far beyond their natural levels, they
trap infrared radiation emitted by the earth's surface, thus
knocking the world's climate out of balance. Moreover, by
eroding the earth's protective ozone layer, they are letting in
dangerous levels of ultraviolet radiation from the Sun. Added
damage from nuclear explosions cannot be discounted. The net
effect has been to produce record heat and drought in many
parts of the planet, resulting in food shortages and mass
starvation. In the polar regions, the warming trend may be
expected to lead to abnormal snow precipitation, building up
snow and ice deposits at the off-center caps to a danger-point
that spells inevitable catastrophe. The extent of the catastrophe, when it comes, will relate proportionally to the size and
weight of the cap as the crustal slippage gains momentum, as
well as to the rise in world temperatures, accelerating the
slippage phenomenon.

Those of us who would stand as guardians of the New Age
should address ourselves actively, and without delay, to this
and a number of other issues that bear not only on the present
welfare of mankind and that of the incoming new race, but on
the well-being of the planet itself as our life-support system.
Consider, for example, the introduction of gene-altered bacteria to increase the production of certain limited crops, without
due consideration being given to the overall side effects on
Nature's inbuilt system of checks and balances. Or the over-
building of dams that can destroy a whole ecosystem in the
twinkling of an eye. Or the destruction of the rain forests in
wanton disregard for their vital role in climate control, as well
as the part they play in providing the exotic ingredients essential to a countless number of important medicines. The list goes
on and on . . .

We live in an age of rapid transformation, which is too
often carried forward precipitously on a rising tide of materialism.

Biotechnology, where scientists have taken to playing
God, is probably the most alarming example. A shortage of

human organs has been advanced as an excuse for proposing anew the implantation of animal organs in humans, following a failed attempt in 1984. The latest scientific proposal, perhaps to test current public reaction as much as anything else, has been to suggest the use of a baboon's heart to ride "piggy-back" on an imperfectly functioning human heart. (That little item was picked up on CBS Evening News on December 6, 1987. No further word, to date.) But if the experiment has been held in cautious abeyance, the talk grows ever bolder. More recently, Dr. Eric Rose, heart transplant program director at Columbia University, has been quoted as saying, "I think implantation of chimpanzee hearts into humans is inevitable; the only question is when."[11]

Alas, the Atlanteans could have set the good doctor straight on that sadly misguided concept. We return to Cayce's warning words, cited earlier in this book: "All flesh is *not* one flesh!" It took man many millennia to free himself fully from the bestial mixtures, and woe unto those who would re-introduce such mixtures willfully . . .

Genetic engineering is quite obviously an area where science and technology are rushing blindly forward without proper regard for spiritual considerations or moral restraints. The splicing, combining, addition and deletion of genes seems on the very face of it to be too hazardous to justify. But when it comes to the swapping of genes between species, violating the natural integrity of each, and again raising the dark spectre of Atlantean mistakes, we must agree wholeheartedly with the chief critic of the biotechnicians, who is said to believe that genetic engineering "is a monstrous idea whose time should not have come."[12] His name is Jeremy Rifkin, referred to as a "biotech gadfly." We hope he keeps on buzzing loudly until the whole abhorrent business is stopped. But *will* it be?

From the Cayce perspective, the entry of a soul into the earth plane through a given body is a matter of the soul's own choice, whether that body is flawed or perfect, black or white, male or female, well or diseased. It all relates to the entity's best means of meeting self in that specific incarnation. Mind, moreover, is the builder of the soul's temple; and any externally induced change or restructuring of the edifice, if it does not occur in coordination with the builder and the occupant as full and willing participants, becomes a violation of spiritual law. In the light of that interpretation of events, genetic manipulation with even the most benevolent of intentions borders on criminal intrusion into the divinely bestowed rights of the individual, particularly if performed on a fetus or a child. And if it means implanting mouse or monkey genes into a human body for any reason whatsoever, it is downright mischievous. Such an act may be presumed to carry heavy karmic consequences for its well-meaning perpetrator. Even as a healing modality, it is illegitimate, and may seriously disrupt and delay the soul's progress. The search for health is of course fitting and proper, but only by proper means. The best means of all is a holistic approach, such as Cayce recommended, simply because it complies with the higher laws, and offers the best hope of permanency. There can be no imbalance in the results when body, mind, and soul are treated as one, in a coordinated healing process. Cayce successfully treated many an inherited ailment in this manner, and he insisted that there are *no* incurable conditions.[13]

Science, in endorsing the controversial subject of genetic engineering, seeks to justify itself by reverting to Darwinian terms, arguing in favor of the survival of the fittest. But in acknowledging the validity of that concept in respect to the animal kingdom, Cayce made it clear that it does *not* apply to man. "Let all read history," said he. "Which has survived—brute strength or the development towards God?"[14] The question was strictly rhetorical. As he noted, it answers itself.

High-tech developments are reshaping our lifestyle, not necessarily for the better. Looming on the horizon is a supercomputer that replies 1,000 times faster than current models. But to what end? Are we to become the victims of our own technology run amok in some sort of dehumanizing "computopia" of tomorrow? Shakuntala Devi, one of those "human calculators" who can produce out of her head in 50 seconds the 23rd root of a 201-digit number, says it is "terrible the way we let machines do our memory work for us." A Tufts University psychologist, David Feldman, lecturing on child prodigies, told of a ten-month-old boy named Adam who startled his parents one day by requesting of them, "Please teach me logarithms. I understand the characteristic but I don't understand the mantissa..."[15] It is assumed, with such prodigies, that some sort of processing, akin to calculation, must be involved. But Devi, for one, insists that the numbers just pop up in her head. Clearly it is a psychic phenomenon. Which is precisely the point. One is reminded of Edgar Cayce's youthful ability to sleep with a textbook under his pillow and awaken the next morning with its whole contents memorized—and not a single page turned! Said the adult Cayce: *All* knowledge is at the hand of *every* individual.[16] (To tap into it, we are enjoined to turn to the Divine within.) Will the children of the new root race be psychically gifted far beyond ourselves, so that they will find our supercomputers outmoded? I tend to think so. I tend to believe that their more spiritually attuned generations will look upon most of our present hi-tech marvels and laugh at them, seeing them as nothing more than old-fashioned gimmicks used by their backward ancestors, who were not yet fully awake to their unlimited spiritual potential. As for themselves, never doubting their true identity as the children of God, they will not hesitate to seek out their heritage as co-heirs with the Christ and co-rulers, with Him, of the universe. Indeed, as He moves abroad in their midst, they will walk and talk with Him freely, and open their hearts to receive His promises. Even now, we may personally rejoice with them. For who will they be, these enlightened souls of tomorrow, but ourselves returning on a higher evolutionary spiral?

Excitement reigns today among the world's official star-watchers. For the very first time in recorded history, astronomers are able to report visual evidence of "planet-like objects" orbiting distant stars within our galaxy. What was formerly no more than fanciful speculation has now moved into the realm of scientific fact.

In separate reports to the International Astronomical

Union on August 3, 1988,[17] American and Canadian astronomers announced their independent findings based on advanced observation techniques in the field of color shift analysis. A combined total of ten planetary sightings, out of nineteen
stars under study, led the head of the Canadian team to suggest
that the majority of stars may have planetary companions,
adding that it could be interpreted as a sign that there are other
habitable earths in the universe besides our own.

Once again, science is beginning to catch up with psychic
wisdom.

Back in the 18th century, in a little treatise titled *Earths in the
Universe*, the noted Swedish scientist-turned-psychic, Emanuel
Swedenborg, embarrassed his ex-colleagues in the scientific
community by stating in unequivocal terms his conviction
"that there is a plurality of worlds," and "that the human race is
not from one earth only, but from numberless earths"![18] He then
backed up his conviction with personal testimony of psychic
visitations in the etheric state to a number of the planets within
our own solar system, which he was able to reach and penetrate
by means of modifying, in each instance, the vibratory rate of
his own etheric form to coincide with that of the specific planet
he was visiting. He found human-like spirit inhabitants in
each, and communed with them. From these experiences, he
was able to ascertain to his own satisfaction that time and space
are relative concepts, which take on reality only in the mind of
the sensual man and have little if any meaning in the realms of
spirit.

Elsewhere, in a mystical passage in the same book, Swedenborg tells us that "the entire heaven resembles one man," or
the Christ. It is an esoteric concept also to be found, with some
elaboration, in the 16th-century writings of the Swiss philospher Paracelsus. "Heaven is man, and man is heaven,"
writes the latter, "and all men together are the one heaven, and
heaven is nothing but one man." Then, in a further observation,
Paracelsus manages to provide us with an astrological key that
links up wondrously with the psychic revelations of Edgar
Cayce: "Therefore," he adds darkly, "the starry vault imprints
itself on the inner heaven of a man."[19]

A full interpretation of the preceding passages, in the light of the Cayce readings, must begin with our understanding that each of us is part and parcel of the Universal Consciousness, or God. This includes, we are told, the stars, the planets, the Sun and moon.[20]

While retaining our individuality, we also have our oneness with each other, and with Mind the Maker, or the Christ, whose *individual selves* we are—"corpuscles in the *life flow* of thy Redeemer," as Cayce metaphorically expresses it.[21]

Concerning earth's planetary companions, our psychic source says of these that they represent "phases of our consciousness," and each in its individual sphere bears a relationship to us.[22] That relationship becomes specific in a marvelous psychic reading that tells of the passage of our Wayshower through those various phases, or stages, of consciousness in His own soul development, as also becomes necessary in ours.[23] (For, without passing through every stage of development, the evolving soul-entity cannot reach the proper vibration or gain sufficient mastery of the universal laws to move on, passing at last from this solar system to the outer spheres.[24]) In the developing from plane to plane, then, as the Wayshower's experience demonstrated, flesh provides the "testing portion" for the soul. For the soul's original transgression was the descent into flesh-form in the beginning, as was commanded not to be done;[25] and it is the flesh, in the last analysis, that must be overcome.

In Mercury's environs, the spirit-entity learns to master those mental forces needed by the evolving soul in its earthly rounds, for weal or woe. Venus' lessons apply to the love-principle. Cayce called love "the oil of salvation"; it enables the forgiving nature to get out from under the karmic wheel more quickly, and pass under the protective law of grace. (Karma, for those unfamiliar with the term, is simply the law of cause and effect, carried forward from one incarnation to another.) In Mars' forces, the harsh schooling-ground inculcates courage under adversity, and the overcoming of wrath. In Jupiter is found strength, coupled with the ennobling forces. Saturn is that sphere to which the spirit-entity is banished when the soul fails in its lessons, and must begin over again, erasing the past. In Uranus, the psychic development occurs, while in Neptune the mystic forces reveal their secrets to the soul. Pluto (called Septimus in readings Cayce gave before Pluto's rediscovery by modern science, in 1930) appears to relate to the evolving of the higher, or cosmic, consciousness of an entity. It is named as an exit-point out of this solar system.

As for the Wayshower's exit, we are told that He went on to Arcturus following His Ascension. Interestingly enough, the renowned Bible scholar and mystic, E. W. Bullinger, tells us that "Arcturus means *He cometh.*"[26] It is a star twice-mentioned in the Book of Job, which, as already noted, was authored by Melchizedek. Cayce identifies Arcturus—"that *glorious* light"—as the star of the Christ-child, which led the journeying magi to Bethlehem.[27] Reading 5749-14 terms it the central Sun of our universe.

Does each soul, like the Christ, have a star with which to identify, perhaps? This surprising possibility is intimated in a life reading given by Cayce, wherein he speaks of "the entity's own activities as a new star in the universe..."[28]

In our three-dimensional earth, we find that time, space, and patience are the "stage props" of our ongoing development. Other worlds, other dimensions. But spiritually perceived, we are told, these differing dimensions are used only as puppets to educate the evolving soul toward its full, spiritual self-awareness. (In the interior consciousness of the Eternal Now, all dimensions meet as one.)

Meanwhile, where does the next turn in the river take us before our evolutionary journey brings us Home? Man, it is clear, is not made for this world alone. All worlds, we are assured, are the work of the Lord's hand, and are ours to possess, ours to use, as one with *Him.* For the Maker has given to the souls of men—and *women* (for they are as one)—the abilities to subdue not only the earth but the universe.[29]

As for our ultimate destination, it is sure. The end is where the beginning was. It is beyond the bounds of the visible universe we see around us. In that place, in that kingdom, there is no need of the Sun, nor of the moon, nor the stars. For the Lord is the Light thereof.

Christ is the last word of evolution, as someone once said,

because He was the first. The Alpha is also the Omega. His Word brought the many into being, and His Word leads the many back to the One.

NOTES _____

PROLOGUE
1. Edgar Cayce Reading 5023-2.
2. Ref. Quatrain 87, Century I, *The Complete Prophecies of Nostradamus*, Translated and edited by Henry C. Roberts (Nostradamus, Inc.: Jericho, NY, 1978).
3. Page 233, *Meister Eckhart*, A Modern Translation by Raymond B. Blakney (Harper & Bros., New York, 1941).
4. Cayce, 364-9. (Redefined in 364-10 as simply "being close to nature.")
5. Page 275, *Walden and Other Writings*, by Henry David Thoreau (Modern Library; Random House: New York, 1950).
6. Cayce, 2072-10.
7. Page 105, *The Universe and Dr. Einstein*, by Lincoln Barnett (William Sloan, Associates: New York, 1957).
8. Page 98, *Cosmic Religion, with Other Aphorisms and Opinions*, by Albert Einstein (Covici Friede: New York, 1931).
9. Cayce, 2630-1.

CHAPTER 2
1. Cayce, 3508-1.
2. Ibid., 1770-2.
3. Ibid., 262-52.
4. Ibid., 2872-3.
5. Ibid., 5756-10.
6. Page xli, "Introduction"; Vol. l, *The Secret Doctrine*, by H. P. Blavatsky (Theosophical University Press: Pasadena, Calif., 1963).
7. Cayce, 364-9.
8. Ibid., 5681-1 & 281-9.
9. Isaiah 14:12,13 (KJV).
10. Page 299, Vol. l, *Isis Unveiled*, by H. P. Blavatsky (Theosophical University Press: Pasadena, Calif., 1960).
11. Cayce, 443- series. Also 440-13.
12. Pages 174-8, *The Apocryphal New Testament*, Translated by M. R.

James (Oxford University Press: London, 1975 ed.).

13. Page 91, "The Forgotten Books of Eden," *The Lost Books of the Bible and the Forgotten Books of Eden* (The World Publishing Co.: Cleveland, Ohio, 1962 ed.).

14. Luke 10:18 (KJV).

15. Revelation 12:7-9 (KJV).

16. Cayce, 3037-1.

17. Isaiah 45:6,7 (KJV).

18. Cayce, 412-9.

19. Ibid., 524-2.

20. Ibid., 900-16.

21. Ibid., 900-70.

22. Ibid., 262-89.

CHAPTER 3

1. Page 98, Vol. l, *The Secret Doctrine*, Blavatsky.

2. Page 191, *The Symbiotic Universe*, by George Greenstein (William Morrow & Co., Inc.: New York, 1988).

3. John 12:32 (KJV).

4. Cayce, 5757-1.

5. Page 429, Vol. l, *Isis Unveiled*, Blavatsky.

6. Ref. *The Symbiotic Universe*, Greenstein.

7. Cayce, 262-52.

8. Ref. article, "Cosmic Strings," by Alexander Vilenkin; *Scientific*]

CHAPTER 4

1. Cayce, 262-57.

2. Ibid., 2072-8.

3. Luke 21:19 (KJV)

4. Ref. article, "Two Primeval Galaxies Believed Detected"; *The Washington Post*, January 14, 1988.

5. Ref. article, "Universe Is Over 70 Billion Years Old"; *San Francisco Sunday Examiner & Chronicle*, December 24, 1972.

6. Cayce, 254-67 & 5749-5.

7. Ibid., 900-422.

8. Ibid., 699-1.

9. Ibid., 900-70.

10. Ibid., 3384-2. Also 137-81 (re: "the mind of each atom").

CHAPTER 5

1. Cayce, 3491-1.

2. Ibid., 262-114.

3. Ibid., 3744-4.

4. Ibid., 262-80 & 900-31.

5. Ibid., 262-88.

6. Ibid., 262-52, 262-119, & 254-67.

7. Ibid., 262-99.

8. Ibid., 262-56.

9. Ibid., 262-99.

CHAPTER 6

1. Cayce, 1554-6.

2. Ibid., 5749-14.

3. Ibid., 3660-1.

4. Ibid., 5755-2.

5. Ibid., 900-348.

6. Ibid., 699-1.

7. Page 190, Vol. 2, *The Secret Doctrine*.

8. Quoted on p. 750, *A Treasury of Traditional Wisdom*, Edited by Whitall N. Perry (Simon & Shuster: New York, 1971).

9. Cayce, 900-89 (also 699-1, re: "gods in the making").

10. Ibid., 1201-1.

11. Ibid., 689-1.

CHAPTER 7

1. Cayce, 364-13. (Also ref. 364-4, re: pre-Atlantean demise.)

2. Ref. *The Lost Continent of Mu*, by Col. James Churchward (William Edwin Rudge: New York, 1926).

3. Published by the Theosophical Publishing Society, London, 1904.

4. Cayce, 2665-2.

5. Ibid., 364-13.

6. Ibid., 281-25.

7. Ibid., 5748-6.

CHAPTER 8

1. Ref. *The Collected Dialogues of Plato*, Edited by Edith Hamilton and Huntington Cairns; Bollingen Series LXXI, Bollingen Foundation (Pantheon Books: New York, 4th printing, 1966).

2. Page 171, *Atlantis, The Eighth Continent*, by Charles Berlitz (G. P. Putnam's Sons: New York, 1984).

3. Cayce, 364-4, 364-6, 262-39, & 470-22.

4. Ibid., 958-3.

5. Ibid., 5750-1.

6. Pages 172-4, *The Books of Charles Fort*, Published for the Fortean Society, with an Introduction by Tiffany Thayer (Henry Holt & Co.: New York, 1959).

7. Cayce, 1219-1 & 884-1.

8. Ecclesiastes 1:10 (KJV).

9. Cayce, 364-1. (Also ref. Genesis 10:25, KJV.)

10. *A Dweller on Two Planets*, by Phylos the Thibetan (Harper & Row: San Francisco, 1987).

11. Cayce, 364-4.

12. Ibid., 364-10 & 364-11.

13. Ibid., 364-4 & 364-10.

14. Pages 284-5, Vol. 2, *The Secret Doctrine*.

15. Ibid, pages 262-3.

16. Cayce, 2390-1 & 364-7.

17. Ibid., 364-7.

18. Ibid.

19. Ibid., 364-4.

20. Page 221, *A Dweller on Two Planets* (Borden ed., 1952).

21. Cayce, 2072-10.

22. Ibid., 5750-1.

23. Ibid., 440-5.

24. Ibid.

25. Ibid., 2072-10.

26. Ibid., 5755-1.

27. Ibid., 364-3.

28. Page 278, Vol. 2, *Isis Unveiled*.

29. Cayce, 364-4.

30. Ibid., 1859-1.

31. Ibid., 364-11 & 262-39.

32. Ibid., 364-8.

33. Ibid., 263-4.

34. Ibid., 440-5.

35. Ibid., 640-1.

36. Ibid., 621-1.

37. Revelation 2:14 (KJV).

38. Cayce, 823-1.

39. Ibid., 3271-1.

40. Ibid., 602-7.

41. Ibid., 2794-3.

42. Ibid., 3184-1, 3031-1, 3069-1, 3029-1, & 2850-1.

43. Ibid., 2794-3 & 3029-1.
44. Ibid., 440-5.
45. Ibid., 378-16 & 3976-15; also 958-3.
46. Ref. *The Books of Charles Fort*, with an Introduction by Tiffany Thayer (Published for the Fortean Society by Henry Holt & Co.: New York, 1959 ed.).

CHAPTER 9
1. Ref. article, "Did Stone Age Hunters Know a Wet Sahara?", *The Washington Post*, April 30, 1988.
2. Cayce, 364-13.
3. Ibid., 5249-1, 3976-15, & 826-8.
4. Quoted on Page 294, *The Path of the Pole*, by Charles H. Hapgood (Chilton Book Co.: Philadelphia, 1970).
5. Excerpted from Foreword to the First Edition, by Albert Einstein. Ref. Page xiv, *The Path of the Pole* (cited above).
6. Cayce, 5748-6.
7. Ref. article, "The Moon's Ancient Magnetism," by S. K. Runcorn; *Scientific American*, December 1987.
8. Ref. article, "Ancient Magnetic Reversals: Clues to the Geodynamo," by Kenneth A. Hoffman; *Scientific American*, May 1988.
9. Page 31, *Exploring Our Living Planet*, by Robert D. Ballard (National Geographic Society: Washington, D.C., 1983).
10. Cayce, 364-8.
11. Ibid., 5748-4. (Note: See entire 5748 series for detailed information on the Council of 44, with date correction given in Reading 262-39.)
12. Ibid, 5249-1.
13. Ibid., 5748-6.
14. Ibid., 294-142.
15. Ibid., 5748-4.

CHAPTER 10
1. Ref. Cayce, 364-13, for detailed presentation of five racial groupings and their significance.
2. Cayce, 390-2.
3. Ibid., 3121-1.
4. Ibid., 1391-1 & 254-91.
5. Ibid., 3744-4.
6. Ref. *A Commentary on the Revelation*, based on 24 psychic discourses by Edgar Cayce (A.R.E. Press: Virginia Beach, Va., no date).
7. Cayce, 338-3.
8. Shambhala Publications, Inc., Berkeley, Calif., 1971.

9. Quoted from edition published by Harper & Bros., New York, 1959, based on group translation of original Coptic text. (Logion 11.)

10. Cayce, 288-29.

11. Ref. pages 23-24, "Adam (Higher Aspect)," *Dictionary of All Scriptures and Myths*, by G. A. Gaskell (The Julian Press, Inc.: New York, 1969 ed.).

12. Cayce, 2067-7.

13. Ibid., 3976-9.

14. Ibid., 5373-1.

15. Ibid., 3188-1.

16. Pages 177-179, *Atlantis: The Antediluvian World*, by Ignatius Donnelly (Harper & Brothers: New York, 1949 revised ed.).

17. Ref. "Adam," *The New Smith's Bible Dictionary* (Doubleday & Co.: New York, 1966).

18. Cayce, 364-13.

19. Ibid., 5023-2. (Cross-ref.: Page 399n, *Mysterium coniunctionis*, by C. G. Jung.)

20. Cayce, 5748-5 & 281-42.

21. Ref. Cayce, 294-151, and two-part article, "As Above, So Below," by W. H. Church, *The A.R.E. Journal*, Virginia Beach, Va., Vol. IX, Nos. 3 & 4, citing Jung and other sources to corroborate Enoch-Hermes connection, and attribution of Great Pyramid to Hermes.

22. Cayce, 1179-2.

23. Ibid., 2126-1.

24. Ibid., 2481-1.

25. Ref. "The Istanbul-Chicago Universities' Joint Prehistoric Project– 1980 and 1981," *Research Reports*, Vol. 21, The National Geographic Society, and subsequent news releases on Cayonu project by The University of Chicago (1986, 1987).

26. Ref. Chapter 6, "The Lucy Caper," *The Bone Peddlers*, by Wm. R. Fix (Macmillan Publishing Co.: New York, 1984).

CHAPTER 11

1. Cayce, 294-147.

2. Ibid., 5755-1.

3. Ibid., 294-151 & 294-147.

4. Ibid., 281-42.

5. Ref. Chapter 5, *Many Happy Returns: The Lives of Edgar Cayce*, by W. H. Church (Harper & Row: San Francisco, 1984).

6. Cayce, 1021-3.

7. Ref. pp. 78-79, *Many Happy Returns: The Lives of Edgar Cayce*, for documentary data linking Hermes to Enoch.

8. Cayce, 5755-1.

9. Ref. Cayce 294-151, and page 218, *Secrets of the Great Pyramid*, by Peter Tompkins (Harper & Row: New York, 1971).

10. Ref. Chapter XXXVII, *The Secret Teachings of All Ages*, by Manly P. Hall (Philosophical Research Society: Los Angeles, 1972).

11. Pages 201-202, *Aion*, by C. G. Jung; Vol. 9, "Collected Works," Bollingen Series XX (Princeton University Press: Princeton, N.J., 1959).

12. Page 243, *The Secret Books of the Egyptian Gnostics*, by Jean Doresse (The Viking Press: New York, 1960).

13. Page 534, Vol. 2, *The Secret Doctrine*.

14. Cayce, 1662-2.

15. Ref. "Uriel," *A Dictionary of Angels*, by Gustav Davidson (The Free Press: New York, 1967).

16. Cayce, 262-57.

17. Ibid., 281-25.

18. Ibid.

CHAPTER 12

1. Cayce, 877-10.

2. Ibid., 2067-4.

3. Ibid., 877-10.

4. Ibid., 877-10 through 877-12.

CHAPTER 13

1. Cayce, 1472-10.

2. Ibid., 364-13.

3. Ref. "Aryan," *The Encyclopaedia Britannica*, 11th ed. (1910-1911).

4. Cayce, 294-152.

5. Ibid., 870-1. (*Note*: In this reading, a date of 858 B.C. was initially recorded by Edgar Cayce's secretary, Gladys Davis, but in a subsequent footnote she amended the date to 8,058 B.C. When personally asked about it by the author, she explained that she had only come to realize later on, based on data contained in other life readings on the Persian period, that Mr. Cayce must have said "*eighty* fifty-eight" on that earlier occasion, rather than "eight fifty-eight," as she had set down in her shorthand notebook at the time. This revised dating not only coincided with information in several life readings implying a fairly quick return from the Egyptian period to the Persian experience,

but was confirmed in more general terms in Reading 962-1, wherein the reign of Croesus II, whom Uhjltd conquered, was said to have occurred "some seven to ten thousand years B.C.")

6. Cayce, 364-7. (Also see 288-6 & 288-48.)

7. The author's source has been the authoritative 11th edition of *The Encyclopaedia Britannica* (cited above).

8. Cayce, 1258-1.

CHAPTER 14

1. Ref. Introduction, *The Great Journey: The Peopling of Ancient America*, by Brian M. Fagan (Thames & Hudson, Inc.: New York, 1987).

2. Ref. pp. 465-7, *The Ancient Maya*, by Sylvanus G. Morley & George W. Brainerd; Revised by Robert J. Sharer (Stanford University Press: Stanford, Calif., 1983; 4th ed.).

3. Cayce, 5750-1.

4. Ibid., 1215-4.

5. Ibid., 3253-2.

6. Ref. article, "Riddle of Costa Rica's Jungle Spheres," by James O. Harrison; *Science Digest*, June 1967.

7. Cayce, 2438-1.

CHAPTER 15

1. Cayce, 364-3.

2. Ibid., 470-22 & 364-4.

3. Ref. June 16, 1986 issue. (Article summarized in "Science Notebook," *The Washington Post*, June 23, 1986.)

4. Cayce, 262-55.

5. Ibid., 364-4.

6. Ibid., 1998-1, 315-4, & 1681-1.

7. Ibid., 3541-1.

8. Ibid., 1489-1.

9. Ibid., 2365-2.

10. Ibid., 470-2.

11. Ibid., 3611-1.

12. Ibid., 1909-1.

13. Ibid., 2686-1.

14. Ibid., 4713-1.

15. Ibid., 2887-1.

16. Ibid., 1681-1.

17. Ibid., 1859-1.

18. Ibid., 1616-1.

19. Pages 128-131, *Flying Saucers: A Modern Myth of Things Seen in the Skies*, by C. G. Jung (Routledge & Kegan Paul: London, 1959).

CHAPTER 16

1. Cayce, 262-28.
2. Ibid., 281-63.
3. Ibid., 262-28.
4. Ibid., 364-9.
5. Ibid., 115-1.
6. Page 333, *Symbols of Transformation* (Vol. 5, Collected Works).
7. Ref. Genesis 12:1.
8. Ref. "Jerusalem," *The New Smith's Bible Dictionary*.
9. Cayce, 364-9.
10. Ibid., 364-7, 5023-2, 362-1, & 5749-14.
11. Page 17, *An Introduction to the Cabala*, by Z'ev ben Shimon Halevi (Samuel Weiser, Inc.: New York, 1972).
12. Hebrews 7:3 (KJV).
13. Cayce, 5749-14.
14. Genesis 12:7 (KJV).
15. Cayce, 3744-3.
16. Ibid., 262-55.
17. Ibid., 3976-15.
18. Joshua 10:12-14 (KJV). (*Note*: China's ancient Bamboo Annals tell of a day nearly 3,000 years ago "when the day dawned twice at a place called Zheng." A conjectural date, perhaps? Anyhow, we think of Ahaz' sundial... Or could it, in fact, have been an event historically coincidental with Joshua's halting of the Sun at Gibeon? In Reading 470-22, the date of the Exodus is placed at 5500 B.C., which, if correct, would mean that Joshua's battle at Gibeon a half century later was far ahead of that solar phenomenon at Zheng some 3,000 years ago. But in an apparent correction, Reading 3976-26 refers to the time of Joshua as "3200 years ago." That revised dating also accords with biblical reference sources. Close enough to the Bamboo Annals to merit our consideration.)
19. Isaiah 38:7,8 (KJV).
20. Cayce, 1929-1, 333-2, & 518-1.
21. Ref. King James Version. (*Note*: The 117th Psalm, in the King James Version, is not only the shortest, but also the *central*, chapter of that particular translation of the Bible, for whatever esoteric significance that may carry for some. It constitutes the 595th chapter, with exactly 594 chapters on either side, totalling 1188 chapters between them.

Another way to express Psalm 118, Verse 8, would be 118:8. Meaningful? Perhaps. Meanwhile, taking note, as we have done, of the 22nd verse in Psalm 118, which is identified with the Christ, any student of numerology knows that 22 is a master number specifically associated with the Christ. For verification on this point, refer to pp. 176-7, *Numerology and The Divine Triangle*, by Javane and Bunker. Finally, research discloses that the Book of the Revelation consists of exactly 22 chapters and 404 verses (404 may be reduced to the master number 44). Verse 8, of the opening chapter, has the Lord identifying Himself as "Alpha and Omega, the beginning and the ending." This identification is reiterated in the closing chapter as well—Chapter 22. Reverting briefly to 595, mentioned earlier, it is a number reducible in numerology to One. So, too, is 118. So, too, is 1189, representing the combined total of chapters in the King James Version, inclusive of the 595th. Sheer coincidence? Quite possibly. But possibly, too, it represents the occult handiwork of some Bible translator familiar with the symbolism of One.)

22. Cayce, 5023-2.

CHAPTER 17

1. Page 364, Vol. 1, *The Secret Doctrine*.
2. Page 199, *The Mound Builders*, by Robert Silverberg (Ohio University Press: Athens, Ohio, 1986 ed.).
3. Cayce, 5750-1.
4. Ibid., 3528-1.
5. Ref. article, "Jews May Have Beat Columbus," *San Francisco Chronicle*, October 19, 1970.
6. Cayce, 1298-1.
7. Ibid., 3528-1.
8. Ref. article, "8,000-Year-Old Genetic Link Found," *The Washington Post*, May 6, 1988.
9. Cayce, 1434-1.
10. Ibid., 3179-1.
11. Ibid., 884-1.

CHAPTER 18

1. Cayce, 438-1.
2. Ibid., 1298-1.
3. Ibid., 583-3.
4. Ibid., 1210-1.
5. Ibid., 3651-1.

CHAPTER 19

1. Cayce, 3976-18.

2. Ibid., 1602-3.

3. Ibid., 5748-5 & 294-151.

4. Ibid., 826-8.

5. Ref. GD footnote of 12/20/34, Reading 3976-15.

6. Cayce, 1152-11.

7. Ibid., 470-35.

8. Ibid., 3420-1.

9. Ibid, 3976-29 & 900-272.

10. Ibid., 1352-4.

11. Ref. article, "Animals as Donors," by Robin Marantz Henig; *The Washington Post* ("Ethics" Supplement), January 26, 1988.

12. Ref. article, "Jeremy Rifkin Is a Little Worried About Your Future," by David Van Biema; *The Washington Post Magazine*, January 17, 1988.

13. Cayce, 3744-1.

14. Ibid., 900-340.

15. Ref. article, "Prodigies and the Arithmetic of Genius," by Michael Kernan; *The Washington Post*, December 13, 1987.

16. Cayce, 333-6.

17. Ref. article, "Scientists Report 10 Planet-like Objects Circling Distant Stars," *The Washington Post*, August 4, 1988.

18. Par. 2, *Earths in the Universe*, by Emanuel Swedenborg (The Swedenborg Society: London, 1970 ed.).

19. Pages 39-40, *Paracelsus: Selected Writings*, Edited by Jolande Jacobi (Bollingen Series XXVIII, Princeton University Press: Princeton, N.J., 1969).

20. Cayce, 2794-3.

21. Ibid., 1391-1.

22. Ibid., 1567-2.

23. Ibid., 900-10.

24. Ibid., 900-16.

25. Ibid., 262-99.

26. Page 42, *The Witness of the Stars*, by E. W. Bullinger (Kregel Publications: Grand Rapids, Mich., 1981 ed.).

27. Cayce, 827-1.

28. Ibid., 1695-1.

29. Ibid., 4082-1, 5755-2, & 1486-1.

BIBLIOGRAPHY _____

ACKNOWLEDGMENT
The author gratefully acknowledges his debt of thanks to the
Edgar Cayce Foundation and the Association for Research and
Enlightenment, Inc., for the valuable research resources made
available to both A.R.E. members and the public, alike, at the
A.R.E. Library, Virginia Beach, Virginia. Transcripts of all of
the psychic readings of the late Edgar Cayce are on file there,
along with detailed index records.

Ballard, Robert D. *Exploring Our Living Planet*.
    Washington, D.C.: National Geographic Society, 1983.
Barnett, Lincoln. *The Universe and Dr. Einstein*. New York:
    William Sloan Associates, 1957.
Berlitz, Charles. *Atlantis, The Eighth Continent*. New
    York: G. P. Putnam's Sons, 1984.
Blavatsky, H. P. *Isis Unveiled*, 2 vols. Pasadena:
    Theosophical University Press, 1960.
___. *The Secret Doctrine*, 2 vols. Pasadena: Theosophical
    University Press, 1963.
Bowen, Catherine Drinker. *Francis Bacon: The Temper of a
    Man*. Boston: Little, Brown & Co., 1963.
Bowen, Charles (Editor). *The Humanoids*. London: Neville
    Spearman Limited, 1969.
Brown, Hugh Auchincloss. *Cataclysms of the Earth*. New
    York: Twayne Publishers, Inc., 1967.
Bucke, Richard Maurice. *Cosmic Consciousness*. New York:
    E. P. Dutton & Co., Inc., 1901.
Budge, E. A. Wallis. *The Egyptian Book of the Dead*. New
    York: Dover Publications, Inc., 1967.
___. *The Gods of the Egyptians*, Vol. 1. New York: Dover
    Publications, Inc., 1969.
Bullinger, E. W. *The Witness of the Stars*. Grand Rapids:
    Kregel Publications, 1981.
Calder, Nigel. *Einstein's Universe*. New York: Greenwich

House, 1979.

Capra, Fritjof. *The Tao of Physics*. New York: Bantam Books, 1984.

Cayce, Edgar. *The Edgar Cayce Readings*, A.R.E. Library Series, Vols. 1 through 22. Virginia Beach: A.R.E. Press, 1973-1987.

Cayce, Hugh Lynn. *Earth Changes Update*. Virginia Beach: A.R.E. Press, 1980.

"Cheiro" (Count Louis Hamon). *Cheiro's Book of Numbers*. New York: Garden City Publishing Co., 1932.

Church, W. H. *Gods in the Making*. Virginia Beach: A.R.E. Press, 1983.

___. *Many Happy Returns: The Lives of Edgar Cayce*. San Francisco: Harper & Row, 1984.

Churchward, Col. James. *The Lost Continent of Mu*. New York: William Edwin Rudge, 1926.

Davidson, Gustav. *A Dictionary of Angels, Including the Fallen Angels*. New York: The Free Press, 1971.

Davies, Paul. *The Cosmic Blueprint*. New York: Simon and Shuster, 1988.

Donnelly, Ignatius. *Atlantis: The Antediluvian World (A Modern Revised Edition)*. Harper & Bros., 1949.

Doresse, Jean. *The Secret Books of the Egyptian Gnostics*. New York: The Viking Press, 1959.

Eckhart, Meister. *Meister Eckhart: A Modern Translation*, by Raymond Bernard Blakney. New York: Harper & Bros., 1941.

Einstein, Albert. *Cosmic Religion, with Other Opinions and Aphorisms*. New York: Covici Friede, 1931.

Evolution, A "Scientific American" Book. San Francisco: W. H. Freeman & Co., 1978.

Fagan, Brian M. *The Great Journey: The Peopling of Ancient America*. New York: Thames & Hudson, Inc., 1987.

Fix, Wm. R. *The Bone Peddlers: Selling Evolution*. New York: MacMillan Publishing Co., 1984.

Fort, Charles. *The Books of Charles Fort*, with an introduction by Tiffany Thayer. New York: Henry Holt & Co., 1959.

Gandhi, Mahatma. *Selected Writings of Mahatma Gandhi*. Selected and introduced by Ronald Duncan. London: Faber & Faber Ltd., 1951.

Gaskell, G.A. *Dictionary of All Scriptures and Myths*. New York: The Julian Press, Inc., 1969.

Gleick, James. *Chaos: Making A New Science*. New York: Viking Penguin, Inc., 1988.

Gospel According to Thomas, The, translation from the Coptic Text. New York: Harper & Bros., 1959.

Greenstein, George. *The Symbiotic Universe*. New York: William Morrow & Co., Inc., 1988.

Halevi, Z'ev ben Shimon. *An Introduction to the Cabala*. New York: Samuel Weiser, Inc., 1972.

Hall, Manly P. *The Secret Teachings of All Ages*. Los Angeles: Philosophical Research Society, 1972.

Hanson, Robert W. *Science and Creation*. New York: Macmillan Publishing Co., 1986.

Hapgood, Charles H. *The Path of the Pole*. Philadelphia: Chilton Book Company, 1970.

Holy Bible. King James Version. New York: Harper & Bros., (no date).

James, Montague Rhodes (Translator). *The Apocryphal New Testament*. Oxford: The Clarendon Press, 1975.

Javane, Faith, & Dusty Bunker. *Numerology and The Divine Triangle*. Rockport, Mass.: Para Research, 1979.

Jung, C. G. *The Collected Works of C. G. Jung*, 17 vols., Bollingen Series XX. Princeton: Princeton University Press, (various dates).

____. *Flying Saucers: A Modern Myth of Things Seen in the Skies*. London: Routledge & Kegan Paul, 1959.

Krajenke, Robert W. *A Million Years to the Promised Land*. New York: Bantam Books, Inc., 1973.

Krishna, Gopi. *Kundalini*. Berkeley: Shambhala Publications, Inc., 1970.

Kyselka, Will, & Ray Lanterman. *North Star to Southern Cross*. Honolulu: The University Press of Hawaii, 1978.

Lost Books of the Bible, The, and the Forgotten Books of Eden. Cleveland and New York: The World Publishing

Co., (undated).

Medawar, P. B. *The Limits of Science*. New York: Harper & Row, 1984.

Mishra, Rammurti S. *The Textbook of Yoga Psychology*. New York: The Julian Press, Inc., 1963.

Morley, Sylvanus G., & George W. Brainerd. *The Ancient Maya*, (Revised by Robert J. Sharer). Stanford, Calif.: Stanford University Press, 1983.

Paracelsus. *Paracelsus: Selected Writings*, Bollingen Series XXVIII. Princeton: Princeton University Press, 1969.

Phylos the Thibetan. *A Dweller on Two Planets*. San Francisco: Harper & Row, 1987.

Plato. *The Collected Dialogues of Plato*, Bollingen Series LXXI. New York: Pantheon Books, 1966.

Prabhavananda, Swami, & Christopher Isherwood. *The Song of God: Bhagavad-Gita*. London: Phoenix House, 1953.

Prabhavananda, Swami. *Vedic Religion and Philosophy*. Mylapore (Madras, India): Sri Ramakrishna Math, 1950.

Roberts, Henry C. *The Complete Prophecies of Nostradamus*. Jericho, N.Y.: Nostradamus, Inc., 1978.

Robinson, Lytle. *Edgar Cayce's Story of the Origin and Destiny of Man*. New York: Coward-McCann, Inc., 1972.

Scott-Elliot, W. *The Lost Lemuria*. London: The Theosophical Publishing Society, 1904.

Silverberg, Robert. *The Mound Builders*. Athens, Ohio: Ohio University Press, 1986.

Smith, William. *The New Smith's Bible Dictionary*. New York: Doubleday & Co., Inc., 1966.

Swedenborg, Emanuel. *Earths in the Universe*. London: The Swedenborg Society, 1970.

Thoreau, Henry David. *Walden and Other Writings*. New York: Random House (Modern Library), 1950.

Tompkins, Peter. *Secrets of the Great Pyramid*. New York: Harper & Row, 1971.

Waite, A. E. *The Secret Tradition in Alchemy*. London:

Stuart & Watkins, 1969.

Walker, Bryce. *Earthquake*, (Planet Earth Series). Alexandria, Va.: Time-Life Books, 1982.

Westwood, Jennifer (Editor). *The Atlas of Mysterious Places*. New York: Weidenfeld & Nicolson, 1987.

Wilson, J. Tuzo (Introductions by). *Continents Adrift and Continents Aground*, (Readings from "Scientific American"). San Francisco: W. H. Freeman & Co., 1976.

Wood, Robert Muir. *The Dark Side of the Earth*. London: George Allen & Unwin, 1985.

About the Author

W.H. Church is the author of many popular and well-researched articles published in the *A.R.E. Journal* over a span of almost two decades. He has also written books on various aspects of the Edgar Cayce phenomenon, of which the most recent is a reincarnation biography, *MANY HAPPY RETURNS The Lives of Edgar Cayce*. Currently a resident of Charlottesville, Virginia, Church is a life-member of the Association founded by Edgar Cayce. His literary career began as an award-winning writer of children's fiction and later as a free-lance journalist for various publications, including Tokyo's leading English-language newspaper, *The Asahi Evening News*.

What Is A.R.E.?

The Association for Research and Enlightenment, Inc. (A.R.E.®), is the international headquarters for the work of Edgar Cayce (1877-1945), who is considered the best-documented psychic of the twentieth century. Founded in 1931, the A.R.E. consists of a community of people from all walks of life and spiritual traditions, who have found meaningful and life-transformative insights from the readings of Edgar Cayce.

Although A.R.E. headquarters is located in Virginia Beach, Virginia—where visitors are always welcome—the A.R.E. community is a global network of individuals who offer conferences, educational activities, and fellowship around the world. People of every age are invited to participate in programs that focus on such topics as holistic health, dreams, reincarnation, ESP, the power of the mind, meditation, and personal spirituality.

In addition to study groups and various activities, the A.R.E. offers membership benefits and services, a bimonthly magazine, a newsletter, extracts from the Cayce readings, conferences, international tours, a massage school curriculum, an impressive volunteer network, a retreat-type camp for children and adults, and A.R.E. contacts around the world. A.R.E. also maintains an affiliation with Atlantic University, which offers a master's degree program in Transpersonal Studies.

For additional information about A.R.E. activities hosted near you, please contact:

A.R.E.
67th St. and Atlantic Ave.
P.O. Box 595
Virginia Beach, VA 23451-0595
(804) 428-3588

A.R.E. Press

A.R.E. Press is a publisher and distributor of books, audiotapes, and videos that offer guidance for a more fulfilling life. Our products are based on, or are compatible with, the concepts in the psychic readings of Edgar Cayce.

We especially seek to create products which carry forward the inspirational story of individuals who have made practical application of the Cayce legacy.

For a free catalog, please write to A.R.E. Press at the address below or call toll free 1-800-723-1112. For any other information, please call 804-428-3588.

A.R.E. Press
Sixty-Eighth & Atlantic Avenue
P.O. Box 656
Virginia Beach, VA 23451-0656